HORSELOPAEDIA

A Complete Guide
To Hor

D0808498

WITHDRAWN

Stewart Hastie MRCVS
and Johanna Sharples

RINGPRESS

600056615

Published by Ringpress Books Ltd,
PO Box 8, Lydney, Gloucestershire GL15 4YN

© 1999 RINGPRESS BOOKS

ALL RIGHTS RESERVED

No part of this book may be reproduced or transmitted in any
form or by any means, electronic or mechanical, including
photocopying, recording, or by any information storage and
retrieval system, without permission in writing from the
Publisher.

ISBN 1 86054 170 4

Manufactured in Singapore

10 9 8 7 6 5 4 3 2

The **Sheffield College**	
Learning Resources - Hillsborough	
☎ (0114) 260 2254	
56615	
Cypher	21.12.03
636.1	£9.95
	SL

CONTENTS

Shelter; Water; Care of the grass-kept horse.
5. Security
6. Choosing a yard: Livery; Renting a yard; A horse at home; Building your own.
7. Grooming and Turnout: Grooming Do's and Don'ts; Grooming kit; Basic grooming routine; Sheath and udder cleaning; Bathing; Clipping; Pulling and trimming; Special occasions.
8. Shoeing: Finding a farrier; When to shoe; The balanced foot; Horn condition; Types of shoe; Removing a shoe; Studs.
9. Feeding: Basic diet; How much to feed; Storing feed.
10. Transport: Types of vehicle; Travelling tips.
11. Horsemastership: Health checks; For the active horse; For the horse at grass.
12. Finding A Service

1. Understanding Health: Routine inspections; ABC of Horsemastership; Daily checks; Common problems; Veterinary examination; Types of disease.
2. The Respiratory System: Related skeletal anatomy; Neurologic control; Effects of evolution and domestication; Diseases of the respiratory system; Degenerative diseases of the respiratory system.
3. The Digestive System: Food and feeding effects; Diseases of the digestive system; Disorders of the digestive tract; Associated disorders.
4. Teeth: Types of teeth; Constituents of teeth; Dental 'jargon'; Teeth formulae with eruption times; A special effect of domestication.
5. The Locomotor System: The foot and the distal limb; Farriery; Common disorders; Foot disease; Metabolic disease causing lameness; Disorders of the locomotor system: The signs.
6. Prevention of Disease: Infection; Tetanus: Worming programme for the control of endoparasitism; Ectoparasitism and other skin disorders; Allergies; Functional and metabolic disorders; Degenerative diseases; Rehabilitation; Saddle fit and related back problems.
7. First Aid At the scene of an accident; The ABC of first aid
8. The Older Horse
9. The End Of The Road

SECTION V: TACK AND EQUIPMENT

1. **Basic Shopping lists**
2. **Choosing equipment:** Specialist tack; Numnah or saddlecloth; The girth; Reins; Rugs; Fly fringes; Safety clothing.
3. **Fitting equipment:** Tips before you start; The headcollar; The bridle; The martingale and breastplate; The saddle; Numnah or saddlecloth; The girth; The stirrups.
4. **Bits and their action:** Types of bit; Fault-finding; Trouble-shooting.
5. **Care and maintenance:** Tack room; Leather cleaning; Tack maintenance; Bits and stirrups; Tack storage; Synthetics.
6. **Rugs:** Fastenings; Types of rug; Rug fitting; Rug maintenance.
7. **Leg Protection:** When and why?; Boots and bandages; Types of boot; Types of bandage; Care and maintenance.
8. **Clothing for Travel**
9. **Schooling Equipment and Training Aids**
10. **Final Checks before Buying Equipment**

SECTION VI: TRAINING AND COMPETING

1. **Assess the Raw Material**
2. **Understanding the Horse's World**
3. **Choose the Right Time To Train**
4. **Learn how Horses Learn**
5. **Riding Basics:** Early lessons; Equine balance and movement; Aids.
6. **Fitness and Exercise:** Schooling; Riding out; Work from the ground; Fitness programmes; Injury and rehabilitation.

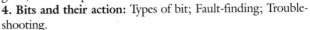

7. **Jumping:** Position: The rider; Position: The horse; Introducing poles; Building grids; Distances; Show jumps; Cross country.
8. **Showing:** Tack and turnout.
9. **Western Riding**
10. **A-Z Competition Guide:** Competition Day Tips.
11. **Problem Solving:** Physical problems; Psychological/Behavioural problems.

SECTION I

INTRODUCING THE HORSE

1. A BRIEF HISTORY

THE ORIGINAL 'HORSE'

Equus caballus, the 'modern' horse, traces its ancestry back some 60 million years to the Eocene Period, the Dawn Age, when a 30cm high, 4 toe-ed in front and 3 toe-ed behind herbivore first emerged. This was *Hyracotherium* or *Eohippus* in Eurasia and the Americas respectively, where identifiable remains have been discovered in terrain which was, in their day, marshy pastures between river and forest.

Eohippus (Hyracotherium) was a scansorial browser who stood on its hindlegs to browse the succulent tips of young trees and bushes. This height not only brought it to its basic feedstuff but also allowed for scanning the limited open spaces from which it could swiftly run for safety into thick undergrowths. It lived in pairs or very small, scattered groups. Its digestion was part enzymatic, from gastric and small intestinal juices on the easily-masticated sugar-rich leaves, and part fermentation of the residual cellulose plant material in a relatively small hind gut of colon and caecum (more porcine than bovine). For this it required plier-shaped incisor teeth and only relatively small molars in a pointed, lightweight skull on a longish neck. The abdomen was relatively small and its legs likewise short.

During the next 60 million years dramatic, if slow, changes occurred in climate

6

and terrain. By around 26 million years ago the forests began to give way to open country of steppes, plains and even deserts, in all of which the vegetation became stemmy and much coarser. The prehistoric horse had to change to survive.

It became a trickle feeder – eating little and very frequently – and a grazing animal, resulting in the digestive functioning specific to the horse. Incisor teeth became pincers to cut (or incise). Molars became progressively much bigger requiring larger jaws with more powerful muscles. The resulting enlarging head, basically a masticatory structure, needed a longer, stronger neck and a different forequarter and trunk to support it. The backbone was now having to support the much larger, more copious and relatively heavier digestive system which had evolved to cater for the increasing importance of microbial fermentation of the mainly cellulose ingesta. It became functionally more rigid for this purpose, although the rigidity was also relative to increasing locomotion speed.

The development of fright, fight and flight as an instinctive survival behaviour depended on an efficient combination of postural muscles, long tendons and strong ligaments, the stay and suspensory apparatus as well as propulsive muscles especially in the hind-quarters (the forehand is said to contribute but 18% of the forward and upward power). The limbs therefore elongated and over many years became solipedal, standing on the tip of only one toe which was encased in a horny capsule, to be ungulgrade in stance within a complicated hoof/foot structure[1].

Eohippus' 'descendants' were not traceable down a family tree, but were many individual subspecies originating from 60 million years ago as offshoots of Eohippus; most struggled in vain to survive and 'disappeared'. The Ice Ages completed the changes in the environments over which many of these subspecies lived and roamed in restricted areas from Eurasia to the Americas, until a sea replaced the original landmass linking Asia with what became Alaska – the Bering sea. The American descendants disappeared altogether for unproven reasons between 800,000 and 10,000 years ago (presumably in the same way as did many other earlier genera), although *Equus caballus* was reintroduced much later, as cavalry horses, when Cortes invaded the South Americas.

EQUUS CABALLUS

About 8,000 years ago the ultimate horse evolved. It was still relatively small, about 12 hands high, but was 'all horse', as we know it today.

Taxonomy (abbreviated): The horse *Equus caballus*

Kingdom	Animalia
Class	Mammialian quadruped
Order	Perissodactyla (odd number-toed ungulate)
Suborder	Hippomorpha (Includes the Rhinocerus and the Tapir)

[1] There is often confusion between hoof and foot. Technically foot (or hand,) as in man, is the length of the distal limb from the hock (tarsus) or 'knee' (carpus) inclusive down to the third phalange of the single middle toe (or finger). The hoof is the specialised horny capsule, a very complicated nail. Both fore and hind limbs, in the horse, are described as having a 'foot', and colloquially 'foot' refers to all the structures within the horny capsule or hoof as well as the capsule itself.

Horselopaedia

Family	Equidae
Subfamily	Equinae
Genus	Equus
Species	caballus

Further natural history facts are:

Herbivorous: Grass-eater (grass is rich in cellulose and so required large strong molars and fermentation chambers in the digestive system).

Gregarious: Herd or group living.

Nomadic: The group moves daily over new grazing areas within a relatively restricted territory; it is cursorial (having limbs adapted for running).

Soliped: The limb extremity is the pedal bone, the 3ins phalange of a single digit – one (odd) toed.

Ungulate: The limb extremity is encased in horn, the hoof capsule.

This was *Equus*. There were 6 species in the genus:

(a) *E. caballus:* the true horse.

(b) *E. asinus:* the wild ass, the North African progenitor of the donkey.

(c) *E. hemionus:* the Asiatic wild ass.

(d) *E. grevyi:* Grevy's zebra.

(e) *E. zebra:* the mountain zebra.

(f) *E. burchelli:* the plains or common zebra.

Equus' herbivorous digestive organs were mainly suspended from its backbone, namely the caudal, thoracic and the lumbar vertebrae, and the total body mass was significantly that of the gut. It was also a relatively fast mover when necessary. As mass multiplied by speed (acceleration) equalled weight, the spine had to be even more functionally rigid, a feature which played no little part in its use to man: it was first put to a chariot but soon became a ridden animal, about 6,000 years BC.

Since the *Equus* did not have a collar bone (clavicle), the shoulder blade (scapula) articulating with the upper arm (humerus) did not have a bony attachment to the chest's breastbone as in man. This permitted the scapula to glide over the ribs producing a more elongated stride especially in the asymmetric gallop gait (including the canter subgait). Locomotion has many gaits (sometimes called paces) but the main ones are:

- Stance.
- Walk.
- Trot.
- (Canter.)
- Gallop.

Plus the variants of leap or jump from out of any gait.

From stance to gallop is a means of increasing speed, yet keeping the limb stride rate approximately the same, despite changing patterns of footfall and stride. Modern equitation has developed variable stride lengths, such as, in the canter 'collected', 'working', 'ordinary' and 'extended' – the speeds increasing from 225 metres per minute at 'working' to 375 at 'ordinary' canter. Collection is the slowest, and extended the fastest, in terms of ground-covering times. In dressage the footfall intervals should be constant regardless of stride length (speed).

Walk and trot are symmetric gaits: the limbs on both sides using identical stride patterns. The canter and gallop are asymmetric, with 'change of leads' possible.

ORIGINS OF THE HORSE TODAY

The progenitors of today's horse were established out of the early *Equus* as it settled in different geographical areas in which they eventually became indigenous. There they developed morphologically or phenotypically to be best suited for the existing climate and the related soil/grazing and terrain. These developments were eventually stabilised as genetic, inheritable features.

There is evidence of four subspecies of *Equus caballus*. Palaeontologists discovered skeletal remains sufficient to record specific bone structures, molar and incisor teeth-shapes and occlusal surface design (the molar tables) to suggest:

Pony type –12-12.2hh: For example, the British Exmoor (which had 7 effective molars in each arcade) and others in North-West Europe, where there was a harsh, wet climate and sparse short stem grazing.
Pony type – 14-14.2hh: (Heavy build.) For example, the Highland and others in Northern Europe in very cold climates.
Horse type – 14.3hh + : (A long narrow body.) For example, Turkmane of Central Asia. Both great heat and extreme cold resistance.
Horse type – 13.00hh: (A refined type.) For example, the Arab strains around the Caspian sea and elsewhere in the middle east. Dry heat resistance.

Natural fortuitous interbreeding took place during intermittent extended migrations of herds of these four types. When semi-domestication by 'herder'-type human tribes began around 5,000 years BC there was an 'unconsciously' controlled interbreeding. Deliberate, controlled breeding gradually evolved from Greek days until a more planned programme began in the Renaissance, and later with the import of Berber and Arab stallions in the 17th century: the origin of the English Thoroughbred. Today there are some 160 breeds and countless subtypes.

Prehistorical findings do not indicate the horse as anything other than a source of meat and hide for clothing. Historical wall paintings and records on stone, then parchment, and the later treatises – most notably that of the Greek general Xenophon whose teachings on horsemaster- and horsemanship still hold to the present day – indicate that onagers (asses) then ponies were harnessed to chariots around 6,500 years ago and 'broken' to being ridden a half century later.

From then until the First World War at least, and despite the advent of the railways in 1840, it could be said that civilisation developed on the back of the horse, and that conquest and inter-nation mixing depended upon the horse to a significant extent both for war and for travel. Having previously existed on berries and dried meat, man, the farmer, learnt to grow cereal crops the seeds of which, grain, could be stored over winter as a source of additional nutrition for himself and his livestock (who had foraged for coarse fibrous 'old' grasses): no longer was there a need to kill off horse and cattle in the Autumn for dubious storage as meat.

Man was quick to see the advantage of the pony and the horse as a vehicle, first to enable him to round up and catch 'wild' herds for food and replacement stock, and then as an advantage in war. Mounted Infantry could arrive at a battle zone less fatigued than if they had marched, and later became cavalry units which journeyed and manoeuvred at the walk in preparation for the final, relatively short-distance, cavalry charge – the warm-up before the exertion of the gallop.

The development of improved grasses over the last 200 years and the formulation of supplementary fertiliser applications not only increased grazing but also its nutrient levels. Such grazed and conserved herbage (first as hay and later as dried grass, silage and haylage) was a boon to the dairy and to the beef farmer, but were a potential risk to his horse until more was known about their soluble sugars, starch and protein content in relation to that of the indigenous grasses to which the horse's digestive and metabolic system had evolved. The mountain/moorland pony has a significantly poorer ability to cope with these than the horse, but the latter must still be managed nutrition-wise with care, even today.

Success in keeping horses, then and now, depended on man knowing about equine lifestyle and on a man 'knowing' his horse's individual peculiarities and temperament.

NATURAL HISTORY: BEHAVIOUR
The horse's digestive functioning meant that on its travels and in winter time it could live off the land by grazing, augmented by grain carried by it or by draught horses, or plundered, along with conserved grass as hay. Provided it was allowed to do so as near to natural eating patterns as circumstances permitted, it satisfactorily survived. No difference to the present day!

As a trickle feeder it grazed at intervals, with short periods of rest, for 12 even up to 18 hours a day. The major part of its digestion, the cellulose fermentation, was on-going, but it did need regular topping up to supply the average 2.5+ of body weight gross feed as dry matter intake per day, seen as necessary for living and working. Appetite in the horse is not a simple matter of having a full stomach, as it is in man, and the horse knows this, even if scientists are not yet sure of the biochemistry involved (all mammals depend upon biochemical stimuli of appetite-satiated centres in the brain).

The solubles, starch and other nutrients, such as oil and protein and micronutrients, to a variable extent present in grass and its conserved forms, were a primary source of energy for the horse, and also for the multiplication of its caecal and large intestinal micro-organisms. These fermented the main source of herbivore nutrition – the structural cellulose – which was 'digested' to liberate volatile fatty acids, the precursors of metabolisable glucose.

The horse needed replenishing water, which was related primarily to sweat loss and other waste fluids, but as grazing usually provided water naturally in growing grasses, some of its requirements were met by this. The wild horse is known to return to 'drinking holes' only every second or third day, except in desert conditions! The domesticated horse required organised access to water to drink – if it wished (hence the aphorism…!). For example, the stabled horse, on average, drinks 10 gallons per 24 hours. What the horse sucked up through more or less closed lips – a filter technique against gross material contamination, unlike the lapping of carnivores – passed quickly through the stomach, sliding down between gastric wall and gastric contents to enter the small intestine. It did not become mixed with the gastric ingesta.

Rest for the horse takes the following forms:

* Standing and dozing or light sleeping.
* Lying in sternal position; short periods of deeper sleep is possible.
* Flat-out in lateral recumbency, allows deep sleep from which it is quickly aroused by noise and ground vibration, or reflexly from a build-up of congested blood flow in the downmost lungs.

Usually in herds, one or more animals stay awake on guard. These variations allow the group to recover from fatigue in a rota but with safety.

The herd leader is usually a senior mare, not the stallion. A group consists of 5 or 6 mares with foal at foot, yearlings and two year olds. Colts are thereafter driven off by the group stallion. As 3-year and older colts they will try to cut out fillies or mares to form their own new harem. Dominance is not the same as pecking order. Horses often pair off; conversely, individuals may develop a negative, aggressive behaviour to another horse. In domestication this behaviour instinctively returns to horses at grass: obtaining conserved feed dropped casually 'over a fence', for example, can create animosity and subsequent injury to the competing feeders.

The gregarious nature of the horse remains strong, even in domestication. Horses need to have companions certainly to be within sight, sound and smell. To deprive them of this can lead on the one hand to temperamental changes and stereotypical behaviour, especially if stabled, and on the other to attempts to rejoin others by dangerous escapes.

A horse reaches physical maturity between 5 to 7 years of age. This varies from breed to breed; ponies surprisingly do not reach maximum height and cannon-bone diameter (the two important parameters) until 7 years of age. Sexual maturity comes much earlier at 2 years but as a rule fertility is later at 2.5 to 3, although exceptions are known.

A mare cycles all year round but 'quietens down', with no ovulation from October to March, with no outward show of oestrus, being in season, on heat or stallion-receptive. Ovarian activity is light-dependent through the optical/brain circuit to the pituitary gland. In the Thoroughbred, where early foals are an advantage, oestrus is brought forward to January/February by artificial lighting and extra feeding. The cycle is one of 21 days. Actual show or oestrus lasts from 10 down to 2 days within that period, being longest in March and shortest in June/July.

Gestation is approximately 11 months but surviving foals may be born 3 weeks early and up to 2 or 3 weeks 'overdue'. This is a reflection of environment light and temperature which possibly also contemporaneously regulates grass growth. Cold weather early in gestation is thought to delay development.

Survival in the wild (and in domestication) depends upon a well-developed instinct of fright, fight and flight. Man makes use of these instincts by 'training' them into alertness, agility, speed and endurance. The instinctive behaviour is a series of reflex actions related to an awareness of a predator – frightened into alertness and flight or, if attacked, into an agile twisting, rearing, bucking and kicking to throw off the attacker and then fight. These will then be succeeded by a fast anaerobic gallop to out-distance the carnivore, followed by an aerobic canter to get well away.

It is not surprising, Monty Roberts aside, that an unbroken horse will resent the restraint of a halter rope, the feel of a saddle and a girth, and then the weight of man and the feel of his legs on its ribs, all reminiscent in instinctive memory, of an attacking carnivore. How important it is, therefore, to accustom the horse to these, to minimise or subdue the associated responses to sight, sound and feel, and to maintain a saddle-fit and a human seat which send acceptable sensory messages, through peripheral nerves, to the central nervous system of the cord and the brain, preferably in a balanced, pain-free horse.

Behaviour is the exhibition of a horse's interpretation of its interaction with the environment – animate or inanimate. The responses are innate or instinctive but become adjusted to acquired and memorised inputs. When in doubt, as on sensing something nearby but out of immediate sight, it will respond instinctively; all 'training' is set aside in favour of survival. Because it will respond irrationally – in man's view – its behaviour is then seen as unpredictable. To the horse, however, it is quite rational and psychologically necessary, even if sometimes mentally and physically injurious to itself and to the rider. Equitation as well as horsemastership are the skills of being able to think like and as quickly as a horse – to foresee features which actually do cause it, or can be used as an excuse for it, to behave instinctively.

For example, in a field a horse will hear and see man approach carrying a bucket. Memory tells it that this is promising of food; instinct tells it it could mean being caught. A sense of smell could advise friend or possible unknown foe. Whilst investigating it will scan the immediate environment with ears and eyes. It may find it necessary to get a better perception by pivoting on its forehand without losing track of the food or to place its quarters between itself and possible approaching danger. Man's known voice and manner of patting will assure the horse and it will eat. An attempt to catch could result in it walking away, head down pretending to graze but placing its head and so its eyes in a position to see behind, ready to walk further or gallop off, possibly as a playful or even a cussed behaviour. Either way it gains time and room to decide.

Likewise, a horse engaged in eating or sleeping while standing should be warned of one's approach by a quiet voice, not an immediate slap on the rump, even in the confines of a loosebox. Such blind spot contact could well invoke a backward kick to repel the 'aggressor' until the horse is satisfied who it is. A horse confined in a box still needs space to consider.

A horse's natural hearing range is that of man's conversational pitch. Much higher could frighten, just higher but for a short spell could warn by drawing attention. Unusual smells and noises will put it on guard. Previously experienced pain or worry will continue to colour its response to seeing, smelling or hearing the associated approach. For example, a view of clippers might alert it; the noise certainly will. Patience and perseverance may decondition it into ready acceptance. Chemical tranquillisation can overcome or subdue its fear for a time. Repetitions may well allow deconditioning.

It is advisable to learn how a horse communicates by facial expression and ear placement as well as the more obvious tail-towards – more importantly, to learn how your horse(s) behave. Ears back, white of eyes showing when they are 'rolled' in the socket and the body turned, is a reaction repeated from a natural response. It may give some horses an unfair branding of bad temper or even dangerousness.

It was many centuries before man realised the reasons for the horse's highly-prized natural attributes which made it suitable for flight and for riding over long distances (stamina), carrying an armed rider (strength) over variable country (agility) quickly (speed) and continuing to do so (durability).

The structures specific to the horse which gave it advantages over other herbivores and made it especially suited to carrying man are:

- The *functionally* rigid thoracico-lumbar spine.
- The solipedal stance or foot/ground support phase of a stride.
- The stay and the suspensory apparatus in the elongated limbs.
- The stifle/hock synchronisation.
- The various gaits and the relationship of respiration with the asymmetric stride of canter and gallop.

Nature evolved these units of locomotion and associated systems to enhance flight. Man, in recent years, attempted to breed in further improvements. Where two breeds were intercrossed, for example, to give better speed with greater stamina, their characteristics did not always 'nick' and weaknesses could evolve. Even when cross-breeding was satisfactory, the abnormal use of the horse and mistakes in its nutrition, training and fitness, could undermine the benefits of these elite structures. They became weak links, the ones most subject to the traumas of over-stress.

ANOMALOUS BEHAVIOUR

This is usually the consequence of boredom associated with confinement in isolation, without adequate exercise. The results are so-called 'stable vices' invoked by neurotic over-stress. They are not really vices and are now called stereotypes or stereotypic behaviourisms. They are essentially a highly repetitive or set form of motion patterns: a displacement activity suggestive of starting an action but being unable to complete it – instead, the start is continuously repeated.

With the possible exception of crib-biting and wind-sucking, which can develop in the bonding activities of the foal copying its dam, such so-called vices are not the result of mimicry; more than one horse in a yard so affected implies that these horses are genetically predetermined or programmed to be stressfully susceptible to common trigger factors.

Types of vices are as follows:

Crib-biting: When the horse 'hooks onto' a solid object with its upper incisors and pulls forward to arch the throat After a period of 'practising' this movement it begins to swallow air – to become a wind(air)-sucker – into the stomach. (Some horses learn to wind-suck without cribbing. Wind-sucking and immediate blowing it out is a variant.) Over a period of weeks much energy is said to be expended with loss of condition. An indigestion and sometimes colic may develop. Very recent work indicates that the sucked-in air gets as far as the throat and is then exhaled. Little, if any, in the majority of such horses, is swallowed. This explains the observed low rate of associated colics and, to a lesser extent, the presumed loss of condition.
Weaving: This is a lateral swaying from one forefoot to the other and back again. The momentum is obtained by swinging the head from side to side. Again an energy-expensive trait which also inflicts unnatural overstresses on the distal forelimb joints.
Box-walking: As the name implies, this is a persistent tramping around the perimeter of the loose box. Energy is expended, eating time is used up and the

constant tight circling overstresses the limbs.

Flanking: This is a self-mutilation by the teeth on the skin of the flank, said to be initially directed at an irritating blanket. Sores which can become infected follow.

Kicking: Usually by one hindleg against a wall. It may continue for long periods at a time. Fractured pedal bone and navicular bone are not an unknown consequence, and the point of hock is often traumatised. The persistent noise gives no rest to other horses or to personnel sleeping nearby.

Foreleg banging: This usually begins as an attention-seeking trick in which the front of the 'knee' (the carpus) or the front toe wall of the hoof is persistently hit against the stable door. Feeding in response only perpetuates the habit which requires the head and the neck to be over the half-door. A grid is a helpful stopper and a padded inside of the lower door masks the sound, lack of which often stops the habit as it then seems unproductive to the horse.

Head shaking: Head shaking is a disease, not a stereotype, but because of its persistence and repetitive motion it is often confused with vice habits, which makes it suitable for inclusion here. Head shaking is an erratic vertical nodding of the head usually at the trot especially after a period of cantering. More so in the ridden horse; it may begin as soon as locomotion starts or even before.

It is most common between May and September and usually requires bright sunlight. In most cases there is a concomitant rhinitis presumably of a (pollen) allergic type. The phototonic/nasal mucosal irritation appears to trigger the head nodding. A rider loses contact with the bit and so the aid through the hand, but there is rarely any attempt to run off; the nodding is a more of a sensitivity-induced action. The causes are still not fully known; the suggestions are many.

Lateral and circular movements in a horizontal plane are more usually the result of ear irritations and are not stereotypical.

FACTORS WHICH INFLUENCE BEHAVIOUR
Instinct
Common to all horses are automatic responses to stimuli from certain situations. It does not learn these responses or think about what and when to make them. Examples include:

- Grazing, drinking, resting (the first and possibly the second is almost certainly originated by seeing its bonded dam do them).
- Reproductive posturing and actions; the olfactory stimuli to the male are pheromones 'collected' by the Flehman positioning of the upper lip and his nostrils which directs the hormone molecules onto the Organ of Jacobson – high in the rostral nares. This contains pheromone-specific olfactory sense endings.
- Herding and other social behaviour.
- Flight from danger preceded by shying and other defensive actions.

The autonomic influences of heartbeating and breathing are constant and so need no trigger mechanism; they reflexly respond to athletic and other demands by accelerating. Conversely, the horse cannot stop these, whereas other instinctive behaviours can be over-ridden by higher nerve centre inputs.

Breed or type

The hot blood in comparison to the cold blood has different characteristics. A speed horse is more likely to have a readily stimulated excitement; the draught a more phlegmatic nature. These are reflections of metabolic processes associated with the transfer of energy into movement.

Within a type or breed there is the individual temperament which can alter the type characteristics: for example, the hot blood can be 'laid back' when not tacked up, while the cold blood may well exhibit explosive behaviour when led in-hand especially the stallion.

Experience and Learning

The horse has a good memory of good and of bad experiences and will react to re-exposure accordingly. Both will influence temperament for good or for ill. 'Breaking', training and management generally should invoke only pleasant sensations whenever possible.

Intelligence

(Recent American work has thrown new light on the possibility of equine intelligently determined behaviour based on solving feed availability problems.)

It is questionable if intelligence enters into a horse's general behaviour. There is still considerable argument whether a horse can solve problems even if they can come to associate end results with patterns of sight and sound which lead up to these. Reasoning as such is based on past experiences. Learning by exposure is therefore essential to its training; they are good at learning and remembering, which often complements instinctive behaviour.

They cannot, however, remember many things in regard to action learning. Some 15-20 commands or aids are said to be their limit. Exceed this and confusion follows and what has been learnt can be erased. Training must be reinforced by reward (positive enhancement) or by punishment (negative reward, not the infliction of pain). Fortunately they seem more responsive to positive enhancement, co-operation and reward than to threats and so-called punishment. Sessions should be short and are best if ended on a good note.

Certain morphological and/or conformation features are said to be guides to temperament or natural disposition:

- Close set, small 'piggy' eyes, as compared to large, well set apart 'generous' eyes, mean an unco-operative nature, a mean streak.
- The convex facial line, the Roman nose, is associated with placidity, as distinct from the volatile Arab with its dished face.
- Pricked, alert and listening ears are said to be signs of good temperament, in contrast to the horse with quickly and frequently laid back ears.

Sex or gender

The gelding is reputed to be consistent in its temperament which is usually biddable and placid. The mare varies with her oestrus seasons, pregnancy and when with foal at foot. Stallions, unless firmly handled from the outset, can be dangerous from exuberance and the desire to show off. They are worse when at stud, especially if running with mares, when they are extremely possessive.

Health

Intercurrent illness will upset normal behaviour. Painful conditions of the mouth, back and feet can make any horse less than co-operative.

Domestication

Isolation, boredom, lack of gregarious stimuli and erratic feeding times will all upset natural behaviour. The horse which switches off when not required for action but persistently and continuously fidgets in work is energy-expensive and less likely to be responsive to aids other than those that ask for 'go'.

Equine Senses

Whether horses have common sense is debatable. The 'sensible' application of instincts may not mean the same to man as it does to the horse. It is reasonable to state that man with his given dominion over the horse should use that to understand the horse and not expect the horse to understand more than man's varying attempts to apply the aids. Some such messages sent through superficial nerve endings can be so subtle, and often the subconscious application of conscious thought, that the horse is given the credit of being able to read the rider's mind.

What a horse does have are finely tuned cranial nerve sensory inputs: the senses. The four main ones have direct communication with their respective brain centres via cranial nerves, and these are:

- Visual
- Auditory
- Olfactory
- Gustatory

The various skin and other 'body' sensations are mostly via spinal nerves and thence to the brain. Muzzle skin and facial tactile hairs, whiskers, lashes etc. all carry 'touch' information direct to the brain. All such sensations can reach the conscious brain but many are via the subconscious centres, where they invoke reflex responses; for example, the muzzle's muscular prowess makes it an efficient reflex 'hand' to the information gathered by the senses.

Proprioception, mainly from muscles, tendons and joint ligaments do not normally reach the conscious level but do play a vital part in feedback reflexes regarding the horse's balance, and its sense of positional contact with and movement over the environmental ground surface.

The horse is very much a 'react first, ask questions later' type of being. It doesn't often stop to think; not at least until it feels safe. Thus sudden defensive or unguarded movements by the handler can immediately invoke panic reaction from an otherwise normal horse.

Vision: It is impossible to accurately assess visual acuity in practical terms. Testing for sight is a very inexact science. It is the sense involved to provide long-range information as a defence against predators. Close vision at speed is required to help evaluate changes in terrain, and closer still for recognising edible vegetation before olfactory analysis is effected. It is believed that the horse evaluates objects at 1.5 times human perception. It has the biggest eye ball of all mammals.

Binocular ability is restricted to 65° but its combined monocular sense gives 190° horizontal and 180° vertical. In bright light the iris contracts to form a horizontal pupil. Effectively the equine vision is 350° with a narrow blind spot in front of its nose and another to several metres behind its rump. The lens does not lend itself to focusing as in carnivores. It was originally thought the horse obtained variable focusing by altering the angle of the head but it is now known that it uses offset monocular 'depth cues' for such a purpose. For this it requires freedom of the head which is not always obtained quickly and sufficiently enough when being ridden – one other explanation of shying.

Colour recognition has not yet been fully defined; red is thought to be difficult. Night-vision power is enhanced by good recognition of size, shape and position rather than by detail acuity. Any change in the outlines of even familiar objects can arouse suspicion; a horse wearing a large rug will appear sufficiently different as to cause concern. The response to darkness is slow but eventually night vision is good. This feature is possible because of the area at the back of the eyeball called the Sapetum lucidum which 'collects' and 'reflects' light down onto the retina; it acts as a light amplifier. Sudden changes as from open country into woodland present difficulty in equitation especially if jumping is involved.

Hearing: 'Speech' or vocalisation in the equine has a small vocabulary but what is said and the nuances therein must be clearly heard and interpreted by other horses. Dangerous noises must also be quickly sensed. The highly mobile ears, the funnel-shaped pinnae, prove good conductors, and one can be moved independent of the other. The horse's hearing is most sensitive in between 2 and 5 KHz – normal quiet human voice – which has importance in the man-to-horse relationship.

The position of the pinnae are also signalling devices to other horses and to man if he looks for and interprets them. If held flat back: sound is shut out, "I'm not listening to you!" – because he can't!

Smell: A vital sensory input to pick up messages left by other horses as well as other animals and plants; a safeguard. It is also a means of decision regarding sexual attraction for reproduction, e.g. the reaction caused by the pheromone exuded via vaginal secretion.

The acuity is not good enough for tracking (compare the canine where the scent is often sparse and diluted with the equine pheromones concentrated in a relatively small area in the air. The horse is, however, sensitive to these even when they are blown down wind a considerable distance.)

Taste: Essential, along with smell – these two work together – in determining what is safe to eat. Ragwort's smell and taste when growing warns the horse off, for example, but when cured in hay these disappear with fatal consequences for a horse offered such contaminated roughage feed. Hunger, due to depleted pasture, may drive a horse to eat noxious weeds – against its better judgement.

A foal will recognise its dam's faeces and will eat these in its early days to populate its intestine with essential fermentation micro-organisms.

Proprioception: The conscious and the constantly 'used' sub-conscious sensory input from the locomotor systems has to be stimulated by use. The reflex response is thereby tuned. Young horses at play in a field use movements which are similar to those required for fright, fight and flight even though predators, other than man, no longer exist. The agility, balance and the speed thus engendered still serve to make it a better athlete.

2. CONFORMATION

All *Equus caballus* look more or less like one another in general outline. Their conformation differs from that of their cousins and these further differ in colour markings, ear size relative to head and trunk size and so on.

To most people a horse's two dimensional appearance, its general shape or conformation, will tell them that it is a horse; to some observers a certain type of horse – pony, light horse or draught animal – and within these are some who will recognise breed. The cognoscenti will recognise the progenitors involved in a crossbred!

The general overall appearance of a horse is the basis of recognising its classification as to genus (e.g. *Equus*), species (e.g. *caballus*) and possibly its breed or subspecies (e.g. Thoroughbred). Once the horse has been remarked in this way, the ground is laid for:

- Objectively assessing its potential within that breed for discipline uses, but less accurately for its ability and durability therein.
- Subjectively estimating its aesthetic qualities, its conformation and condition, 'in the eye of the beholder'.

Over many years breed specifications have been determined – more so in canines and bovines than in equines. Inheriting these could be a guideline for potential excellence; failing to do so could be seen as a warning of lack of athletic potential. Deviations from the ideal were often contradicted by results – handsome is as handsome does – but how long they could continue to do so was an economic as well as a welfare concern.

Whatever else the breed required in detail, the individual had to give the appearance of an overall static balance which would allow self-carriage with a rider in the gaits necessary for the disciplines selected, and which could be confirmed when seen in dynamic mode – ridden or at free exercise.

The most important classification based on conformation is a 'pony', up to and including 14.2hh (147.32cms) and a 'horse', over 14.2hh. The former is not only smaller but is relatively bulkier in body and shorter in limb with a consequently shorter action or stride (compare a terrier with a labrador dog). In the horse there is a distinction between a light riding breed and the heavier draught animal which, of the two, more resembles an 'enlarged' pony.

CONFORMATION AND THE SKELETON
The skeleton is an inherited feature, a genotype and – subject to certain influences before bones mature – is unalterable: nature does not become influenced by nurture in bony anatomy. Malnutrition in the immature animal can particularly influence limb development, because of the impact of mass pressing down on the ground creating displacement changes in the bone's growth plates. The possible results are known as Development Orthopaedic Disease (DOD). The related limb deviation can be amended, but if not corrected is then susceptible to:

(a) Further pressures, leading to Degenerative Joint Disease (DJD), which is a permanent feature after bone growth ceases.
(b) Limb aberrations, leading to limb traumatic interferences and/or deficits in ground support at footfall and in lift-off.

The only part of a limb which continues to grow, and is thereby susceptible to pressure deformation but amenable to correction by farriery, is the hoof – the horny capsule for the pedal bone and related structures.

The conformation is a three-dimensional outline drawn from one 'point' of the skeleton to others. These points are as follows:

- *Point of incisor teeth:* end of muzzle.
- *Point of poll:* posterior high end of skull.
- *Point of withers:* most prominent of the thoracic vertebral dorsal processes; usually 3ins, 4ins or 5ins.
- *Point of croup:* highest part of the inner wing of the pelvic ilium.
- *Point of hip:* widest-out extremity of the outer wing of pelvic ilium.
- *Point of buttock:* posterior end of the pelvis, the tuber ischium.
- *Point of shoulder:* scapular/humerus articulation, actually the dorsal (anterior) projection of the proximal humerus (upper arm bone).
- *Point of elbow:* the highest aspect of the ulnar bone at the elbow joint.
- *Point of knee:* a small accessory carpal bone projection on the palmar (posterior) aspect of the knee (or carpus).
- *Point of stifle:* the dorsal (anterior) aspect of the patella in the front of the stifle joint, the equivalent of the human knee.
- *Point of hock:* the top extremity of the fibular tarsal bone (the human heel bone).
- *Point of fetlock:* the palmar or plantar aspect of the fetlock joint at the level of the ergot.
- *Point of distal hoof wall:* the widest part of the foot in contact with the ground surface.

Some authorities include under 'points' such areas as the shape of the head, the curve of the neck, the bulk of the quarters. These, however, I consider should be recorded as features. They have, of course, an underlying skeleton but some can vary during development, and with muscle fittening and fat deposition.

The soft tissues, muscle and fat, which infill and cover the skeletal framework are very susceptible to variations in feeding, training and disease. The summation of these two which defines the shape of the animal at any one time is 'condition'. It alters the overall 'picture' but does not change the inherent framework which is the conformation. The soft tissues are, in three dimensional assessment, the arbiters of how a horse will fill out, into conditions of:

- Thin.
- Thin but fit.
- Fit but slightly fat.
- Fat, variably fit.
- Obese.

In order to assess conformation it is important to see a horse as a whole three-dimensional, potentially and actually mobile object. The evaluation of conformation is often 'a compromise of' many average features – some good but a very few, if any, bad ones. An inexperienced purchaser may be aesthetically impressed even if only by the eyes or the set-on of the ears; an experienced buyer will look all over whilst the horse is static. An ability to analyse conformation, an eye for a horse, is not quickly developed, let alone the ability to 'see' in a particular breed individual the qualities best suited for a specific discipline. It is perhaps easier to spot faults which could make it unsuitable or lessen its durability therein. By definition a well conformed horse should have most of its structures in keeping or in balance. It should move, when loose in all gaits, in a balanced, self-carriage fashion. (The Thoroughbred race horse is judged slightly differently.)

An important feature of conformation, is that which suggests that work will make it more susceptible to the occupational hazards of over-stresses – such as strain of a flexor tendon or sprain of a hock joint – and other system disorders known to be associated with visible structural deficits. Evidence of previous trauma now healed (i.e. chronic lesion) need not be associated with a primary deficit; even the best conformed of horses can experience locomotor over-stress, related to fitness, terrain and rider's ability, and accidental wrong or inelegant strides. Poor-conformed types are just more likely to be injured under similar conditions of 'nurture' which adds to 'nature's' weaknesses.

It is rare for a less than good conformation on the whole to make a horse useless. Such animals are usually obvious at birth. Those that 'go on' may, however, be:

- Of poor durability.
- An uncomfortable ride.
- One prone to stumble.
- Susceptible to systemic dis-ease (i.e. the animal that is is not 'at ease') and/or acquired defects.

GROWTH

Growth in limb bone length, as in all animals, relates to the time from birth until all the bones' cartilaginous growth plates are ossified. Before that, the bone length at birth 'grows' with the formation of extra cartilage; growth stops or 'closes' when the genetically determined laying down of calcium salts catch up with the band of cartilage or the focal areas in the knuckles of the various bones. Further height in the horse is influenced by the:

- Lengthening of the ribs.
- Increasing bulk of the breastbone and of the spinal vertebrae.
- Lengthening of the dorsal processes especially of the thoracic vertebrae in the wither area.
- Increase in size of the gristle caps of these processes.

All these are relatively small but are significant in summation.

Limb bones vary in their growth potential. From a body height aspect, the main ones 'close' as follows:

Points of the horse

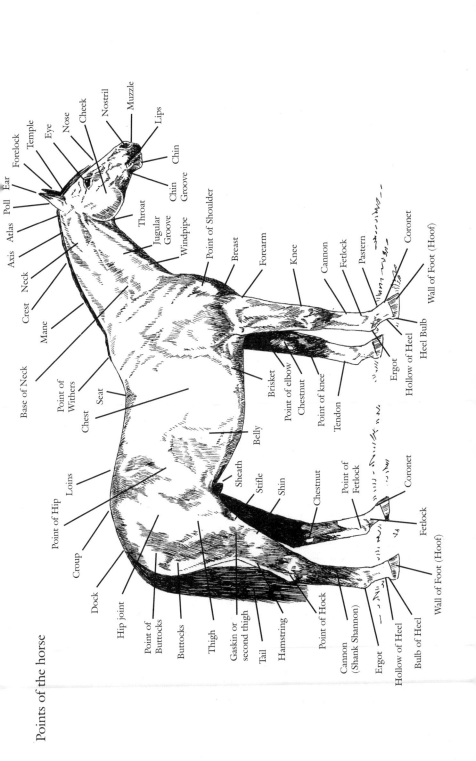

Muzzle
Nostril
Cheek
Nose
Lips
Temple
Eye
Chin
Forelock
Chin Groove
Ear
Chin Groove
Poll
Atlas
Axis
Throat
Point of Shoulder
Jugular Groove
Windpipe
Breast
Crest
Neck
Forearm
Knee
Cannon
Fetlock
Coronet
Pastern
Wall of Foot (Hoof)
Mane
Ergot
Heel Bulb
Hollow of Heel
Base of Neck
Point of Withers
Seat
Chest
Loins
Belly
Brisket
Point of elbow
Chestnut
Point of knee
Tendon
Point of Hip
Sheath
Stifle
Shin
Chestnut
Point of Fetlock
Coronet
Croup
Fetlock
Wall of Foot (Hoof)
Dock
Hip joint
Point of Buttocks
Buttocks
Thigh
Gaskin or second thigh
Tail
Hamstring
Point of Hock
Cannon (Shank Shannon)
Ergot
Hollow of Heel
Bulb of Heel

- Radius or forearm at 3.0 years. A proximal and a distal plate.
- Ulna elbow bone 3.0 years or later. A proximal (and a distal focus).
- Metacarpus or cannon at 1.25 years. A distal plate only.
- 1st phalange or long pastern at 1.25 years.
- 2nd phalange or short pastern at 1.25 years.

Of these, the first are the most significant. The humerus (arm bone) and the scapula (shoulder blade) because of their angulation tend to grow within the ultimate confines of the thorax (the chest) and so do not play a major part in limb total growth.

In practical terms, the distance from the point of the elbow to the posterior point of the ergot (at the fetlock) at 2 years old if radiated up from the elbow gives a good indication of where the point of the withers will eventually be at maturity. A foal's legs grow relatively little from the 'leggy' appearance of the first 6 months; it has to be athletically efficient from day one, unlike puppies and other 'nest'-sheltered neonates who 'hide' for days if not weeks.

The final height at the point of the withers in a horse standing four square but relaxed, is genetically predetermined. Feeding or intercurrent dis-ease may hasten or slow its ultimate growth to this but cannot, except under extreme curcumstances, change it.

In legal terms the actual adult height of a horse is reached at 7 years old and must be measured and certified by two veterinary surgeons. The horse, unshod but correctly trimmed for re-shoeing, is stood up on a certified level floor with the poll no lower than the withers and measured, when relaxed, by a Weights and Measures standards-certified measuring 'stick'. This used to be was read off in 'hands', 4 inches, but is now in centimetres, with approximately 10 centimetres to a hand.

Such exactness is essential for show and jumping ponies and other horses classified by height for competitive classes. In ponies height is a guide to size relative to rider age, height and weight. Height is also one of the 'descriptions' used in identifying horses at time of purchase. Unless this height is officially recorded it must be described as approximate; it is not then a warranty unless out by more than 1ins-2ins either way. A significant marker is 16hh for riding (light) horses, above which value often significantly increases.

The skeleton 'grows' in bone diameter as well as length. Work and related concussive/compressive force, especially on the hard, also encourages the laying down of intramedullary (marrow cavity) bone in a geometrical fashion so as to meet the varying stresses of locomotion. Continuous slow work on persisting hard surfaces stimulates further overall bone diameter increase for that breed – for example, the Thoroughbred relegated to town haulage in days gone by.

The external diameter of mature new bone became a marker for the ability of the horse to carry certain weights. This was particularly important in cavalry and police mounts, hunters, NH eventers and showjumpers and to a lesser extent in endurance horses where there was always a compromise between weight and strength (consider the human marathon runner and the sprinter). It is usually measured at its narrowest around a fore cannon bone. The actual perimeter distance includes the tendons and the ligaments but gives a fair enough estimate of the bone's diameter. At the same time an objective view is made of the 'ideal' flatness of the cannon bone. It is referred to as a particular horse's 'bone'.

Skeletal structure.

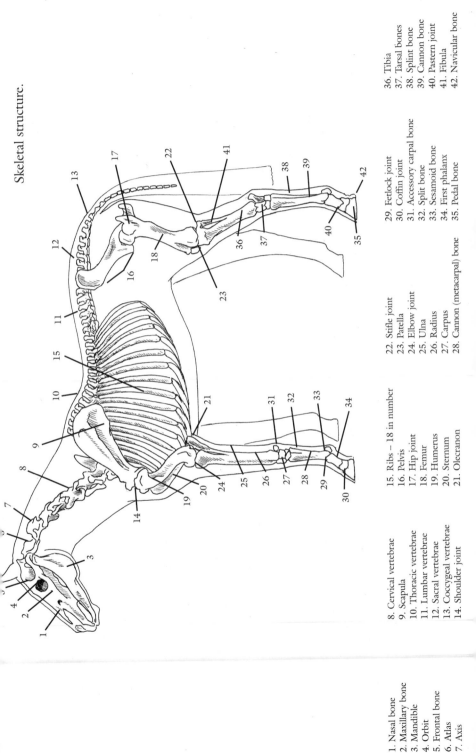

1. Nasal bone
2. Maxillary bone
3. Mandible
4. Orbit
5. Frontal bone
6. Atlas
7. Axis

8. Cervical vertebrae
9. Scapula
10. Thoracic vertebrae
11. Lumbar vertebrae
12. Sacral vertebrae
13. Coccygeal vertebrae
14. Shoulder joint

15. Ribs – 18 in number
16. Pelvis
17. Hip joint
18. Femur
19. Humerus
20. Sternum
21. Olecranon

22. Stifle joint
23. Patella
24. Elbow joint
25. Ulna
26. Radius
27. Carpus
28. Cannon (metacarpal) bone

29. Fetlock joint
30. Coffin joint
31. Accessory carpal bone
32. Split bone
33. Sesamoid bone
34. First phalanx
35. Pedal bone

36. Tibia
37. Tarsal bones
38. Splint bone
39. Cannon bone
40. Pastern joint
41. Fibula
42. Navicular bone

For example a Hunter's ideal bone would be according to its type:

- Light: 8.5 ins
- Medium: 9 ins
- Heavy: 9.5 ins

Ponies, cobs and draught horses have relatively more 'bone' than light horses, but regardless of breed or type, the size should still be in balance with height. A frequent disparity is seen in the 17hh horse with 'light' bone of less than 9ins: the body mass is likely to be too heavy for that bone *and* the associated flexor tendons, and even for security of footfall.

READING A HORSE'S CONFORMATION

As has been said, conformation is the outline of a horse in three-dimension form, determined by bone extremity distances from one point to another. When reading these points, consider:

- The relation of one bone to another as determined by the angle formed at the articulation between them in static position.
- The distance from the ground to a horizontal level (e.g. the height of the knee from the ground compared to the height of the hock).
- The distance from one bone extremity to its 'twin' on the contralateral bone.
- The distance from the most proximal extremity to the most distal within the body as a whole, within the trunk, etc.
- The ratios of these all with each other.

Points, the extremities or tuberosities, which may be a knuckle on its own or part of an articulation, determine conformation. Such points can be clearly identified in the living animal as they protrude or stand out. They are covered by skin, to a lesser extent by fat and never by muscle except at the point of the buttock (the tuber ischium).

Even in the obese animal all the points can be palpated. The dorsal processes in the caudal thoracic and the lumbar region may be countersunk between excess deposits of fat on either side of midline whereby they form a gulley. In a very fit horse the well developed epaxial lumbar muscles have the same morphological effect.

The last pair of ribs play a minor role in estimating one aspect of conformation: the length of the rib cage. By following its palpable line upwards it leads to the 18th thoracic vertebral body which indicates the position of that last vertebra's dorsal process. From the first cranial lumbar to the point of the croup defines the length of the lumbar vertebral span, the loin or coupling where the maximum ventriflexion of the back can occur at the junction of lumbar 6 and sacral 1, the lumbo-sacral articulation, a movement important in 'engaging the pelvis'.

The distance from the most caudal part of the last rib to the ventral prominence of the point of the hip is an indication of 'long or of short back' and so is one marker for weak or strong coupling relative to the pelvis as a whole. Ideally in a 16 to 17hh horse it should be no more than 4ins – a fist of the flexed four fingers. The distance back to the most caudal and upper part of the same tuberosity from the original line of the last rib is a span, approximately 8ins.

The potential 'cubic capacity space' described by bone lengths, joint angles formed, and distances apart, equates with the mass and the contour of the eventual muscle development and variable fat deposition. For example, consider the bulky appearance of the draught horse whose muscles, to be mechanically efficient, should leave their point of origin at a bone (or a fascia) at a wide angle and, via its tendon, insert beyond a joint similarly nearer to right angles. Compare this with the lithe appearance of the racehorse whose muscles are also bulky, especially over the hindquarters, for potential speed, for which efficiency they should leave and insert by their tendon on adjacent bones at more acute angles (they tend to run almost parallel with the long bones involved, especially the proximal one).

In full development these muscles determine the working shape of the horse but this is not true conformation. A fit athletic horse will, for example, have maximum muscle development as seen from mid-crest to the buttocks such as to produce a 'good top line'. The demarcations between neck, back, loins and quarters should be smooth but still recognisable as divisions of spinal skeletal distances and as points of articulation for maximum flexion and extension at cervical vertebra 7 with thoracic vertebra 1 (out of sight and feel) and between lumbar 6 and sacral 1. The overall appearance is that of balanced power; the other ventral and quarter propulsive muscles should also be equally developed.

CONFORMATION POINTS FOR CONSIDERATION

The inferred advantage of a good top line is also dependent on balanced limb conformation to efficiently transfer the potential hindquarter impulsion into forward, elegant locomotion.

The hindleg propulsive power through the iliosacral 'joints' which, in effect, are fixed junctions with the spinal column at S1, is transmitted along the back to the forehand.

The back's 8 cranial thoracic vertebrae are assisted in their stabilisation by the related paired ribs and their attachment to the sternum or breastbone. The caudal 10 pairs are slightly freer because of their unified cartilaginous attachment to the caudal sternum.

The forelimbs have no clavicular or collar bone attachment to the sternum from the shoulder joints; the trunk is slung by muscles and ligaments between the scapulae and the shoulder bones.

It is imperative that the loins are exposed to as little overstress as possible especially from the rider/saddle overhanging onto the lumbar muscles. Basically this area with no support from the ribs should be shorter rather than longer.

In addition one must consider the:

- Set of the head on to the neck.
- Set of the neck onto the trunk (thorax).
- Angle of the shoulder – from point of withers to point of the shoulder joint (the most anterior articular surface of the proximal humerus) and the related parallelism of the foreleg's pastern and hoof capsule.
- Pastern hoof axes in both fore and hind.
- Column of the forelimb support as seen from side and from front.
- Angulation of the hindlimb as seen from side and from rear.

Good conformation.

Well set-on head.

Neck good length.

Strong back.
Not too long or
too short

Flat strong loins

Powerful hind quarters

Barrel, deep with
well-sprung ribs.

Limbs correct length
for body. Big joints
that are well-defined.

These angulations and distances determine the lever action of the limb and the flexor tendon lengths required, and the possible over-stresses which can be exerted on them.

These should all be re-assessed at the walk, the trot in-hand and to a lesser extent at the ridden trot on a 20m circle and wider, and on softer going at the canter past the observer and round him both ways. In all gaits the horse should be assessed seen coming to, going past and going away, to ascertain how well the static conformation and the related condition blend dynamically to give an impression of 'going' in balance and self-carriage. These gaits and movements are also used at 'vetting'.

CONFORMATION TO AVOID
Some deviations in conformation are said to be detrimental to athleticism and can be associated with lameness:

Too big a head and/or **too long a neck:** Gives an overweighted counter-balancing beam leading to the horse becoming 'heavy on the forehand'.

Too heavy on the forehand: As an anatomical feature and only indirectly related to a similar dynamism associated with equitation faults. There is a difficulty in balance and self-carriage putting the horse in a 'downhill position', whereas the impression of 'going uphill' is to be preferred whereby greater engagement of the hindlegs becomes possible with less overstress placed on the forelimbs.

Too upright a shoulder: This through the usually constant shoulder-joint angle brings the elbow back over the thorax and hence the abaxial limb is 'set under'. This can result in problems: unless the back is proportionately lengthened, the fore and the hindlimbs are brought closer together to make for unbalancing and/or limb interference. Also, along with the usually upright pastern the overall straightness predisposes to a jarring action unpleasant for the rider and concussive for the horse; the open angles lose their suspensive effect.

If the pastern hoof axis does not hereditably parallel this or, most especially, if a farrier's attempts to make a 'better' pastern line by hoof trimming throws it out of the parallel, then the asymmetry of the proximal and distal limb angles can inflict additional stresses to those of the basic fault.

The 'too sloping shoulder': This, and the similar angle of the hoof pastern axis to parallel it, will improve shock absorption but tends to throw a greater stress on the palmar (posterior) stay and suspensory apparati including the suspensory ligament and the superficial flexor tendon. Where there is a lack of parallelism and the pastern is upright, once again the asymmetry can lead to insecurity of footfall. Such will be the case if the parallel pastern is associated with a broken forward hoof pastern axis.

'Back at the knee': In the asymmetric gaits particularly, the leading foreleg when in the stance phase of the stride is functionally put into this position. Horses which are genetically developed to be bilaterally back at the knee or acquire this aberrant conformation in one limb as the result of excessive contra-lateral weightbearing, are more likely to be dangerously back of the knee in locomotion. In all cases the deformity is functionally liable to induce over-stress on:

- The accessory carpal bone and its ligmental/tendinous attachments.
- The proximal and the distal check ligaments.
- The superficial flexor tendon.

27

'Sickle-hock': The overbent hindleg, known as 'sickle hocked', leads to a weakness in hock joint stability and a greater strain on the plantar (posterior) ligament at the back of the hock joint which is more liable to strain and form a curb.

'Cow-hock': An often associated inward deviation of the hock, 'cow-hocked', throws greater stress on the medial aspect of the hock predisposing to arthritis of the small bones of that joint – a spavin. The hooves are set apart, splayed, with diminishing ground contact security.

'Upward fixation of the patella': There is argument if the conformation of an overstraight hindleg predisposes to this functional condition. It is possible that since it develops in the maturing horse and particularly one beginning work, that that animal passes through a temporary phase of being upright. Certainly attention to corrective hoof trimming and the use of special shoes with built-up heels do help to ameliorate the severity of the condition during the time that the horse requires to build up muscular power. In some cases surgery, by section of the medial patellar ligament, removes the likelihood of this being over-secured on the thigh bone knuckle which is the basic mechanics of the condition. Most, but not all, horses 'grow out of' this disorder.

NOTE: Farrier help is required for these conditions that can lead to lameness.

The description 'too' is not very definitive and begs the question 'what is ideal?' and how far from ideal is 'too far' with the inferred risk of over-stress? It can be measured in individual cases but even then the assessment of the discrepancy, if any, is really only subjective. In the past, static assessment has suggested that 'ideal' columns of support are those which follow a plumb line from proximal points to ground level at mid hoof. A horse with four such limbs should have a straight (relatively stress-free, interference-free) action, provided the limbs are not 'too' far apart or 'too' close together. Therefore, even with 'ideal' guidelines, the assessment of conformation becomes subjective and based on the success of many horses in work with these 'good' specifications.

One diagram in particular is misleading and that is the line of the plantar (back) aspect of the hindleg: if the stifle, the hock and the fetlock do not face forward and outward, thus making the hoof land and stand slightly toe-ed out, then that limb would not clear the abdomen. It does not mean that the vertical line of the limb should be sloping; the actual line or column of support between the joints must be straight to give maximum support.

A straight, open-angled stifle and its reciprocating hock is beneficial to the sprint racehorse but, in some horses, with not quite good enough alignment of the knee cap with the distal femur, it may predispose to upward fixation of the patella (UFP).

A slight increase in hock flexion (and synchronised stifle) is beneficial to the jumper and to the draught horse as it does increase the potential for 'engaging' the hindlegs. A sickle-hock conformation, which to the layman can resemble the above ideal hock flexion, can be associated with cow hock; if this combination or even the 'sickle' on its own accompanies a narrow hock joint above an overlong canon then there is a great potential for other over-stress of the joint and the associated ligaments as well as the tendons above and below.

Limb deviations can be inherited or acquired. Both can lead to DOD with poor flight action and possible interferences of one limb with another, as well as causing deficits in ground support security.

A further effect of limb deviation would be on the hoof capsule related to 'mass x speed = weight' and downward gravity force, and on ground firmness and upward reaction force. Deformity of the hoof capsule would affect functioning and blood supply of the distal joint and structured integrity, and also security of footfall. This can be corrected by farriery, but it takes time.

It is to these admittedly often slow to develop (perhaps over several shoeings) hoof defects that the horsemaster, along with the farrier, should pay particular attention. The toe-ed in and the toe-ed out horse becomes a greater liability, if it is the result of poor trimming-acquired defects, which often result from a farrier not being given sufficient time for good work but rather being used as a less expensive shoeing smith. If it is a case of an inherited conformation, there is the risk of overstress when attempts are made to correct these natural deviations purely for cosmetic reasons. In all situations, and especially the above, the hoof must be trimmed to follow the 'column of limb support'.

The relative lengths of the various areas of the thoracico-lumbar sacral spine are said to be important influences not only in locomotion but also in pathological disorders arising.

As a guideline, it is emphasised that:

- A long back with a 'loose' loin is a weakness which carries the risk of soft tissue over-stress even if it is beneficial for freedom of movement in certain disciplines.
- A short back with a strong loin, suitable for jumping, tends towards over-stress of the bony spine; a power over-stress rather than the laxity of the long back.

A variety of action disorders, from limb lameness to 'wrong in the back' as in the acute stages of any associated morbidity and to loss of action or a vague stiffness in the more chronic phases of either of these disorders can develop. Where there are bony changes the morbidity is much more serious.

Distal limb deviations including those of the hoof, are seen at stance or in motion when viewed from in front, from behind and laterally; they can lead to traumatic limb interferences and to deficits in stance support and lift-off. These changes are often subtle and require the diagnosis and advice of joint farrier-veterinary attention. Failure to recognise and to treat those deficits which lead to support weakness can also invoke over-stress of the ligaments and joint surfaces in the three distal areas.

Reference again to conformation and the suggestion that a 'square profile' and the ratios of point measurements within, draw attention to the fact that deviations could cause over-stresses induced by the horse being out of balance or by the subsequent counter-balancing actions. Certainly the units of locomotion both axial and abaxial can develop compensatory action, but the basic weakness will remain; such cannot be anatomically corrected, nor in themselves are they susceptible to a variety of therapies. Some of the effects of the imbalances, such as muscle spasm and units of locomotion tension, can respond to a variety of complementary disciplines, but in the long run such lack of basic balance can preclude maximum performance and certainly will require good equestrianism.

No scientific work has yet been authenticated to prove that certain conformation, in part or in whole, is linked clearly to a horse's success in its chosen discipline. The morphology of breeds and types obviously catalogues them as draught, racing, long distance etc., but within these, 'handsome is as handsome does'. 'Expert' opinion on poor conformation is frequently justified not so much on ability as on durability i.e. susceptibility of certain conformation defects to the effects of (repeated) competition stress – the cumulative over-stresses of concussion, compression and stretches.

A description, now somewhat outmoded, which was 'sound in eyes, heart, wind and action', placed the emphass on sound, meaning free from morbidity. With regard to wind it referred to degenerative disorders of the throat (dorsal displacement of the soft palate) and the larynx (recurrent laryngeal neuropathy – paresis of the glottis) as the two major problems. Their presence would interfere with air flow. Conformation-wise this all-important airflow naturally in the horse was a reflection of the diameter of the larynx, which in turn reflected the space between the upright rami of the mandibles. This bony conformation is an inherited feature of the horse. Its measurement is critical in the galloping horse even if variable by only a centimetre.

SOME EQUINE BIODYNAMICS

Security of stance or at footfall's ground support phase is obtained by an interlocking of joint/ligament structures. In the foreleg, the extension lock in both fores at stance cannot be released until the average 60% bodyweight load normally on the forehand is reduced by a lifting of the head and the neck, whereby some of this weight is transferred caudally. This lock is then released unilaterally by the horse lifting the heels to initiate flexion up the limb and so permit subsequent elevation and protraction of it. The other forelimb can then follow after the diagonal hindleg steps forward.

The extended 'lock' position of all four limbs is called 'at the halt' for which postural muscles are much involved to augment the bone/ligament interlocking.

In the 'at rest' stance in which the head and neck is supported by the very strong neck ligament, the ligamentum nuchae, the bodyweight falls forward over the forehand inducing full extension and locking of the forelimbs from the elbow inclusive downwards. This mechanical position spares the muscle effort of all of the posturals. During this posture the hindlegs alternately utilise the stifle hock interlocking mechanism which involves the 'hooking up' of the patella on the distal thigh bone to bear weight with minimal muscle effort and almost complete relaxation of the other hindleg which bears nominal weight on the tip of its toe. They swap position at regular short intervals. It is the stay and suspensory apparati of all the limbs but particularly that of the fore that play a major role in this specific ability.

The foreleg has no bony articulation with the spine nor with the breast bone, i.e. it has no collar bone, but the manner in which the trunk is suspended between the shoulder blades, supported by the extensive ligamental content of the muscles of that region, compensates. The hindleg, of course, does have a bony connection to the spine at the sacro liliac (functionally non-mobile) articulation.

In dynamic situations the foreleg extension lock mechanism plays a big part in the security of footfall particularly at the asymmetric gaits and at landing after jumping. The distal joints and in particular the fetlock are released from this lock by the co-ordinated action of the flexor/extensor muscles and are 'let down' first to absorb concussion and secondly to build up kinetic energy for lift-off.

It is essential that a horse landing from a jump makes contact with one foreleg fractionally ahead of the other to allow lift-off of the first from footfall security before the second foreleg takes over. Failure to do this will result in a full extension lock of both limbs causing the horse to pitch forward on to its nose.

In work, the horse minimises the time of onset of fatigue by 'gear shifts'. Thus from walk to trot to gallop. Within this last asymmetric gait the speed is usually reduced to that called canter. Further minimising is obtained by the horse's ability to 'change leads' in the asymmetric gaits, thus alternating the different stresses implicit in the leading and trailing foreleg.

When a horse starts to lie down, it instinctively circles the area tightly with intermittent half flexions of the limbs and rising again, before almost flopping down – usually with a grunt. The four legs remain flexed up beneath it momentarily before it leans on to one side or the other. The underneath hindleg stays slightly flexed 'up'; so, too, may the underneath foreleg or it can be extended out in front of the body. The upper legs are variably extended laterally or flexed.

The head can be held up or it can be rested in a downward position either suspended by the neck ligament or, occasionally, with the chin resting on the ground. It may turn the head and neck sideways to allow the head to rest on the horse's chest or flank. These various postures in the semi-upright position are known as sternal recumbency.

From the above position the horse can lean right over so that it is resting on one side of its neck, forehand, trunk and quarter with all four legs extended outwards. This is lateral recumbency.

Deep sleep can be obtained in either posture. It is more common in the young animal but it is the least safe of all resting positions because it takes longer for the horse to get to its feet. The duration of lateral recumbency is controlled physiologically by pressures within the vascular system, particularly of the chest, to avoid congestion of the underside lung. A horse can be stimulated out of this flat-out position by vibrations from the ground as well as by 'noises off'.

By a system of reflex movements beginning in the semi-circular canals of the ear and followed by reflexes in the neck, legs and trunk, the horse rises forehand first into a dog sitting position. (The quicker and the higher the head gets the better it is to see and hear potential danger signs.) It then propels itself to its feet by hindleg action in a rather ungainly fashion which propels it forward on to its forehand, oblivious to any humans nearby who must look out for themselves. The mare with foal at foot is much more careful.

The various self-locking mechanisms play other important roles in locomotion.

In the hindleg the stifle/hock reciprocal ligaments stabilise these two joints into a more or less rigid single lever to maximise propulsive force in these limbs. Apart from the rise and fall of the fetlock and the radial movement of the hip joint, the hindleg works like the spoke of a wheel to reach forward for a footfall prior to propulsion which takes place after the limb passes the vertical position.

In the foreleg the 'freedom' given by the non-bony connections in the shoulder blades allows the muscular girdles of that area to act as effective shock absorbers to assist those of the stay suspensory apparati. Importantly, the freedom also allows a sweeping movement of the shoulder blade over the sides of the thorax whereby the stride length can be increased to absorb the increasing propulsive efforts of the hindlegs to produce an acceleration.

The contraction of a flexor muscle usually causes a joint to close up or to flex. It is the pull via a tendon on to a distal bone which induces the lever movement.

The extensor muscle gives in a steady progressive fashion until flexion is obtained to the stretch force on it. It then takes over reversely to open or extend the joint if required. On 'footfall with support' both muscles exert a balancing effect on each other to effect a 'hold' or stability on the various abaxial joints for a limb support phase. The related joints are then said to be in the position of maximum stability.

As said above, muscle force is relayed via its tendon which inserts into the bone distal to the joint to be moved. All tendons have an element of elasticity or stretch. In a horse's superficial flexor tendon this feature permits about a 4ins stretch when the horse bears weight on that leg during faster asymmetric gaits. This stretch absorbs a kinetic energy which, when tension is relaxed, recoils or crimps up to its normal length, thus inducing a lift into the distal joints of that leg and so playing a part in the propulsive effort of the foreleg.

A tendon in its passage over a joint area is held in juxtaposition to the flexion surface of the joint by an annular ligament. Its movement there is through a tendon sheath filled with lubricating synovial fluid. In some situations a tendon on passing over a bony promontory is cushioned by a synovial filled bursa lying between it and the bone.

The joint, and the related tendons and their sheaths and ligaments, are known as units of locomotion. In the limbs they are seen as vital areas because their synovias are prone to penetrating wounds.

SECTION II

CHOOSING AND BUYING

1. Where to Look
2. What to Look For
3. Guide to Types
4. Understanding the Advertisement
5. The Questionnaire
6. Pre-Purchase Examination
7. Step by Step Summary of Buying
8. Insuring your horse
9. Time to Let Go

1. WHERE TO LOOK

When you are sure you have got the time, the money, the energy and the commitment required to own a horse, there are several ways of starting the search:
- Look for advertisements in local newspapers, tack shops, feed merchants and the equestrian press. Consider placing your own 'wanted' advertisement.
- Word of mouth.
- Professional dealer.
- Local yards and riding schools.
- Studs, if you want a particular breed or type.
- Sale rings, markets and auctions (not recommended for first-time buyers).
- Rescue centres – if you can trust your heart not to rule your head, and accept that many of the animals will have suffered physical or psychological trauma.

NOTE: If you do business with a private vendor, remember that your rights as a consumer are not protected in the same way as they are when you buy from a professional. Horses from a professional yard may be slightly more expensive, but you should be paying for a better service and they are likely to come with some sort of satisfaction guarantee. The prospective purchaser would be wise to acquaint themselves with the legal aspects and warranties concerned with making this type of purchase.

2. WHAT TO LOOK FOR

Horses come in all shapes, sizes and colours, and the breed or type you choose is down to personal preference and your individual requirements.

All breeds fall into three separate categories depending on the horse's origin: hot bloods, warm bloods and cold bloods. Hot bloods are of Oriental or Eastern origin, and are typified by the Arabian, Thoroughbred and Anglo-Arab. Cold bloods are the farm workers, bred for size, strength and pulling power, and often make kind and docile riding horses. Warm bloods are a mixture of the two, and should exhibit the good points of both.

As a rule, hot bloods such as Thoroughbreds and Arabs are fast, alert, responsive to training, have good stamina, plenty of spirit and are excellent for adding quality when crossed with other breeds. However, they may be temperamental, sensitive and less robust than other breeds. They are generally not suitable for beginners.

The heavier warmblood type is renowned for its more extravagant paces and powerful jump; it doesn't have the Thoroughbred's speed or alertness but is strong, calm, bold and highly trainable.

There are numerous native and pony breeds which are even-tempered, sure-footed, tough and intelligent, although with a tendency to laziness and weight gain. Cross breeds will have a mixture of characteristics which hopefully reflect the qualities of both parents while minimising their faults. Many of the horses you look at will not be pure-bred – but don't allow unknown parentage to put you off!

Remember, these are broad generalisations and each horse must be looked at as an individual. In your search for the perfect horse you may well find plenty of fat, lazy Thoroughbreds and sensitive, highly strung cobs!

PREPARING TO LOOK

Before you go anywhere near a horse, you will need to sit down with a piece of paper and consider the following.

1. **Your size and weight**
    You must look and feel right on the horse, and it must be physically capable of carrying you in whichever equestrian activities you wish to pursue. It is the build, not the height of the horse, which reflects its weight-carrying ability. A short, stocky type with a good width of bone and muscular back, neck and quarters, such as a cob or native breed, can carry more weight than a tall, spindly Thoroughbred. Your shape will also dictate whether you feel more comfortable on a broad or narrow horse, and the depth of the horse's barrel must suit your leg length.
2. **Your ability and level of experience**
    Don't make the mistake of 'over-horsing' yourself. It will stop you enjoying horse-ownership to the full and may well damage your confidence into the bargain. Generally speaking, 'hot-blooded' types such as Thoroughbreds and

Arabs do not have temperaments suitable for beginners. 'Cold-blooded' types, on the other hand, do not have the speed and athleticism required in a competition horse.

3. **Stable management routine**

    Before you start looking, you need to know where and how you are going to keep your horse, as this will influence the type you buy and the maintenance costs involved. For instance, owing to their desert ancestry, 'hot-blooded' horses are thin-skinned and fine-coated, which means they need extra feed, care and possibly stabling in winter; whereas the robust and hardy native type which has adapted to survive in a colder, tougher climate, should deal better with adverse weather conditions. See Section II for advice on livery options and appropriate stable management.

4. **Future plans**

    The horse must have the ability to match your ambitions, but beware of buying one which is over-qualified. As well as the possibilities of the horse growing bored and not realising its full potential, any points or prize money accumulated with previous owners may exclude you from the more novice classes that suit your riding ability.

5. **Your budget**

    A well-bred, good-quality horse will be expensive, as is any well-mannered animal who is reasonably schooled and has a good temperament. Cheap horses are invariably a false economy, unless you are very experienced and prepared to take the risk. On the other hand, a sentimental owner may place a higher price on their horse than its actual market value, so study advertisements in newspapers and the equestrian press to get a realistic idea of prices. As well as the actual purchase price (and VAT), you need to allow for the considerable cost of kitting a horse out with suitable tack and clothing.

6. **Age**

    For 'age', read 'experience' – which also depends on the horse's level of training. A well-schooled five-year-old could bring you more pleasure than a green eight-year-old. Likewise, you could have years of fun ahead of you with a sound teenage horse who knows the ropes. Or you may seek the rewards of backing and bringing on your own youngster, in which case you need a horse between weaning and three years of age. See 'The age factor' below.

7. **Sex**

    Mares or geldings are the horses most commonly used for riding. Which you choose is largely a matter of personal preference, unless the mare is a particularly good one and you intend to breed. However, some mares can be 'hormonal' at certain times of the month which can affect their performance, while geldings are usually credited with being more consistent. There are obvious complications with the management of stallions, which should not be taken on lightly. Although stallions can make intelligent and talented riding horses in the right hands, it is probably best to stick to a mare or gelding unless you are very experienced or plan to breed.

8. **Colour**

    Generally a secondary consideration for most people looking for a fun horse. However, for showing purposes a breed society may specify which colours are acceptable. Other people may actively seek an unusually coloured or marked horse, such as the piebald, skewbald, palomino, Appaloosa or Pinto, which have their own showing and competition classes.

THE AGE FACTOR – FURTHER CONSIDERATIONS

YOUNG HORSES

Tempting though it is to buy something 'unspoilt', young horses and novice owners are an unwise combination. Breaking in a youngster is not easy (although some horses are easier than others), and the problem pages of equestrian publications are full of the horror stories and bad experiences of people who have failed to heed this advice.

However much you like the idea of bringing up your own baby, the fact is that youngsters are best handled, ridden and trained by experienced people. The horse's future value and happiness depend on getting a good start in life, and it will gain an enormous amount from confident, competent riding in the early days. Your confidence and safety as a rider are also at stake if you take on a young horse which is obviously going to be less predictable, obedient and balanced than a trained horse.

Having said all that, someone who lacks experience or technical brilliance as a rider but has the time, patience and confidence to make up for it, could well make a good job of bringing on a young horse, particularly if the animal were fairly co-operative, trusting and relaxed by nature.

If you definitely plan to take on a young horse, ask yourself if:

- You are doing it for the right reasons. Even though you won't have other people's mistakes to put right, having a blank page to work on is not always an advantage. An impressionable youngster is a great responsibility. What if you simply teach it all your bad habits, or allow the horse to get away with something that later blows up into a serious behavioural problem?
- You can afford the hidden extras. A young horse may be less expensive initially, but may well cost more in the long term, by the time you've paid its upkeep for a couple of years, provided it with new tack and clothing, had extra lessons, etc.
- You have enough time. Everything takes longer with a youngster and it must be taught to do all the things you take for granted with an older horse – tie up, lead correctly, stand for shoeing and clipping, wear rugs and other items of horse clothing, load into a horsebox or trailer easily, etc. – in addition to ridden schooling.
- The horse's temperament suits you. Some youngsters are more flighty and difficult than others, and no amount of training will change their character.
- You accept it may be years before you can enjoy your horse to the full.
- You have the right type of experience. Ten years of weekly riding lessons does not mean you have ten years of experience with youngsters! You should have ridden and handled a number of different and more challenging horses.
- You are committed to being an effective, sympathetic trainer. There are some particular training tips about how and when to train a young horse in Section V.

OLDER HORSES

These have a lot to recommend them and just because a horse is well into its teens, it should not be dismissed – provided the horse is sound enough to do the work you require. Older horses are considerably cheaper than those in their prime, yet many work hard and compete happily into their twenties and beyond. They can be priceless in terms of giving confidence and having fun.

However, the price of experience is that they need the greater care and attention due to any older animal. Like a car, their soundness and reliability really depends on how well they have been looked after over the years and how many miles there are on the clock! They may be less resilient to changing ground and weather conditions, take longer to get fit and be slower to recover from injury or exertion. You must also consider whether it is fair or even possible to sell the horse on in a few years time when it is older still, or whether you have the facilities to keep the horse in retirement. With an ex-competition horse, check it is not over-qualified for the level of competition you wish to compete at. If the horse has won points in affiliated competition, you may have to pay to downgrade it or compete 'hors concours'.

3. GUIDE TO TYPES

While it is unwise to generalise, certain types and breeds have definite characteristics which act as a guide to help you find a suitable horse. The more highly strung and temperamental a horse is, the more sensitive, skilled handling it requires. Its work and stable routine must be carefully managed to prevent undesirable behaviour arising from boredom or frustration, and your riding ability must be up to the challenge.

The starting point when choosing a horse is to decide which physical type will be suited to the work you intend to do, then judge each individual animal on its temperament when the time comes.

Hunter: This is a type, not a breed, and for show purposes there are three different categories – light, medium and heavy weight. This refers to the amount of weight that a horse is capable of carrying for a day cross country, judged by the thickness of the bone below the knee.

Cob: The stocky, short-legged cob should be between 14.2hh and 15.1hh, with quality as well as weight-carrying ability. They are reputed to be sensible, generous types and are usually comfortable rides.

Mountain and Moorland: Britain's nine native pony breeds are described collectively as 'Mountain and Moorland' breeds, and their physical hardiness and good temperament make them a popular choice.

Riding horse: Riding horses fall into two basic categories – small (between 14.2hh and 15.2hh) and large (over 15.2hh). They need to be well schooled, good movers and suitable for anyone to ride out.

Hack: Hacks also come in two categories – small (between 14.2hh and 15hh) and large (between 15hh and 15.3hh). The hack must not only be a pleasure to ride, but a pleasure to look at. They need good conformation, action and presence, as well as impeccable manners both in-hand and under saddle.

Driving: Whilst any horse can be broken to harness, a number of breeds are particularly adept in terms of action and temperament. The Cleveland Bay, Welsh Cob and Hackney are regularly seen between the shafts depending on the type of class.

Sports horse: This is a recognised type, and is a horse bred to suit the requirements of the serious competitor. It may not be pure-bred but is generally from a long line of talented performers, with a high percentage of Thoroughbred blood.

Family all-rounder: The assumption is that such a horse is well-schooled and gentle enough to be safe for the smaller members of the family, yet has sufficient weight-carrying ability for an adult male. The actual breed is not important, but it is likely that such a horse will have native or cob blood.

4. UNDERSTANDING THE ADVERTISEMENT

Most of the descriptions used in advertisements are obvious; for example, a 'Riding Club all-rounder' would be a horse ideally suited to all Riding Club activities. You may also see 'perfect first pony', 'event prospect', 'ride and drive' etc. By law, the horse must match the description given. For instance, the 'ideal first pony' should be suitable for a young child in terms of size and temperament. Some descriptions are less obvious; for example, 'in training' refers to a horse which has been specifically prepared for commercial racing, while a horse which has come 'out of training' is one which has left the racing industry. An inexperienced horse may be described as 'green', while one which has been 'lightly backed' has only had a preliminary introduction to saddle and rider, and should not be considered to be properly broken. Where a competition horse is advertised, any prize money or points won in affiliated competition may be listed to give the buyer some idea of the horse's current standard and potential. If a horse has particularly impressive breeding to make it a more attractive or valuable prospect, these bloodlines may also be mentioned. A horse is said to be 'by' the father and 'out of' the mother, e.g. 'Two year-old filly by Tempest out of Quality Street'.

5. THE QUESTIONNAIRE

Prospective purchasers have always asked searching questions of the seller. The more experienced the buyer, the more exacting the questions and the better the interpretation of the answers by him/her and/or a veterinary surgeon if involved.

The experienced buyer and especially the novice purchaser, even with help, is well advised to have a (checklist) questionnaire. The answers, whether complete nor not, should always be signed as a warranty of the horse's present temperament and behaviour and of its history regarding any disease of structure and/or functioning from the past. Such a warranty is particularly important if the vendor is not a dealer.

The veterinary surgeon will welcome these answers in advance of a pre-purchase examination by him. American veterinarians are strongly advised to obtain a Seller's Statement and a Purchaser's Statement. These broadly equate with the British Questionnaire as well as providing the pertinent facts from the prospective purchaser, albeit the latter is usually in note form rather than signed for. In the USA both documents should be with the veterinarian *before* he examines the horse.

RELEVANT QUESTIONS

There are certain diseases which do not lead to clinical signs discernible within the remit of the vet's examination or may not be otherwise suspected, such as those which are seasonally or intermittently recurrent and so potentially worrying, and others which leave no clinical clues once 'healed to all intents and purposes'. Some may have been 'forgotten' by the dealer, not thought important or not known of by him.

Moreover, the vet's professional opinion on eyes, the heart and on hoof balances must be such as to make up for a dealer/vendor's possible but understandable lack of expertise in these features. A comprehensive warranty with specific answers is of valuable assistance, especially if any future legal action is required. Much more so if the vendor is 'private'.

Established unwanted behaviour patterns can be blanked out during the 'adrenaline flow' of the examination; the so-called stable vices (stereotypes) can be automatically suppressed during the same period when the horse's attention is otherwise engaged.

Opinions differ as to the effect of a 'vice'. Many horses crib and wind-suck for example without apparent detrimental effect. When it comes to putting them into livery or to resale not everyone is so understanding or tolerant. The seller must answer the relevant specific questions accurately. Their appearance after purchase becomes legally important only if it can be proved that the amateur 'seller' knew of their existence. The dealer also must be asked these pertinent questions because stereotypes do not fall within a dealer's responsibility to declare. It must be appreciated that with regard to stereotypes the warranty is to the effect that the vendor is stating that the horse has not displayed such 'faults' to date – a history of freedom from them – not that the horse will never do so.

This questionnaire is not intended to be definitive or conclusive; the questions are guidelines which, in the authors' experience, cover most of the post-sale difficulties, not just the specific veterinary ones. It is a legal answer to legitimate questions about 'goods for sale', and a living one at that!

A veterinary surgeon is not responsible for:

* Obtaining warranties.
* Discussing valuation – except in extremes which, if not commented upon, could be construed as neglect.
* The horse's ridability – unless he is aware of potentially dangerous traits in the horse or of serious deficiencies in the rider when seen riding the horse, failure to comment upon which could again be construed as neglect.
* The horse's innate, trainable and trained ability to perform any discipline.

The aim is not only to establish warrantable historical facts as a background to the present pre-purchase examination but also to remove the vendor/purchaser responsibilities from the veterinary surgeon: on the day he is required only to ascertain any present medical and physical defects and to prognose on them vis à vis the declared use and future aspirations by a known purchaser and/or rider.

At the initial discussion it is essential for the prospective purchaser to ask the questions listed below. The implication of missing answers can be discussed by the veterinary surgeon and the prospective purchaser before the pre-purchase examination.

The signed answers form a warranty. This record can be useful to the seller as well as to the buyer in any dispute regarding the horse's subsequent capability and fitness to do what the buyer clearly explained to the vendor, viz. that at the time of the purchase it had no known history which would render it possibly unsuitable.

A SAMPLE QUESTIONNAIRE
SECTION 1
1. Name and address of legal owner plus telephone number.
2. If applicable, name and address of agent.
3. Address of stables where horse can be seen and tried.
4. Name and address of previous owner.
5. How long in present ownership?
6. Breeding details and records if known, including any passport or identification documents.
7. Reason for sale.
8. Past use/work of the horse.
9. Present use/work of the horse.
10. Is it fit enough to be strongly exercised?
11. When last shod and is it shod at present?
12. Has it any HTA points, BSJA winnings etc.?
13. Is it insured now and for what?
14. Has it ever been refused cover?
15. Has 'loss of use' been paid on it?

Most of these can be answered at the initial phone-call if the conversation is with someone in authority, or later if not, along with Section 2.

Section 2 need not be answered until the horse has been seen and tried but the vendor should be told in advance what the questions will be.

A signature will be required for both parts.

SECTION 2
The important part of the warranty.
16. Name and freeze brand, if any, of horse. Registered name and number, if any.
17. Description.
18. Prospective purchaser's intention of use.
19. Any reason why this horse is possibly not suitable for that purpose.
20. Any legal/official facts to prevent it competing under any discipline rules.
21. Has it ever suffered any recurring lameness or disease or any seasonal disorder?
    For example:
* Allergic respiratory distress.
* Bouts of colic.
* Laminitis.
* 'Set fast' (ER).

- Sweet itch.
- Head-shaking.
- Others, including any food allergies, hypersensitivity to drugs and vaccines.

22. Has it been subjected to any surgery?
23. If a mare, has she bred?
24. Could she be in foal now?
25. Does she cycle regularly and/or is she difficult when in season?
26. Has it received any medication during the last month? If so why, and for what?
27. Vaccination status and worm programme.
28. On the ground, is the horse easy to
- Groom, clip, prepare?
- Tack up, shoe?
- Lead in-hand?
- Load and transport?
- Catch in field and stable?

29. Is it aggressive to
- People?
- Other animals?
- Property?

30. When ridden, has it been known to
- Bolt?
- Seriously buck?
- Rear?
- Roll?
- Nap?

31. Bitting used.
32. Is it traffic-shy in-hand or under saddle?
33. Stereotypes (vices): – has it been seen to
- Crib-bite and/or wind-suck?
- Box-walk?
- Weave?
- 'Flank' at self or its blankets?
- Kick the walls?
- Tail rub?
- Gnaw woodwork regularly?

34. Signature of seller/owners.
35. Date signed.

6. PRE-PURCHASE EXAMINATION

Though not compulsory, when considering the purchase of a particular horse, it has become common practice to enlist a veterinary surgeon to carry out the 5-stage Veterinary Examination on behalf of the prospective purchaser – the Pre-Purchase Examination (PPE). In the USA a vetting is called a Purchase Examination. There is considerable similarity in the two countries' requirements. Both relevant advisory bodies stress that the examination should follow a non-dictatorial pattern or protocol which should be explained

to the purchaser and to the seller. Also, exclusion of one or more parts of the recommended five stages must be noted, together with the reasons why, in writing. There are a few minor variations in the methods of examining and of documenting findings, especially for 'in file' records. Both authorities emphasise that they are not giving exact instructions for the work on the day; such, it is rightly argued, could be detrimental. Each veterinary surgeon will have his own techniques based on experience, although the aim is the same. Differences in getting the correct information must not be seen as, or be usable as, potential points of litigation.

Basically, the pre-purchase examination consists of a series of clinical appraisals of the overt signs of the structure and functioning of all the systems of the body – in which the vet hopes to find no disorders – as evinced at:

- Rest.
- The walk and the trot in-hand.
- Strenuous, exerting but not exhausting, ridden (or driven) exercise.
- Subsequent exercise recovery period and a period of rest.
- A second walk and trot examination and more detailed examination of the feet.

If, however, some disorders are detected, these will be considered by the veterinary surgeon in the light of the expressed requirements for that horse's future use (and of the purchaser's admitted experience and ability), regarding their potentially detrimental effects. He will then give his opinion as to the horse's suitability from a veterinary aspect and record all his findings in the certificate – an identifiable document regarding the horse and the veterinary surgeon.

The examination is to establish veterinary faults regarding the state of the horse's health and its physical ability as determined on the day, but with a reasonably long forecast if used as declared.

Case law has ruled out the use of the long-established statement 'this horse is sound' (and so suitable for purchase). Such a state is finite and is incapable of incontrovertible assessment by overt clinical examination (what can be detected from the outside!).

It is not ideal to use the phrases 'pass' or 'fail', although in the mind of both the vendor and the purchaser, the more acceptable descriptions 'satisfactory' and 'not satisfactory' carry these implications. Legally, there are important differences. A horse can be judged as 'satisfactory to purchase' only if:

(a) No defects likely to be detrimental have been identified, or
(b) Any defects as noted are, *on the balance of probability*, not likely to prejudice the animal's declared future use within the declared limitations of the new rider.

This will be explained and discussed with the purchaser. The balance of probability is a recognised method of helping the purchaser decide to purchase, despite there being an element of risk. The professional opinion or prognosis can never be accurately quantified. The horse is to be used physically, i.e. exposed to athletic hazards, and one with certain defects is more at risk than one without them. The probability of a relapse or a recurring trauma on an already damaged tissue increases with the severity of the athleticism and to some extent with the rider's horsemanship. The veterinarian's opinion will be set accordingly.

If insurance cover is required, underwriters will seek the advice of their veterinary adviser who, from a distance, might not be quite so tolerant. It is important to realise that insurance companies require the examining veterinary surgeon's *opinion of the horse* and not of its suitability for insurance cover; that is their decision. In disputed cases negotiation between the two veterinarians will occur and, if necessary and feasible, conditions can be temporarily placed on the policy cover.

The veterinary surgeon must not be expected to give his opinion that this horse 'is lame because...' It is either lame or not. It would be natural for him to wish to diagnose the cause, but ethically that is a matter for the vendor's veterinary surgeon. There is no obligation to discuss even his unqualified opinion with the vendor unless his client's permission to do so is given. He can qualify the opinion only to his client and thereby suggest if continuing interest in the horse is worthwhile.

If so, a further transaction can be negotiated if and when a diagnosis and a satisfactory prognosis is given on the original defect. However, a further full pre-purchase examination usually by the original veterinary surgeon will be necessary for a 5-stage certificate. There are variations in this which the purchaser can select but these are a matter for discussion (and underwriters' consultation if relevant).

In most situations, and usually to the satisfaction of both the parties, a blood sample will be taken for examination for non-normal-nutrients: active drugs which could mask lameness and misleadingly alter the signs of other conditions, for nefarious purposes. A decision for immediate laboratory investigation may be made. A 'hold' sample – when reasonable work at the buyer's premises is carried out until the effect of the drug has worn off and the suspected hidden condition, if any, is revealed – is an alternative agreement.

The question of ancillary aids carried out by the purchaser's veterinary surgeon must be decided between all the parties. It must be remembered that one-time positive radiological and ultrasonographical findings are historical facts and do not accurately foretell what will happen with ongoing work. (Radiographs in particular can be confusing, even misleading.) With expensive horses underwriters may request these tests as a routine. The cost of replacing shoes removed for radiography is the responsibility of the prospective purchaser whether the horse is bought or not.

It is, on occasion, helpful to use blood samples (with the vendor's permission) for:
- Haematological appraisal for the presence of certain sub-clinical diseases.
- Metabolic profiling for functional (physiological) disturbances.

Other samples may be taken from skin, bowel and airway as considered necessary.

The veterinary surgeon has a duty of 'care' for the
- Purchaser — moral and legal
- Horse — moral and professional
- Vendor — moral only

when he
(i) Carries out a competent, diligent and thorough 5-stage examination, and
(ii) Completes the certificate in which he
(iii) Gives an unbiased opinion, having taken into consideration the purchaser's expressed hopes and the vendor's warranties and/or condition of the contract. He will discuss his opinion with the purchaser (his client) and, if necessary, any insurance underwriters involved, before the transaction is completed.

PREPARATION

The 5-stages should not be arranged until the examining veterinarian has been assured that:

1. The horse is suitable and physically fit to be examined in-hand and at ridden (or driven) exercise.
2. It has no intercurrent disease as far as is known to the vendor.
3. It is well trimmed and shod within the last 3-4 weeks.
4. A competent handler/rider will be available, suitably hatted and booted (and similarly for a driver and a vehicle or simulator).
5. There are suitable facilities, which are namely:
- A box which can be darkened.
- A flat hard area of about 30m x 6m for in-hand trotting.
- A non-slip softer area of 20m diameter for trotting in a circle in-hand.
- A suitable exercising area where the horse can be exerted at the asymmetric gaits.
6. The vendor or a suitable agent will be present.
7. Preferably but not necessarily, the purchaser will be present as well. If not, where and when possible, that person should be in telephone contact to discuss any opinion before the veterinary surgeon leaves the premises and, with permission, possibly to advise the vendor.

The horse should have been stabled overnight and given its last feed two hours previous to the arranged visit time and the haynet removed at the same time. It may be groomed but its feet should not be oiled. It should be left in its box.

The actual clinical examination is effected:
- Visually including ophthalmoscopic viewing of the eye.
- By touch for contour, consistency and temperature changes and for (painful) reaction to digital pressure on and 'through' the skin. Hoof testers will be used on the hoof.
- Auditory with stethoscopic help for heart and airway investigation.
- Body temperature will be recorded by thermometer.
- By observation, for behaviour, static and dynamic (action); and conformation as it may affect fitness for use (not aesthetically).

The height can only be estimated. Age is definitive only if there is identifiable evidence of that horse's date of birth available, otherwise it is only an estimation from an inspection of the teeth; the accuracy drops from 6 years old onwards.

It is not the duty of the veterinarian to comment upon:
- Value.
- Suitability.
- Ability.
- Trainability.
- Usefulness.

THE PROTOCOL EXAMINATION

Here follows a *sample* structure of a 5-stage vetting to give the horse owner and potential purchaser an idea of what to expect. It must be emphasised that this is a recommended method only – veterinary surgeons, through professional experience, each develop their own procedures and techniques designed to exact the correct information.

STAGE I

Preliminary examination, when the veterinary surgeon will:

1. Check that it is the horse in question and that there are no insurance reject freeze brands.
2. Explain to the handler/rider what will be required.
3. Have rugs removed, leaving horse loose in the box.
4. Make a general inspection of:

- Its attitude and interest.
- Its movements.
- Note bedding and presence of droppings, consistency and colour.

5. Have it headcollared.
6. Inspect eyes and nostrils for discharge.
7. When settled, record respiratory rate excursion and lung sounds.
8. Take pulse and listen to heart.
9. Take temperature.
10. Check teeth for age and palpate the bars and commissure only at this stage.
11. Examine eyes.
12. Have it brought out and 'stood up' at the halt.
13. Identify or record markings and tattoos etc.

Thereafter the static inspection will include:

14. Hands-on over entire body surface, limbs and feet regarding condition and superficial abnormalities especially along back, legs, distal joints.
15. Check carefully for muscle group symmetries.
16. Apply spinal reflex tests.
17. Examine hooves for presence of dried dirt, stones etc. on or in the sole, in grooves and under shoes which could influence action temporarily at this stage – a possibly misleading unlevelness.

STAGE II

He will see it move on the hard:

18. At walk, straight line, in-hand with turn on forehand on the right and return.
19. At trot, straight line, in-hand with turn on forehand on the left and return.
20. At trot on 20m diameter circle both ways in-hand.
21. Consider flexion tests if deemed helpful.

STAGE III

22. Tacked up (observe reactions to this).
23. Mounted: ridden walk and sitting trot on hard, then on alternate diagonals riding trot, both reins. Strenuous exercise on a suitable surface:
24. Warm up, walk loose rein, then trot collecting up over 10-15 minutes both reins, both diagonals.
25. Note action.
26. Listen for coughing.
27. Canter wide as possible both leads working up speed until breathing hard, exert, not exhaust the horse.

28. After some 5-10 minutes according to fitness bring in to 30m circle at canter to pass close to the veterinary surgeon (alternate leads).
29. Listen for any adventitious respiratory noise especially on inspiration.
30. Pull up through short trot and walk, repeat listening with head held. Take pulse.
31. Stethoscope examination of heart and lungs for rate and adventitious sounds.
32. Warm down slowly over 5-10 minutes going wide at walk.
33. Return to 30m circle trot, both reins, both diagonals for action assessment (one or two circles both ways should be sufficient).
34. Have it taken back to stables. Replace tack with headcollar, tie up (no food or water). Rug loosely if thought necessary.
35. Palpate tack areas including mouth during this time.
36. Auscultate heart and lungs. Block nostrils to induce deeper respirations. Palpate laryngeal muscles. Apply slap test.
37. Examine molar teeth and the oral soft tissues (use gag if necessary, with permission and with suitable precautions to horse and handler).
38. Palpate limbs carefully from shoulder and quarters to coronary bands for any new lesions or exacerbation of old ones.
39. Look for interference marks on distal limbs.
40. Take pulse and respiratory rate to check for return to resting normal at 10-minute intervals up to 30.
41. Palpate back along central area and girth ventrally. Induce spinal reflexes again.

STAGE IV
After 30-40 minutes rest. The second trot and foot examination:
42. In halter without rugs trot up the 30m and back, then walk the distances for actual lameness, asymmetric footfalls, stride discrepancies. Any weakness or ataxia.
43. Turn both ways on forehand, back up, trot away for some 6-10 metres.
44. Thorough hoof examination:

- Visual.
- Palpation.
- Hoof tester.
- Search sole and round walls, grooves and frog for bruising and other trauma.
- Remove shoes if thought necessary – with permission (buyer may have to pay for re-shoeing!).

STAGE V
45. Note all features already seen. Special note if one or more stages missed and why.
46. Complete certificate and give written opinion; whatever the result, discuss with purchaser. Sign.
47. Take blood sample and explain what will be done with it.
See to horse's comfort and thank helpers.

FURTHER COMMENTS
1. There is no legal necessity to give this opinion to the vendor unless purchaser agrees or has previously agreed to this, but whatever the decision, the vendor may only be told the opinion *after* the purchaser has been.

2. Once the examination is complete, notify underwriters if relevant, by fax in first instance.
3. The vendor is not entitled to a copy of the certificate even if the horse is unsatisfactory but an alternative shortened version can be issued for 'Not recommended for purchase' for both parties. It is doubtful if the vendor will want a copy!
4. The veterinary surgeon *has the right, the duty, to stop the examination at any time* if and when he considers it would be detrimental to the horse to continue, e.g. lameness.

FURTHER READING
The British guidelines have recently been updated in the form of *Notes for PP Examinations* published by the Veterinary Defence Society (VDS) in co-operation with the British Equine Veterinary Association (BEVA). The latter will be publishing a more technical text early in 1999. The *Veterinary Clinics of North America* (Sauners) published in 1992 is a very informative handbook on the subject, the first three articles of which are relevant to all parties. At the 1997 AAEP Congress, one speaker emphasised inter alia the need for exact written information and agreement between the three parties to a horse purchase transaction. Whilst all these publications are directed to the veterinary profession, they are, in a legal sense, common property inasmuch as a veterinarian is well-advised to use them for his/her own sake, and/or as evidence to the seller and to the buyer of what is common and required sensible practice.

GUIDELINES FOR VETERINARY PURCHASE EXAMINATION IN THE USA
Guidelines recommended for reporting purchase examinations in the USA are as follows.
   Do not furnish the buyer a written report of a purchase examination unless the seller and buyer or an authorised agent for the seller or buyer answers and signs a statement presented by the examining veterinarian containing the following questions and statements.

A. SELLER'S STATEMENT
1. Seller's name, address, telephone number.
2. How long have you been acquainted with this animal?
3. How long have you had this animal under your care?
4. Do you have knowledge of past or present:

- Lameness.
- Diseases.
- Vices.
- Neurectomies, colic, surgery or bleeding.
- Use of medications.
- Disabilities.
- Claims regarding any of the above.

If your answer to any of the above questions is 'yes', please give details.
5. Use to which you understand the horse will be put?
6. Any knowledge of past performance of this horse for the proposed use?

7. Estimate of the suitability of this horse for the proposed use?
- Unique.
- Exceptional.
- Adequate.
- No opinion.

8. I am present at purchase examination.

9. I GIVE PERMISSION FOR THE PERFORMANCE OF ANY TESTS CONSIDERED NECESSARY BY THE EXAMINING VETERINARIAN AND AGREE TO HOLD HIM OR HER HARMLESS FOR THE CONSEQUENCES THERE-OF.

10. Date.

11. Signature.

B. BUYER'S STATEMENT

1. Buyer's name, address and telephone number.
2. To what use do you intend to put this horse?
3. What is the age, size, ability, and experience of the intended buyer?
4. How long have you been acquainted with this horse?
5. Have you tried this horse? If so, in what fashion?
6. Of what relevant importance are the following to you? (Rate as Very Important, Important or Not Important)
- Appearance.
- Blemishes.
- Performance.
- Temperament.

7. How do you rate the suitability of this horse for the intended purpose?
- Unique.
- Exceptional.
- Adequate.

8. What type of care (stabling) is anticipated for this horse?
- Intensive (continual care and supervision).
- Average (stabled daily for feeding).
- Other – please specify.

9. I am present at the purchase examination.

10. SAID VETERINARY PURCHASE EXAMINATION DOES NOT WARRANT THE SUITABILITY OF THE HORSE FOR THE PURPOSE INTENDED AND IS EXPRESSLY LIMITED BY MY STATEMENTS AND INSTRUCTIONS ON THE DEPTH OF THE EXAMINATION DESIRED, THE SPECIFIC TESTS WHICH I HAVE REQUESTED TO BE PERFORMED, AND THE FEE I HAVE AGREED TO PAY.

11. Date.

12. Signature.

All reports should be in writing and should be accompanied by signed Seller's and Buyer's statements.

The report should contain

(a) A description of the horse with sufficient specificity to fully identify it.
(b) The date, time, place of examination, and the names and addresses of all persons present during the examination.

The veterinarian should list relevant findings discovered during the examination and give his or her opinion as to the effect that these findings are likely to have on the use of the horse for the purpose intended.

The veterinarian should qualify any findings and opinions expressed to the buyer by making specific reference to tests not performed on the horse (radiographs, endoscopy, blood, drug, ECG, rectal, nerve blocks, laboratory studies, etc.) which have not been requested by the buyer after being informed of their availability by the veterinarian.

The veterinarian shall make no determination as to the suitability of the horse for the purpose intended; this remains the responsibility of the buyer.

A complete record of all the examination procedures performed should be kept in the veterinarian's file but should not be listed in the report to the buyer.

7. STEP BY STEP SUMMARY OF BUYING

1. Start looking! See 'Where to look' (Section II,1), and be prepared to wait for the right animal. It may take several months to find it!
2. Write down a specification for your ideal horse and decide on a price limit, so that you are not swayed by emotion when you go to try one.
3. Spread the word that you are ready to buy, and circulate your specification among local horsy contacts.
4. Have a comprehensive list of questions to ask on the telephone so that you know as much as you can about the history and suitability of any horse before travelling too far. Be honest with the vendor about your own ability.
5. Take someone along to act as a witness to verbal agreements (see Section V, Questionnaire). If they are an experienced horse person then by all means listen to their views, but remember – this horse is for you, not them!
6. See if you like the overall look and temperament of the horse in the box, then ask for it to be walked and trotted up in-hand. If you are experienced you may wish to check its teeth and look for odd lumps and bumps, but ultimately this is a job for the vet.
7. Watch as the horse is tacked up or do it yourself, and see it ridden at all paces and over jumps (unless you definitely do not require a jumping horse).
8. Try the horse yourself in a number of different situations, such as out on the roads and in a school. Choose somewhere with good facilities, even if it means boxing it to a cross country course or suitable area.
9. If you don't like a horse, admit it immediately. If you do like the horse, go home and sleep on it before informing the vendors of your final decision. It's unusual to be allowed a trial period, but it's worth asking.
10. Always get the horse vetted before purchase (see Section II,4 Pre-Purchase Examination).
11. If the horse passes the vetting, check that any comments made on the veterinary certificate will not result in exclusions on your insurance policy – most

companies exclude obvious problem areas or previous injury sites, but the exact nature of the exclusion should be detailed on the policy.

12. If the horse fails the vetting it may not be the end of the matter – you may decide that you can put up with whatever faults were found and renegotiate the price. However, you may not be able to insure the horse without a vet's certificate and the horse will also be difficult to sell on.

13. Check that paperwork, such as breed papers, registration documents and vaccination certificates, is in order.

14. Discuss how and when you intend to pay the vendor, and ask for a receipt and warranty if not yet obtained.

15. Arrange transport and make arrangements for the horse's arrival at its new home. You will need to have stocked up on its usual feed, hay, bedding etc. and arranged insurance for the horse, beforehand.

8. INSURING YOUR HORSE

GUIDELINES

While every care has been taken to render this information as accurate as possible, it is emphasised that these are guidelines only, and in the event of insurance queries or disagreements etc. readers should seek advice from professional individuals specialising in this field.

As a living animal, subject to illness and injury in the course of its work, a horse's intrinsic value can be suddenly and dramatically altered. Circumstances in which value may be altered include:

- Death.
- Incurable illness or injury, i.e. permanent loss of use, or where the cost of treating an illness or injury will be such that the expense involved is well outside budgeted running costs.
- Theft (of the horse, its tack and transport) is always a possibility.
- Moreover third party 'injury' as the result of your horse's activity may be cripplingly expensive.

A horse's value is that which the 'market' can justify. It does not include sentiment or potential consequential emotional damage to the owner and family. To knowingly over-value can be illegal. The 'market' has a fair estimate of all types of horses' value. It relates to:

- Breed or type.
- Height.
- Age.
- Sex.
- Capability – meaning potential, to a limited extent grading up through levels of discipline competitions, and proven success (records held by discipline authorities).
- Past history of illness and/or injury (which must be declared).

The premium to obtain insurance cover will reflect capital value required, risks involved in use, and other environmental factors such as where the horse is kept, owner's experience, etc.

The schedule of premiums will consider the type of cover required. There is no such thing as a bargain policy although there are some advertised as cheap or cheaper than others. Some underwriting syndicates, either to attract business or because of business success, can offer an 'edge', but none are running a charity. *It is actuarially driven.* Brokers or Insurance Agents occasionally 'throw in' loss-leading inducements such as free tack cover, loss of trailer, refund of competition entry fees and so on out of their commission. It is essential to read the small print, ask and get answers to any point not clear to you – particularly with regard to 'vets' fees' and 'loss of use' covers.

The categories for horse insurance are variable within narrow limits but generally they are as follows.

Pleasure horses: Includes horses used for riding, driving, Pony or Riding Club functions, etc.

Working horses, low-level activity: Includes horses used for hunting – certain packs are 'extra' – polo (not high goal), horse trials below advanced level, dressage, show jumping, long distance riding competitions.

(Both above types attract standard rates but related to value.)

Elite athletes: Includes horses for higher levels of competition such as Advanced and above horse trials, 'A', 'B' and 'Open' jumping, Grand Prix dressage, racing (Point to Point and National Hunt), high goal polo.

(Rates usually 10-15% of the value to be covered.)

Breeding animals: Thoroughbred animals are in a separate specialised group, but for non-Thoroughbreds there are policies to cover:

- Loss of the foetus by abortion.
- Loss of the foal – still birth.
- Loss of the foal – during first 30 days of life.
- Loss of mare during/immediately after foaling.

Related covers: Such as Third party liability and indemnity; Theft of tack and trailer; Fire.

The applicant for insurance cover completes the proforma as a legally binding warranty with special reference to:

- History of illness and/or injury – particularly any that is seasonal and allergic in nature, or repetitive.
- Present physical and medical status.
- Presence of conformation defects likely to make the horse a greater risk. An amateur owner is not expected to be au fait with these, but if it can be shown that these (a) had been pointed out to him by a farrier or at a veterinary examination as at pre-purchase, or (b) had already caused problems, the underwriters can legally withdraw from the contract or refuse payment.

The applicant has a duty to be truthful and open.

In high(er) value animals the underwriters will require a 5-stage veterinary report and in some cases evidence of radiography and ultrasonography. Such a veterinary opinion as to purchase does *not* carry any legal weight regarding underwriters' willingness to cover. Their veterinary adviser will make that decision in the light of the vet's certification.

A horse owner can seek insurance cover:

- Direct from a Lloyd's equine syndicate.
- Direct through British agencies with a USA underwriter's office.
- Through an Insurance Company which has access to several syndicates.
- Through a registered 'broker' who can be more selective and will act as the owner's agent. He should have a reputation for experience in horse insurance.

The various covers available are as follows.

All risks mortality

- Accidental lethal injury.
- Illness with fatal outcome.

(These are all subject to acts of omission and/or commission on the part of the owner applicant.)

- Humane euthanasia required for incurable injury or illness, or if the treatment for either is unjustifiable on welfare grounds.

(These policies often include proven theft cover.)

'Accidental injury', 'death only' or acknowledged euthanasia on humane grounds

A veterinary surgeon must certify the correctness of these claims, may have to support it from autopsy findings and, except in serious welfare considerations, or 'out of Lloyd's or agents' hours', seek agreement before carrying out euthanasia. Such professional involvement is at the expense of the owner even if the horse is covered for vet's fees.

These two covers are the ones most commonly held by owners of pleasure horses and low-level activity working animals.

The next two covers can be separate from all-risks or accident only mortality cover.

Loss of use cover

This is usually 75 per cent of capital but is negotiable vis à vis the premium. Owners of elite-value animals can be faced with injuries and sometimes illnesses which are sub-lethal but may leave the horse incapable of performing in a discipline for which it is insured; it is no longer of use for that work. To replace it at the same level would be expensive. Such inability must be both (a) claimed by the opinion of the owner's veterinary surgeon often with expert or orthopaedic specialist opinion, and (b) agreed to by the Underwriter's veterinary adviser.

Sometimes the opinion can be expressed at the time of the injury; in other situations a reasonable and welfare-acceptable time must elapse both to assess response to treatment and to observe the level of physical recovery clinically and/or as the result of work.

It is wise to ascertain that such a time lag, if it goes over the period of cover, will still be honoured. Further general cover must be renewed.

Once again the cover can be:

- All risks.
- Accidental injury only.

In both categories, loss of use may be as a result of
- External trauma.
- 'Internal' orthopaedic over-stress and/or strain.

NOTE: Loss of use does not mean temporary inability to work, as in convalescence.

Loss of use claims can be controversial. It is wise to have the cover's 'i's dotted and its 't's crossed at the start.

VETS' FEES

When taking out insurance cover, particular attention should be paid to the cover's insurance against vets' fees incurred by treatment of the horse. Some underwriters require this to be linked with Loss of Use cover. Both are relatively expensive.

The premium should be such as to give cover for potentially major surgery, such as that involved with some colics, plus a period of hospital post-operative care. Currently this must be £3,500 to £4,000. It is important to be clear whether this sum is for all claims in a given year or is in part or in whole for more than one claim. Some may not cover transport costs to veterinary clinics and/or hospitals, or a vet's travelling expenses.

Should the owner wish 'to continue using the horse at a lower level' to be an acceptable possibility, this must be written into the policy. If the veterinary surgeon decides that complementary discipline help is necessary during a course of treatment, permission must be sought in individual circumstances, if this was not part of the policy.

No cover under fees is related to routine work such as the costs of vaccination, helminth (worm) control, dental care and elective surgery. Where elective surgery is concerned, e.g. castration, the horse can be insured against consequential illness or 'injury' by arrangement during the period of cover; this is also applicable to injury and illness associated with foaling.

At all times, the use of a general anaesthetic should be notified in advance, except in emergency situations.

In all covers the underwriters have an excess clause whereby either a fixed sum or a percentage sum, as in elite animals, is discounted from the payment.

INSURANCE IN THE USA

In 1990 the AAEP published (as a 2nd edition) a handbook on the 'Veterinary Role in Equine Insurance'. This was in association with inputs from the major equine insurance companies. As with their 'Vetting' handbook this makes essential reading for both professions and should be made available to clients. Several pages of 'Questions commonly asked', together with the answers, will go a long way to avoid unnecessary difficulties when claims arise – and if claims are refused.

Once again, the broad principles and practices of insurance the UK and the USA are similar. The American book emphasises

- The need for a true and honest declaration from the insured, not only at the time of application, but also at any later time when an illness or an injury is suffered during a period of cover.
- That the insurance covers against a 'fortuity', i.e. the likelihood of something that might happen in the future as opposed to something that will. This relates

to the warranty expected from the insured owner that the horse is physically acceptable for the use intended of it.

American insurance cover may be built around the 'Mortality Policy' which is similar to the British version except that it cannot, as a rule, be only for accidental death. 'Loss of use' endorsement is a special addition to the above policy to cover against an animal developing a physical condition which renders it permanently incapable of performance for the stated use intended, but short of humane slaughter. (It does not, in this edition, include medical reasons for loss of use: there is, in both countries, a fine line of distinction as to a medical condition such as chronic obstructive pulmonary disease (COPD) being so bad as to warrant euthanasia; it is a manageable condition even if the sufferer would be a poor competitor.) The brood animals' covers are essentially similar.

All the above require variable prior veterinary certificates in addition to the owner's warranties. There are specified (restricted or limited) perils which must be named on the policy. In Great Britain these are 'Acts of God' – lightning, flood or other natural occurrences. In the USA to these are added:
- Smoke, collapse of bridges and earthquake.
- Limited transportage cover for road accidents and when loading or unloading from aircraft.
- Theft, but not straying (as in Great Britain).

Optional perils endorsement can be added for accidental shooting, electrical faults, building collapse, attacks by dogs. No prior veterinary examination is required for these specified covers.

'Vets' fees' are discussed under
- Surgical insurance.
- Major medical insurance. Cover may require prior veterinary examinations.

These are basically similar to the British 'Vets' fees' cover.

The American covers are subject to specified limits which vary from company to company but include:
1. A minimum premium of $160.
2. A cover limit of $6,000 in the aggregate per animal insured.
3. The fees must be reasonable for the geographical location.
4. Veterinary fees must be reasonable for veterinary care necessitated by accident, injury or illness.
5. There is an excess of $300 for each separate claim.

Exclusions – no cover is offered for:
- Those conditions contracted before commencement of insurance or any recurrence thereof.
- Any elective or voluntary medical (and surgical) procedures.
- Expenses of travel, vet and/or patient.
- Normal preventative measures, e.g. vaccination.
- Osteochondroses-related condition.
- Any performance-enhancing treatments.
- Racehorses' accidents.

- Vets' fees incurred after 60 days from the commencement of the treatment's fees already being claimed for.
- Orthopaedic conditions referable to osteochondroses which are seen as hereditable and usually congenital if radiographically 'looked for'.

The premium is active from day one; no part is returnable, even if a situation changes following treatment. It is wholly earned as it is in Great Britain. They are intended to:

- Reimburse the owner (the Assured) for reasonable and customary fees for surgical procedures to save the life of the horse.
- Pay for reasonable and customary after-care while the insured animal is kept post-operatively at the premises of the surgical intervention.

These are all subject to the maximum amount identified in the endorsement to the scheduled policy. The after-care is limited to 50 per cent of the surgical fee and no more than 15 days from the time of surgery.

In addition, a deductible 'excess' of $150 will be applied to each separate claim. The claim, fully supported, must be lodged within 21 days with copies of invoices. No cover is offered for unqualified (i.e. as a veterinary surgeon) surgery or if carried out in a non-recognised clinic. All operations in this optional endorsed policy must be under a general anaesthetic. It will not include elective or voluntary procedures. There is *no* death benefit or costs for autopsy.

9. TIME TO LET GO

Another important responsibility of every horse owner is knowing when the time is right to pass the horse on. Perhaps you realise you have bought the wrong horse, your requirements have changed, the horse is not achieving its full potential or your circumstances have changed so that, however much you love the horse, it is no longer practical for you to keep it. There are a number of options for owners, and a fit, healthy, well-mannered horse should not have too much trouble finding a good home.

Selling
Advertise through the equestrian press, local feed merchants and tack shops, riding schools and word of mouth. Ask a realistic price and be prepared for it to take time to find the right home. If you don't think a potential buyer is the right person for your horse, you are within your rights to say so and refuse to sell them the horse.

Working livery
A number of riding schools, training centres and agricultural colleges take suitably schooled horses on working livery. However, you would have to accept that a number of riders of differing standards would be riding your horse.

Gift

You can give a horse away to a friend who you trust to give the horse the right kind of home and work. Make sure the home is genuine and that the horse's limitations are clearly understood. If you are 'gifting' the horse because you specifically do not want to sell or loan it – maybe because you wish to retain some control over its future welfare – then clarify this in a written agreement, otherwise the new owner is within their rights to use or dispose of the animal as they wish. Don't hand your horse over to an equine charity and expect them to take the responsibility – they are already over-stocked with needier cases.

Loans

Loaning a horse is worth considering if you doubt your ability to meet the time constraints and financial commitments of owning a horse, but do not wish to sell. You may also agree to loan a horse 'with a view to buy', or use a loan period to gain experience before buying your first horse. There may be a fee for loaning a very valuable horse for breeding or competition, but generally there is no charge and the loaner and loanee come to an agreement about who pays certain bills instead. Done properly with a responsible loanee, you get the best of both worlds; done badly, you can end up having expensive battles over who is responsible for the animal when things go wrong.

Word of mouth is usually the best way to find a good loan home for your horse, but many people also advertise in local tack shops or the equestrian press. In such cases, make sure you 'vet' the prospective home carefully before handing over your horse. Horror stories abound! There are also several loan agencies which specialise in matching up horses and riders, taking a lot of the hard work out of successful loaning.

Always ask for a written agreement, even (or especially) if you are loaning to a friend. Agreements need to be tailor-made, but consider the following points:

- Duration. Is there a maximum or minimum loan term? When is the renewal date? What notice is required for cancellation? Do you want special terms to apply if you become unhappy about the horse's condition or anxious about its welfare? If you are the loaner, beware that the owner can always take the horse away from you, even if you have become attached to it.
- Money. Make it clear who is paying for feed, livery, farriery, veterinary costs, insurance etc. The horse's running costs are nearly always met by the borrower, but under what circumstances might other costs be shared? Even if the horse is insured against vet's bills, who will pay the excess? If a competition horse wins money, who keeps it?
- Stipulate which vet or farrier should be used, if you have a strong preference.
- Ensure there is personal accident and third party insurance cover for horse and rider.
- Use of the horse, and the type of work it is capable of. Do you mind your horse competing?
- Tack, rugs and their maintenance.
- Visiting rights – regular inspection is a good safeguard, but the owner must not interfere with the loaner's enjoyment of the horse.

Sharing

Sharing is usually a more casual arrangement than loaning, where perhaps a friend looks after your horse at weekends in return for rides. If you still pay all the bills then you have the advantage of halving the work load while retaining control of your horse's welfare. However, you will also retain the responsibility of being its owner, and may have to foot the bill if anything untoward happens, even if it is the sharer's fault. As with loaning, it is wise to have the exact nature of your agreement in writing.

SECTION III

STABLE MANAGEMENT

Horses come in all shapes and sizes, and successful stable management lies in considering each animal's individual requirements as well as your own lifestyle, before making a decision on how you're going to organise the horse's routine. Remember you want to enjoy your horse, not resent the demands it makes on your resources or the considerable impact it will have on your life.

In removing the horse from its natural environment we take away its ability to attend to its own needs. These then become our total responsibility. It's up to us to keep our horse fit and well, for our own sake as well as the animal's.

The horse's health requirements are both physical and mental. Physically, every horse has a basic need for food, water, shelter and exercise. As a domestic animal, it also has a right to be free from disease, pain and discomfort, which means that in addition to the basic needs outlined above, the human responsible for a horse's welfare must attend to such things as sharp teeth and overgrown feet, and implement an effective worming and grooming programme. For its mental health, the horse needs the company of other equines and regular periods of complete liberty in an open space. It also has the right to be treated with respect and kindness.

Being completely responsible for a horse's mental and physical welfare is a big commitment, but just how big depends on your personal circumstances. Vets' bills are expensive, while horse care is time-consuming and can even be disappointing, if you are unable to reap the rewards that having a sound and healthy horse can bring. How much time, money and energy are you prepared to give? Is this going to be sufficient to meet the requirements of the particular horse you're planning to buy? The fact is that a horse is one of the most expensive and labour-intensive pets you could ever hope to own, but the type of horse and management routine you choose can alter the workload considerably.

1. STABLE MANAGEMENT SYSTEMS

Whichever system you choose, it is important that it suits both your needs and those of the horse. The basic choices are as follows.

Stabled full-time
Advantages: Stabling means that the horse is clean, dry and available for work at a moment's notice. You also have precise control over its food, drink, exercise and environment.
Disadvantages: More expensive than having a horse at grass in terms of bedding, hard feed and forage. Time and labour-intensive – a stabled horse requires a great deal of knowledgeable care. Unsuitable for all but the hardest-working horses, although even they should be allowed at least a couple of hours of freedom each day.

Turned out full-time
Advantages: A healthy option, provided the horse has sufficient grazing, water, shelter and company. Low maintenance for the owner, with fewer additional feed and bedding costs.
Disadvantages: A large area is needed if horses are to be self-sufficient. Weather-dependent for most breeds. Can be difficult to monitor the horse's diet and prevent a 'good doer' becoming overweight. May be discordant with hard work in winter, as the horse needs a least some of its winter coat for warmth and protection, yet this may lead to overheating when ridden.

Combined system
For example, stabled at night, turned out during the day.
Advantages: The best (and worst) of both worlds. You can control the horse's diet and environment to a greater degree without the expense and restrictions associated with a fully stabled animal.
Disadvantages: Double the accommodation – you need to find and maintain both stabling and turnout. Once the horse is used to coming in at night or has been clipped for the winter, it is too late to change your mind and leave it out full-time!

Yarding
Advantages: Horses have access to a covered yard (preferably bedded) opening onto pasture or a turnout area, and can come and go as they please. Living with a number of other horses, this is a very natural and comfortable existence for the horse, and low daily maintenance for the owner.
Disadvantages: Horses must be compatible to prevent bullying and fighting. Can be awkward to single out animals for individual attention. Difficult to feed horses

varying rations or to control diet. For practical purposes the bedded yard is often deep litter, which is back-breaking to clear out when you eventually need to! The system is often used for groups of youngsters, which would actually benefit from more day-to-day handling.

2. CHOOSING A SYSTEM

THE HORSE'S NEEDS

If the horse is to be kept happy and healthy, its breed, temperament, age, condition and the level of fitness required, must obviously influence your decisions about where the horse is to live, how it is to be cared for and how much exercise it needs. Before you buy a horse, therefore, you need to consider your needs and lifestyle in relation to these points, in order to find an animal to suit you.

1. **Breed:** If your horse is going to live out, it's no good purchasing a fine-coated Thoroughbred which needs stabling in winter, even if it fulfils all your other requirements for the ideal horse! The horse you choose must be physically capable of living comfortably in the environment in which you intend to place it. Generally, native types and cross breeds cope well with living out provided they are allowed to grow their winter coats. However, these are also the types that become dangerously overweight if left out at grass all year round with insufficient exercise.
2. **Temperament:** Some horses are more highly-strung or energetic by nature than others. These types may not thrive or remain pleasant and well-mannered if cooped up in a stable for long periods. On the other hand, the more excitable types tend to be 'blood' horses such as Thoroughbreds, which are equally unsuited to weathering long hours out in the field. It's a question of compromise and careful management.
3. **Age:** Old horses cope less well with wintering out and often need extra feed, care and stabling in poor weather; however, they can stiffen up if kept in all the time and will benefit from the gentle exercise which regular turning out gives them. Young horses need to spend as much time out as possible to develop strong muscles and a tough skeleton. Those under the age of three which have not yet been broken to ride, certainly need the freedom to graze and play, preferably twenty-four hours a day. Even finer types such as the Thoroughbred generally winter out well as part of a group of youngsters if fed plenty of hay in the field and allowed to grow a full coat.
4. **Condition:** Like humans, some horses lose and gain weight more easily than others, and grass is particularly fattening in spring and autumn. It is easier to control what the horse eats if it lives in; however, it will use less energy keeping warm and mobile than a horse at grass. A horse in poor condition will certainly benefit from being turned out on good grazing, but in the absence of a decent layer of insulating body-fat it must be protected from the elements by shelter and rugs when appropriate.
5. **Level of fitness required:** If you wish to keep a horse fit for hard competition, it will almost certainly need to be stabled for a least part of the time to allow it

to rest and recuperate. The facilities at your yard must also be sufficient to allow you to keep the horse fit enough for your purposes; for example, you may want a floodlit arena, a horse-walker or set of show jumps. On the other hand, if the horse is a family hack and only ridden at weekends, it will either need to be turned out every day or kept full-time, so the yard must have acceptable turnout facilities.

THE HANDLER/RIDER'S NEEDS

In addition to the horse's physical and mental needs, the rider or handler's ability and experience, support crew, time, money, inclination and the time of year, are decisive factors when choosing a yard and stable management routine.

1. **Ability and experience:** Caring for a horse's every need is a complicated task and one which first-time owners may not have sufficient knowlege or confidence to take on alone. It is therefore wise to keep the horse at a place where you can seek help and advice when necessary. Even if you know your stuff, it's always reassuring to seek a second opinion in times of crisis. Also, consider the ability and experience of others who will be riding or handling the horse, such as friends or children. It's very restrictive to have an animal which only you can handle – everybody needs a holiday sometime!

    Also bear in mind that being a good rider does not automatically make you a good owner. Years of perfecting your technique in the saddle won't prepare you for the day-to-day care of a horse. Get some hands-on experience.

2. **Support:** If you have lots of knowledgeable friends or horsy relatives who can step in and care for your horse in times of holiday, sickness or unexpected late nights at the office, then fine. If not, it is well worth going to a yard where this support will be available to you, even if you have to pay a little more or travel a little further for it.

3. **Time:** There is no doubt that horses make labour-intensive pets, and the management routine you adopt will certainly affect your enjoyment of your horse. Generally speaking, keeping your horse as close to its natural free-roaming, constant-grazing lifestyle as possible, is the best way to ensure you have a happy and healthy horse to deal with every day with minimum effort. Horses which do not require stabling can be kept at 'grass livery' – i.e. only grazing, no stable – which is a cheaper option but could raise problems if the horse needs stabling due to illness, injury or a long period of foul weather. A compromise, if you are short of time, might be working or part livery (see Part 6, 'Choosing a Yard').

4. **Money:** Quite simply, you can pay someone else to do all or just part of the work if you lack the time, knowlege, skill or inclination to do it yourself. You will have peace of mind and your horse should get the regular routine and careful handling it needs. However, experienced professionals do not come cheap, and for many people caring for their own horse is part of the fun.

5. **Inclination:** There are many dedicated owners who manage to keep a horse fit, clipped, competing and happy, as well as holding down a full-time job, but there is no doubt that it is a considerable commitment and leaves little time or energy for anything else! You may not wish to devote a minimum of four hours a day to such high-maintenance horse care. However, low-maintenance horse care generally only works with tougher, native types which can cope with

living out at grass with minimal care – so choose your horse according to your inclination!

6. **Time of year:** A horse in summer is much less work and cheaper to keep than a horse in winter, if it is turned out, so it's your chance for a holiday too. Winter, however, can be a long, hard slog for the working owner who is doing everything for a stabled or part-stabled horse. You may need to pay for extra help or the use of facilities such as an all-weather manège, if the weather is bad or daylight hours short. Compare the care of the stabled horse to the care of the grass-kept horse, below.

3. STABLING

While it is never advisable for a horse be kept stabled constantly, the domestic horse (particularly a competition horse) is often stabled for at least part of the time, for greater convenience. The environment the horse is kept in can make all the difference to its health and well-being; well-designed stables not only add to the value of a property but can also significantly improve quality of life for both horse and carer.

There are two basic types of stable – a yard of traditional loose boxes with additional tack and storage spaces, or an American barn which covers a large area and is partitioned within into individual boxes. The latter is entirely under cover, so is highly convenient for the stable staff, and is also cheaper to construct if a large number of boxes are required. On the other hand, ventilation and access to daylight are more limited for the horses, and there is a greater risk of cross-infection. There is generally enough room to drive a tractor or small digger down the inner aisle for mucking out purposes.

The ideal stable:
*   Is solidly built in brick, stone, blocks or timber. The walls should preferably be double thickness and well insulated to retain warmth and reduce condensation.
*   Has a well-fitting, wide, outward-opening, solid door with strong hinges and bolts top and bottom. It should be hung slightly above floor level to allow it to swing easily, and to prevent it from absorbing water from the stable floor and rotting. It needs a metal anti-chew strip along the top edge of the lower half, and a means of securing the top half of the door open.
*   Is warm. Warmth is provided by the body heat of the horse being trapped by a sound, well insulated, weather-proof building. In general no additional heating is required within a stable, although infra-red lamps are sometimes installed in racing yards, high-class stud farms or veterinary practices.
*   Is dry. As well as having a water-tight roof, walls and windows, a large overhang over the stable door, and preferably around the entire stable, will allow the horse to stay dry as it looks out, prevent driving rain entering the box and protect walls and windows.
*   Has dry foundations and good drainage. If wet and urine can run freely away, the risk of dampness in the bedding and atmosphere is greatly reduced.
*   Has good ventilation but no draughts. The horse's respiratory system is under

constant threat from the dust and ammonia present in even the most well-kept stable, but careful provision of air inlets, windows, vents and an ever-open top door will ensure that air can circulate and will not grow stale. Louvred windows which encourage upward air movement are the best, allowing good air flow without a direct draught. It is important that the horse's necessary warmth and protection from the elements is not gained at the expense of fresh air; it is far better to add another rug than to shut the horse in.

- Has both natural and artificial light. Daylight is essential for the horse's wellbeing, particularly sunlight which provides essential vitamin D. Lack of natural light causes depression and hormonal imbalance. However, artificial light is also essential for the owner's sake, and to allow the horse to be attended to in winter and after dark. Generally, lighting in loose boxes is by fluorescent fittings which need to be unbreakable and moisture-resistant. Bare light bulbs can reach a sufficiently high temperature to ignite dust or other combustible material, and should not be used without a protective cover. A qualified electrician should do all wiring and should make sure all the electrics have a tough, rodent-proof cover; switches should be designed for outdoor use and be out of the horse's reach. You should also consider exterior lights in the yard and surrounding buildings, for both convenience and security.

  Windows should be made from safety glass or a shatterproof plastic, protected internally by a galvanised metal grille.

- Has an electricity supply. As well as the need for artificial light mentioned above, there are numerous other tasks which require electricity such as clipping, kettle boiling, heat to prevent burst pipes, etc.

- Has a water supply. Horses drink several gallons of water a day even in winter. Water is also needed for washing, hosing, hay-soaking and hygiene purposes.

- Is accessible but secure. Being miles from any sort of habitation may sound idyllic, but it also means you're miles from any kind of veterinary help, farriers, emergency services, feed and bedding deliveries, etc. Close neighbours can be useful to keep a look out for you, but on the other hand, there are security risks associated with stables whose location lays them constantly open to public attention. Some sort of compromise between access and security is necessary.

- Is designed to minimise labour. Horse-keeping is labour-intensive enough as it is, and the design of the stable yard can significantly contribute to or alleviate the workload. Practical considerations might include having the stables close to the turnout area, allowing plenty of storage space for feed and bedding, creating a suitable area for the muck heap near to the stables, keeping a clean covered area for grooming, tacking up, hosing etc., or investing in automatic waterers to save on bucket-filling and carrying time.

- Is safe, with no sharp projections or hazards such as exposed wires, sockets, switches or light bulbs. Horses are notoriously accident-prone and vets' bills can be very large where stitches and anaesthetic are concerned. Blemishes also devalue a horse, even if they do not affect performance. There are some fittings which are desirable and necessary in a stable, such as tie rings, rings for hay nets or a hay rack, mangers, saltlick-holders and possibly a bucket-holder or automatic waterer. Make sure all fixtures are securely fitted, of good quality and designed for stable use.

- Allows the horse plenty of room to move around, lie down and roll in comfort.

The more time the horse is to spend confined to the box, the bigger it should be for its psychological as well as physical wellbeing. If the box is too small, the horse may get 'cast' as it tries to roll (i.e. become stuck on its back against a wall, unable to free itself).

The exact dimensions of the stable obviously depend on whether it is to house a Shetland pony or a Shire horse! There should be adequate head room (at least ten metres). The minimum size box for a large horse is 3.7m x 4.3m (12ft x 14ft), and for a pony 3.7m x 3m (12ft x 10ft); for a foaling box, 4.6m x 4.6m (15ft x 15ft) is the minimum size for safety and comfort. Stalls should be at least 1.8m (6ft) wide, with at least 1.8m (6ft) behind them for people and other horses to walk past without being in danger of getting kicked. The stable door should be at least 2.4m (8ft) high and 1.2m (4ft) wide to allow the horse easy access.

BEDDING

A good deep bed on a non-slip floor is essential to encourage the horse to lie down in comfort, to insulate against cold, to absorb wet and to protect the horse's feet from excessive wear and disease. There are several types of bedding available; whichever you choose, it must be clean and free of dust, which can cause great damage to the horse's respiratory system. If your horse is kept in a livery yard, your choice of bedding may depend on the yard owners.

Straw, wood shavings, paper and rubber matting are the most commonly used bedding materials, although various other vacuum-packed 'super-absorbent' materials are starting to appear on the market. These tend to be expensive to set up initially but relatively cheap and labour-saving to maintain thereafter.

When deciding on bedding, take the stable flooring into account – rubber matting requires a particularly well drained floor to work well, for example. Your choice will also be influenced by time and your horse's habits: 'deep litter', for instance, where the droppings and obvious wet patches are skipped out daily and fresh bedding put on top, is very quick to do, but is unsuitable for a particularly wet or dirty horse.

STABLE HYGIENE

Stables are dirty places, and although horses may appear to be big, tough creatures, their immune systems are certainly lowered if they are made to live in unhygienic surroundings, leaving them prone to illness and disease. In particular, the equine respiratory system is vulnerable to the excessive amounts of dust and airborne diseases which abound in most stables.

It is quite possible to significantly cut down the chance of a horse picking up a disease or infection, by keeping down dust levels (e.g. by using good-quality or dust-free forage and bedding) and maintaining good stable hygiene. Regular mucking out is not enough. Stable floors, walls and food and water containers should be washed regularly with a disinfectant solution. Many normal disinfectants are inactivated by organic material such as that found in every corner of the average stable, so look for one specifically approved for stable use. Periodic pressure-hosing or steam-cleaning of hard-to-reach corners is also advisable. Steam-cleaning is the most effective, as most infections are more readily killed by heat than cold.

Hygiene is particularly important when a horse moves into a new box. Even apparently healthy horses may be carrying diseases to which they are immune but others are not. Stables should always be thoroughly disinfected and cleared of old bedding before new arrivals take up residence.

In addition to the stable and feed buckets, the horse's tack, clothing, grooming brushes and the horse itself need to be kept clean. Horse boxes and trailers are another hotbed for disease, especially those used commercially, and the added heat and stress of travelling, coupled with poor ventilation, makes the horse particularly prone to picking up nasties in transit. Again, a regular washdown of the vehicle with an approved disinfectant is called for.

In addition to the above measures, an outbreak of serious contagious disease may mean that a horse has to be isolated from others. An isolation box should be at least 300 metres away from the rest of the yard, preferably downwind. If the affected horse is still being ridden, it needs separate tack, grooming kit etc., and its rider/carer must not handle other horses without disinfecting hands and boots, and changing clothes first.

As well as preventing the spread of serious disease, good stable hygiene also reduces the risk of low-grade health problems such as coughs and runny noses, and will certainly improve your horse's health and reduce the total number of vets' bills on a long-term basis.

WATER

Stabled horses should have a constant supply of cool, clean water which is usually available from a bucket or automatic waterer. A bucket is easier to clean and you can keep an eye on how much your horse is drinking; not all horses like to drink from automatic waterers, but they are certainly labour-saving. Ensure all water pipes are well lagged to prevent freezing and bursting in winter; routing pipework away from external walls and cold draughts, where possible, also helps prevent freezing in all but the sharpest frosts. Alternatively, trace heating can be installed around water-pipe work within equine buildings. Keep all pipe work and insulation out of horses' reach to avoid chewing, particularly if trace heating is being used.

The stabled horse can be expected to drink at least 25 litres of water a day at rest; more in hot weather or after strenuous exercise. Lactating mares may drink three times this amount. It is incorrect to deprive a horse of water, even before strenuous exercise.

CARE OF THE STABLED HORSE

Since it is a total captive with no control over its environment at all, the stabled horse requires a lot of care. It is important to remember that horses are creatures of habit and are most content with a set daily routine. Obviously this is something you will work out according to how much time you have, how much work the horse needs and how many stabled horses you have to care for; but an example of a good yard routine, where people are available to feed and skip out etc. during the day, might be as follows:

7am: Tie horse up outside box with small feed and hay while mucking out. Leave doors and windows open and bed thrown up against sides of box to air.

7.30am: Brush off horse and prepare to ride.

8-10am: Exercise horse.

10.15am: Return to yard, allow water and hay while you thoroughly groom or wash horse down.

11am: While horse dries off, put its bed down and put in fresh hay and water.
11.30am: Rug the horse as appropriate and return to box for main breakfast. Clean tack and sweep yard.
2pm: Feed and skip out. Turn horse out for at least a couple of hours if possible, or perhaps ride a second time.
6pm: Feed, top up hay and water and prepare bed for the night. Add fresh bedding and change rug if necessary.
10pm: Take it in turns to do a late night check if possible.

NOTE: Feeding, grooming, exercise, health checks, worming, farriery, clipping, tack and horse clothing are covered in detail in later sections.

FEEDING TIPS FOR THE STABLED HORSE

Feeding is covered in more detail later, in Part 9. However, there are a few facts which are particularly important to the owner of the stabled horse.

Since the horse literally has no idea where its next meal is coming from, and because the equine digestive system requires an almost constant passage of food through it in order to stay healthy, depriving a stabled horse of food for any length of time causes real anxiety and can result in serious physical upset such as colic. Just as your stomach starts to rumble around your usual meal times, the horse's body clock becomes primed for feed times. For most horses, but particularly the stabled animal, this is the highlight of their day. The horse's world revolves around its stomach, which is why it is only fair to keep to a strict and regular routine.

There is only so much concentrated feed (e.g. mix or nuts) a horse can take, so more of this is not going to prevent your horse from growing hungry; however, you can divide the daily ration into smaller, more frequent portions which will help alleviate boredom as well as being more compatible with the horse's digestive system. The routine above is based around four feeds, which is already more than is practical for most owners, but the more you can fit in, the better. Very often at least fourteen hours go by between the last feed at night and the first one in the morning. If you live on site and can give the horse its last feed late at night and its morning feed as early as possible, so much the better. It is also possible (but expensive) to install automatic feeders which work on a timer and release regular rations around the clock. Remember it is not the quantity of feed that must increase but the frequency of meal times, to emulate the horse's natural 'little and often' grazing pattern.

A plentiful supply of low-energy fibre such as hay is what is needed to keep the horse occupied and content, and its digestive system in good working order. In the field, a horse will graze almost constantly to satisfy its need to chew, but when this option is removed by stabling it may well turn to eating bedding or any suitable wood around the stable, if hay supplies are limited. So before you get annoyed and plaster all surfaces with anti-chewing preparations, consider why the horse has adopted this destructive habit. A hay net with really small, tight holes is effective at slowing greedy eaters; turnout for a few hours on sparse grazing will also have a therapeutic effect without unwanted calorie consumption!

Remember to allow at least one hour, preferably two, before riding the horse after feeding. If you want to feed something but do not have time to wait for full digestion, compromise with hay and a handful of hard feed or chaff before riding, then feed the rest of the ration later.

STABLE VICES

When horses are badly managed and kept stabled for long periods without sufficient exercise and correct nutrition, boredom and frustration can lead to a number of behavioural problems such as box-walking, weaving, rug-tearing, wind-sucking, door-kicking and crib-biting. If allowed to continue, these signs of frustration may become habitual in the long term, so that even if the horse's management routine is changed, it continues to exhibit the so-called 'vices'. They are difficult to cure once established.

Although their appearance initially indicates mental stress, stable vices will eventually compromise the horse's physical health. For example, its teeth may become worn and its digestive system upset with constant wind-sucking; leg joints may be damaged by weaving or door-kicking. It was also once thought that other horses in a yard would learn to copy or mimic a horse exhibiting such behaviour, but recent research has proved this to be untrue. If other horses in the yard start exhibiting stable vices (or stereotypies as they are now called), it is more likely to be because they are subject to a management system similar to their unhappy neighbour's, causing them to be equally frustrated.

Prevention is always better than the numerous cures on the market, and common sense also plays a part. If your horse is ripping its rug, for example, is it because it is too hot or uncomfortable underneath it?

Also see the feeding tips above. A high-fibre diet keeps the horse mentally and physically occupied and content, and can help prevent the development of vices. Although they may be greedy at first, most horses learn to regulate their fibre intake if they are given a near-constant supply. Ensure that the horse is not suffering pent-up energy from too much hard feed, and that it gets sufficient exercise and freedom to socialise with other equines.

FIRE SAFETY

One of the greatest fears of any horse owner has to be fire in the stables. With so much flammable material about, a stable fire will spread with frightening speed and is very difficult to stop or control once started. The most obvious and easily eliminated hazard is smoking around the stables or storage areas, but a more common cause of a stable fire is actually an electrical fault: plug sockets, exposed wires, light bulbs and faulty or abused heaters make prime suspects. Self-combusting hay barns and muck heaps are next on the list, followed by poorly maintained vehicles or appliances igniting flammable material lying on or near them. Sadly, good security is also needed to deter the arsonist.

Fire safety check list

- Put clear signs banning smoking near the yard or barns, and enforce the rule rigidly.
- Keep brightly-coloured hoses, clearly marked, reeled onto a drum under a frost-proof cover. They should stretch to the furthest points of the yard.
- Place fire extinguishers at strategic points around the yard and tack room.
- Think carefully about heating in the tack room – not all heaters are suitable for drying rugs and clothing. Never place items over a convector-type heater to dry, and ensure that anything left near a gas or electric heater cannot fall onto it.
- Keep the yard, stables and outbuildings clear of dust and cobwebs, and do not

allow loose hay and bedding to pile up. These flammable materials create a potential hazard and allow fires to spread more quickly.

- Write up an evacuation procedure for the horses in case fire does break out, and display it in a prominent position.
- Get a qualified electrician to do the wiring and make sure all the electrics have a tough, rodent-proof cover. Mice love to gnaw on wiring and once they are through the cable casing, sparks will fly.
- Switches should be designed for stable use and should be out of the horse's reach.
- Always use low-energy light bulbs with protective covers. They are much cooler and cheaper to run than ordinary bulbs, which can heat up to over 250 degrees centigrade and set dust, cobwebs or loose straw alight.
- Hay bales, straw stacks and muck heaps generate a large amount of heat and if improperly managed, can self-combust. Make sure hay is properly baled, keep stacks well away from the stables (preferably in a brick building rather than an open-fronted barn) and ask a local farmer or fire service to check the centre of stacks for excess heat with a special probe if you have any doubts.
- Do not park hot tractors, cars or horseboxes in a barn with loose straw or hay about.
- When planning your stables, bear in mind that a fire appliance needs at least a three metre gap to get through.
- Deter potential arsonists (the second most common cause of stable fires in the UK) with good security.
- If the stable is isolated or difficult to find, write the address with any helpful information or obvious landmarks on a card by the telephone, so that whoever calls the emergency services can give clear directions.

QUICK-RELEASE KNOT

Whenever you tie a horse up, in the yard, stable, field, horsebox or trailer, use a quick-release knot tied to a piece of breakable twine or string. Horses fighting an

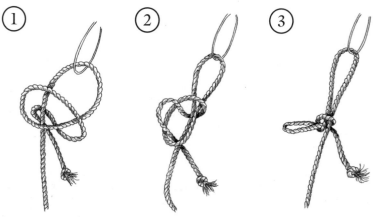

Quick-release knot: The safe way to tie up a horse.

indestructible rope will often panic and damage themselves or break the headcollar before giving up, so it is better to risk the string breaking and the horse getting loose. In the case of an accident involving the trailer or horsebox, a horse which is unable to free its head faces additional trauma.

4. GRAZING AND PASTURE MANAGEMENT

Horses evolved to roam over an extensive area in herds, eating a constant supply of low-quality fibre, and this is the lifestyle we should allow them to emulate as far as possible. Under such circumstances, the horse is able to regulate its own food and water supplies, get several hours of light exercise a day, wear down the overgrowth on hooves and teeth, and seek company and shelter where necessary. In addition, this nomadic lifestyle reduces worm infestation because the horse is not forced to graze alongside its own droppings.

Provided they have adequate food and shelter, with warm, weatherproof rugs when necessary, every horse is better off turned out to graze as nature intended. However, horses are wasteful grazers and metal-shod feet can soon ruin pasture, particularly in winter. It is not economical or practical for most people to have the amount of land necessary for a domestic horse to be self-sufficient, so in order to make the most of what land you have and to ensure that it serves the needs of your horse, it is necessary to maintain it properly.

PASTURE MANAGEMENT
You don't need green fingers to maintain safe and healthy grazing for your horse. Here are some of the measures you can take to keep the pasture in good condition.

- Worm all animals at the same time and pick up dung twice weekly in summer and autumn, and once weekly in winter. This is the single most effective way of reducing parasites and keeping flies at bay.
- Apply protective woodcoat to wooden gates, fencing and fence posts once a year.
- Do a daily check for weak fencing, contaminated water, poisonous plants and rubbish.
- Split the land up and allow one part to rest while the horses graze the remaining area.
- Mix horses with other livestock if possible. They will eat the grass rejected by horses and aid parasite control. Donkeys can be lungworm carriers, however, so ensure they are healthy and properly wormed before turning them out with horses.
- Keep horses off wet land whenever possible.

The more technical side of pasture management is something which the average horse owner can't be expected to know too much about, unless they have an agricultural background. It's essentially a job for the experts, who will be able to analyse your soil, assess the pasture and advise on suitable fertilisers etc. A local farmer may also be willing to help, and is likely to have the machinery to make such things as topping, harrowing, reseeding and fertilising a quick and painless procedure.

Harrowing: Aerates the soil, breaks up and scatters piles of droppings and roots out dead grass, encouraging new growth. However, unless environmental conditions desiccate the exposed larvae, harrowing is counter-productive for worm control. Its other uses are important.

Topping: Reduces rank areas of longer grass which horses will not eat.

Fertilising: Adds nutrition for strong, healthy grass growth, but beware of making grazing too rich for the horses' good. You will need to keep the horses off the grazing while certain chemicals wash into the soil.

Reseeding: Covers bare patches, such as around the gateway or water trough, in spring. Make the seed merchant aware that it is for equine grazing as the seed mixes suitable for dairy cattle provide grazing that is too lush for horses.

Drainage: To prevent land becoming poached and unusable in winter. Horses also like somewhere relatively dry to lie and rest. Having a drainage system installed is disruptive and expensive, but if the land belongs to you or is on long-term lease, it is worth it.

Weed control: Weeds are of poor nutritional value to the horse, rob the soil of valuable nutrients, and prevent the growth of good-quality grazing. Good pasture management can control or prevent their growth, and in the UK some are covered by the Injurious Weeds Order, which legally obliges the land owner or occupier to control particular weeds.

Common weeds and measures to control them are as follows:

- *Nettles* are best cut or sprayed when they are growing vigorously. Many horses enjoy nettles and they are believed to have some therapeutic properties, but they should not be allowed to take over a paddock.
- *Creeping thistles* require spraying at the 'early bud' stage.
- *Docks* may need spraying in spring and autumn.
- *Chickweed* can be sprayed at any time, but preferably in the seedling stage.
- *Buttercups* are mildly poisonous if eaten fresh in quantity. They are most common on wet or overstocked land and should be sprayed before flowering.
- *Ragwort* must be treated before the flowering stem emerges. It is highly poisonous when dead, so mature plants should be pulled up by the roots and disposed of outside the field. Cutting ragwort simply encourages more vigorous growth.

NOTE: When using sprays always follow manufacturers' instructions regarding time needed to elapse before returning horses to the treated grazing.

POISONOUS PLANTS

A number of grassland and hedgerow plants are poisonous to horses. While horses often avoid them in the fresh state if they have an alternative, they can become more palatable yet still be poisonous when wilted or in hay.

While it may seem like the ideal solution to a keen gardener, it is also unwise to feed grass cuttings to horses as they quickly ferment and may cause choking. As well as pasture and hedgerows, check that overhanging trees are not going to provide unsuitable snacks. Yew is particularly deadly, as are acorns which, due to the sheer size of old oak trees, can easily fall in great quantities even over a boundary fence.

FIELD SIZE

One acre per horse is the minimum amount of space needed for satisfactory turnout, although the larger the area allowed per horse, the healthier both land and horses will remain as long as the grazing is not too rich. (This can sometimes be the case if the pasture has been seeded for cattle rather than horses.) If your horse has a weight problem, you can section off the main field into smaller areas using electric fencing, or introduce other livestock such as cattle and sheep to reduce the grazing to a healthy level. Mixed grazing is also recommended for the control of parasites, since the life-cycle of the worms which affect horses are disrupted when they are ingested by cattle and sheep.

If you are combining daily turnout with stabling, smaller turnout areas are acceptable for leg-stretching purposes, but beware of turning out too many horses in too small an area; as well as ruining the grazing and sending worm egg levels sky-high, it leads to fights and injury.

FENCING

Ideal horse fencing is post and rail, but this expensive and needs regular maintenance. For more mature animals, money can be saved by making it a two-rail fence, one at the top of the fence post and the other halfway down, especially if the fence has a secondary barrier such as a hedge behind it. Ideally three, four or even five rails should be used, especially where extra security is needed such as on a stud. The bottom rail should be low enough to prevent the horse getting wedged underneath it if he rolls close to the fence; around 30cm is normal but this may be reduced to as low as 15cm on a stud to prevent sleeping foals getting stuck. The top rail should be at least 120cm high to discourage the horse from jumping out, with the rails flush with the inside of the posts to present a smooth barrier with no projections. With a stallion or horse which is in the habit of jumping out, an extra rail or line of electric tape run above the top rail will increase the height still further and act as a deterrent. Other options are electric tape, rubberised webbing and thick hedging. The latter should be at least five feet high and two feet wide at the base to make a stockproof barrier, and weak spots lined with timber or wire to prevent horses pushing through. Although it is cheap and often seen in fields intended for horses, plain and barbed wire are not recommended. Sheep wire, with square wire holes right down to ground level, is the most dangerous of all as feet can so easily get caught. Also consider the gate – it's important that this is strong but easily manoeuvred by someone holding a horse with one hand! It should also be at least as high as the rest of the fence and wide enough to allow the horse to pass through without catching the rug or banging his hips. Around 1.2m, the approximate width of a stable door, is adequate, but you may wish to lead more than one horse at a time through the gate for convenience, in which case it should be at least 1.8m wide.

SHELTER

Horses can regulate their temperature and remain comfortable in the coldest conditions provided that they can get out of the rain and wind. A purpose-built field shelter with a high, wide entrance (at least 5.5m), facing away from the prevailing wind, is the ideal. In poor weather it can be bedded down and kept stocked with hay, but ensure every horse gets a fair share – horses will not wish to enter a shelter with the herd bully. Thick trees, hedges, banks and land undulations also offer some natural shelter depending on their position, but are insufficient for horses kept out all winter.

Rugs (covered in Section Five) come in all shapes, sizes and weights, and are essential for the comfort of most grass-kept animals in winter.

WATER

As long as it is fresh and easily accessible, the water source can be natural or artificial. Obviously you have more control over a trough than a pond, and it is easier to clean and maintain. An automatically filling trough is ideal. Large plastic dustbins also make suitable water containers but need regular topping up as horses may not be able to reach the bottom. They are also light enough to fall or blow over when empty, so consider roping them upright to a fence. Old sinks and baths can be used but taps must be removed and sharp edges padded or boxed in. A natural water source must be clean and have a shallow edge with a firm base to allow easy access and safe paddling.

CARE OF THE GRASS-KEPT HORSE

A grass-kept horse's basic requirements are:

- Sufficient, suitable and well-maintained grazing.
- A clean water supply.
- Safe fencing.
- The company of other horses.
- Shelter from the elements.
- Regular worming, tooth and foot care.
- Access to a salt and mineral lick.

DAILY ROUTINE

Horses kept at grass are relatively low-maintenance compared to stabled animals, but they still need checking at least twice a day for injury, basic grooming and a quick health and condition assessment. You also need to allow time to check the field's fencing, water supplies, any new hazards that have appeared overnight and to clear droppings. Horses which are ridden regularly may need extra feed, for which they will need to be separated from others in the field to avoid fighting.

If you think this sounds like fairly hard work for a supposedly low-maintenance system, remember you may not always have to do the twice-daily check yourself – your horse should be turned out with others, so it's often possible to organise a rota with other owners.

ADDITIONAL CARE

This depends on the weather, time of year and type of horse. Feeding and grooming requirements are covered later in this chapter; use common sense for other seasonal requirements. For example, in summer the horse will be more comfortable with a daily squirt of fly repellant, while in winter you need to check that its rugs remain dry and comfortable. It can be doubly difficult to spot disease or injury through a thick layer of hair and mud too.

While it is in every horse's best interests, both physically and psychologically, to spend several hours a day at liberty with equine companions, all too often in practice too little exercise and the richness of intensively managed pasture leads to many domestic horses becoming overweight, particularly in the spring and summer when grass is at its most nutritious. As well as putting additional strain on the heart, lungs, joints and tendons, the overweight horse becomes prone to other potentially fatal diseases such as laminitis (see Section IV). This is something that you need to be aware of, particularly if you have a hardy, native type of animal rather than a less thrifty 'blood' horse. Finer types, bred for speed or athleticism, have naturally thinner coats and less of a fat layer, and may not thrive if kept out all winter. They will certainly require more food, good rugs, shelter and possibly partial stabling in winter.

THE HERD HIERARCHY

Understanding the herd system is an important part of horse ownership. In the wild, horses live in herds for companionship, safety and breeding purposes, but the strict hierarchy within each herd also ensures that youngsters are taught basic social graces and discipline. The head brood mare will see to this in no uncertain terms. It is cruel and unnecessary to deny your horse the companionship of others, both in and out of the stable; if you have a youngster, it is positively harmful to its development not to turn it out with others to play and learn. If a youngster learns to respect the herd leader and rules of equine society, it will find it easier to transfer that respect and understanding to you and your rules.

Horses have their own way of deciding who's who in the hierarchy and there may initially be a few scuffles between strangers; allow nature to take its course but keep an eye out for real bullies who may present a threat to the welfare of other horses, particularly when there's food about.

A stallion should only be turned out with his own brood mares and their youngsters, or on his own in a secure paddock preferably out of sight and earshot of other colts or in-season mares. Organising a stallion's work and social life require a great deal of experience and careful management on the part of the handler, but like all horses, he should never be denied the company of others. His behaviour should not present a problem if he is kept content and properly disciplined.

5. SECURITY

It's a sad fact that horses and their paraphernalia make rich pickings for thieves. A well supervised yard with security lights, a well advertised alarm system and limited access is the best way to keep your property safe. It is wise to padlock the main gate to the yard to prevent horses and vehicles being easily removed; horse boxes and trailers can also have wheel locks or better still, be kept in locked buildings. Your insurance company may also have specific requirements regarding security. In addition to insurance cover for your horse and property, there are several other measures you can take to deter thieves.

Protecting your horse

There are various methods of identification which will make your horse less attractive to a thief. These include branding, freeze-marking, micro-chipping and hoof-marking. Most are linked to a national database which may offer a reward and aid recovery if the horse is lost or stolen. Horses kept outdoors can be more vulnerable to theft (unless they are difficult to catch!), particularly if the field is isolated.

You should have posters in obvious places warning thieves that property and horses are marked. The most important thing is to deter thieves with good security and to keep recent pictures and records of your horse to hand, so that you can give an accurate description if the horse is stolen. While some pure- and part-bred horses have official papers and are registered with their relevant breed society, many horses and ponies have no such records. As well as the size, age, sex, colour, breed or type, you should also note white markings on the face or legs, old scars or injuries, whorls (where the hair changes direction) or the odd muscle indentations known as a prophet's thumbprint.

Field security

Always use capped hinges on the gate or have a chain and padlock at both ends to prevent it from being lifted off the hinges. Ensure that fencing is secure, and avoid leaving headcollars on the horses or near the gate. Check the horses at least twice a day so that you can alert police immediately if anything is amiss. Hedges should be as thick and prickly as possible. Be particularly careful if rights of way cross your land; ensure that gates cannot be left open.

Stable security

This is more difficult as it is very unwise to actually padlock a horse into the stable, due to the fire risk. However, it's a good idea to padlock the main gate to the yard so that even if a thief gets a horse out of the box, they will be unable to get it out of the yard easily.

Security lights with an infra-red sensor activated by movement are relatively cheap to install around the yard and stable and make a good deterrent. Also, make your routine unpredictable with irregular patrols, late night checks or dog walks around the yard, and ask anybody living nearby to keep a look-out. There are a number of alarm systems on the market that will go off if the stable door is opened. With a very valuable horse, closed-circuit television surveillance may be an option.

Protection for tack and equipment

Even a single horse owner may have many thousands of pounds worth of equipment stored in the tack room and it is often a prime target for thieves. Access should therefore be through one door only, which should be robust and set into a solid frame with a minimum of two locks. Windows, if there are any, should be as high as possible and have security bars or grilles fixed on the inside. Many tack thefts occur through the ceiling or roof construction, so a sandwich layer of steel mesh reinforcement is advisable, as is an alarm system which is clearly advertised outside. As a final deterrent, tack can be individually security-marked by police.

Don't leave rugs and other items of clothing lying around the yard, and clearly mark rugs in large, bright letters with your name or post code. Beware also when you are away from home or at a show – it's easy for people to pick up your belongings if you leave them on the grass outside your horse box while you are competing. Insurance companies are unlikely to compensate you for goods lost under such circumstances.

CCTV

Closed-circuit television is not found in many private yards but is widely used in commercial yards and studs both for security and for observation; for example, a brood mare can be left in peace to give birth while being closely watched for signs of distress. For security purposes, cameras can be positioned to overlook key areas such as the yard entrance, field gate or tack room. Individual boxes, such as foaling boxes, can be observed by putting a camera inside the actual box with a monitor set up in a nearby sitting-room.

6. CHOOSING A YARD

When you have taken on board all the information so far and decided how you wish to keep your horse, the search for a suitable place to keep it begins.

LIVERY

There are many commercial livery yards around, offering different services and facilities. You rent a stable in the yard, and grazing is usually shared with other owners. Sharing a yard with others makes it easier to ask for advice, ride out in company and get back-up support if you go on holiday or are sick. However, you can't choose who you share with! How much you have to do for a horse kept at livery pretty much depends on how much you want to spend.

Full livery

Absolutely everything is done for the horse, and the owner can simply turn up and ride at will. Full livery should include mucking out, grooming, exercising, tack cleaning and turnout, but the owner is usually charged for extras such as worming, farriery and vaccination boosters. This is a good option if you can spare the money and have insufficient time, knowledge or confidence to look after the horse yourself. Choose a reputable yard and determine exactly what is included in their full livery – some charge extra for tasks such as mane and tail pulling.

Do-it-yourself

A cheaper option, where you do absolutely everything for the horse yourself. Depending on the yard, hay and bedding may be provided, but you usually have to provide your own hard feed. Some big yards offer DIY livery but will carry out some tasks for an extra charge, e.g. turning the horse out. Many owners in DIY yards make their lives easier by job-sharing; for example, one person may turn both horses out in the morning, while the second owner brings them in at night.

Part livery

A compromise between full and DIY livery in terms of work and price. The yard owner may do certain tasks for the owner, such as mucking out each morning, feeding or bringing the horse in at night, but every other aspect of the horse's care is the owner's responsibility. This can be a very helpful system for the working owner who wishes to look after their horse but whose working hours or family commitments make it difficult to be consistently available for the horse at the appropriate times.

Working livery

Often available in riding schools, where the weekly livery fee is reduced because the school has the use of your horse for a specified amount of time each week. You and the school need to be clear about when this will be, and the ability of the people who will be riding your horse.

Grass livery

The cheapest and most basic type of arrangement, suitable for horses which do not need a stable. You rent the grazing alone, but it's essential that there is good shelter, since the horse will be out in all weathers.

Competition livery

A special arrangement where a horse is sent to a professional rider to be produced for competition. It generally includes full livery plus the relevant exercise, schooling and training necessary for competition success. Expenses such as entry fees and transport to events may be additional. Price will vary according to the rider's circumstances and the horse's level of training and talent.

RENTING A YARD

You will have more privacy and be more independent than in a livery yard, but you will need to make your own arrangements for hay and bedding deliveries, upkeep of pasture and fencing, muck-heap removal etc. Depending on its size, a rented yard may not have the same facilities as a commercial yard, and security is compromised if there is only you keeping an eye on the place.

WHICH YARD?

There are several factors you should take into consideration when selecting a yard, in order to get the best out of it for you and your horse.

- Location, not only from your home but in relation to your work place, major roads and access to bridleways. The closer you are to safe off-road riding, without having to ride along major or busy roads, the better. You may have to travel further from home to find a good yard, but it will be worth it.
- Facilities. You may think a basic stable and field are all you need, but your first winter spent struggling without electricity or running water will soon change that! If you don't want horse-owning to be all work and no play, you have to be somewhere with facilities which enable you to enjoy your horse. Does the yard have an all-weather school? Is it floodlit? It may work out cheaper to pay for a yard with a school than having to hire an arena, transport your horse there, etc. Are there jumps you can use? Is there safe parking for your lorry or trailer? Not all yards have toilets or washing facilities, which are helpful if you plan to go straight from the stables to work. Be prepared to pay more for good facilities.
- Turnout options. If grazing is limited the yard owner may not allow owners to turn their horses out all year round. How many horses do they turn out

together? If your horse is prone to becoming overweight, is there an area where its grazing can be restricted? Fencing should also be well maintained and of a suitable type for horses.

- Storage. Ask if the livery yard supplies hay and bedding. If not, is there adequate storage room for you to buy your own supplies in bulk? How much space does each owner have for tack, feed, rugs etc? Is there a rug-drying area? What about parking a trailer or horsebox – is there provision for this and does it cost more?
- Security. It is preferable for your horse to be housed where someone lives on site. Ask the yard owner what their policy is on late-night checks – some are reluctant to have people on site after a certain time.
- Yard maintenance. How are the stables, yards and other areas maintained? Could you and your horse live happily in a disorganised environment? Or is everything unnaturally pristine?
- Condition of other horses. This will tell you a great deal about the yard, and what the attitude of other owners might be towards the welfare of your horse.

A HORSE AT HOME

To keep your horse outside your own back door often appears to be the ideal solution and the realisation of a dream for many horse lovers. However, while it is certainly convenient in terms of proximity, and of course you won't have to pay livery or yard rental fees, there are some drawbacks:

- It can be lonely and unsafe to always ride alone.
- It is more difficult to ask last-minute favours or share holiday cover with other owners.
- A second opinion from others who know your horse can be very comforting in times of crisis!
- It may be more difficult and expensive to obtain the services of vets, farriers, chiropractors, instructors etc. than it is in a yard full of other owners also requiring their services.
- You won't have many of the facilities that are available at a large commercial yard, such as an all-weather school or a number of jumps to practise over.
- You will be responsible for the day-to-day tasks which livery yard owners often take care of, for example, disposal of muck heap, maintenance of buildings, fences and grazing, buying and storage of hay and bedding, etc.

BUILDING YOUR OWN

It may be that your property already has stables, grazing and storage facilities. If not, it may have some land and old farm buildings suitable for conversion. Check the criteria for ideal stabling, grazing and fencing, earlier in this section.

If you intend to build your own stable from scratch, it is best to consult a specialist rather than just contacting the local builders. You will need planning permission, a piece of flat land and a hard surface for the building to be constructed on. A roughened concrete base is ideal but adds considerably to the cost.

Also consider such things as:

- Drainage and smells.
- Power supplies.

- Nuisance to neighbours.
- Fire risk from bedding or other flammable materials.
- Access and frequency of delivery lorries.
- Proximity of major roads if horses escape.
- Sufficient turnout facilities.
- Company for your horse.
- Future equine residents; make the box big enough for any horse, not just your own!
- Future possibilities and extensions. Even if it is unlikely you will want to develop further, the potential is there for others.

PLANNING PERMISSION

If you wish to develop your own property, it is essential that you consult the relevant authorities before you start, because the exact legislation depends on what you plan to do. In the UK, a stable within a garden and more than five metres (15ft) from a dwelling may be constructed without planning permission if it is for private use. However, there is still legislation concerning height and position etc. so it is worth going through the final design with a planning officer before you get started. The rules for a commercial establishment are more complex and your local council will be able to advise you on individual cases.

Planning permission is required for all other stables and field shelters. Bear in mind that with any commercial development of stables, there may also be a need for human dwellings to be built in close proximity and these require additional planning permission. Rights of way running through the land have to be respected and if you don't want people tramping past your horse's stable or through his field, you must design around them or apply to have them re-routed (although this is becoming increasingly difficult). The style and materials of local buildings is also an issue: your stables must not be out of keeping with the area, and there are severe restrictions on the alteration of listed properties. If the proposal involves building or diverting drains, ponds or lakes or the installation of a sewage disposal system, approval may also be required from the national organisation in charge of water courses and drainage.

The yard owner may also have additional legal obligations such as to ensure that health and safety regulations are adhered to on site from construction, throughout the lifetime of the building and, eventually, to demolition. A reputable construction company should ensure that these points are fully explained and covered.

7. GROOMING AND TURNOUT

As well as improving the horse's appearance, regular grooming keeps the skin and coat healthy and provides an opportunity for the owner to thoroughly check the animal and get to know every lump and bump. It's essential for health and hygiene, and horses will do it for themselves in their natural state by rolling, rubbing against trees and posts and scratching each other with their teeth. The human version is a little more refined than this, but the principle is the same – to get rid of scurf and dirt and stimulate the skin.

A gleaming, immaculate horse turned out for the show ring is a beautiful sight, but the effect takes hours to achieve and lasts for a depressingly short time! It's more realistic to reserve such standards for special occasions and settle for a clean, comfortable animal on a day-to-day basis. The precise extent of your grooming routine will depend on the weather, time of year, type of horse or discipline and your management system, but whatever the circumstances you should never put tack, clothing or equipment on a dirty horse. At best he will be uncomfortable, at worst it will rub and cause sores which are invariably slow to heal. If you are short of time there is no need to groom the whole horse – just clean off the areas where equipment will lie.

There are several factors that may influence your grooming routine.

1. **Weather**
   Wet weather can mean muddy horses, and you'll need to go easy on removing the natural waterproofing grease from your horse's coat. In hot, dry conditions, many horses will prefer a cool shower to remove sweat after work and the horn of their feet may dry out and crack without regular watering.

2. **Time of year**
   In summer a hoof pick, sponge and fly spray may be the most you need in terms of grooming kit, but with winter comes mud and an extra hairy coat. If your horse is clipped and rugged-up over the winter it may appear clean beneath them, but its skin will need extra stimulation and clean, well aired rugs to stay healthy. (Also see 'Weather' above.)

3. **Type of horse and discipline**
   If you plan to show or compete with your horse, there are various rules and regulations about what constitutes correct turnout for different disciplines. It is usual to be smartly pulled and plaited or braided for dressage (see 'Pulling and trimming' and 'Special occasions' below) and the upper levels of show jumping, for example. Anything goes for cross country competitions or the speed and endurance phase of an event. Manes can hang loose for Autumn hunting but the horse must be smartly clipped and plaited, with a pulled or plaited/braided tail, later in the season. Likewise, particular breeds and types have their own turnout rules for showing. Trimming hairy heels or pulling the unruly mane of a Welsh Cob would be considered scandalous in the showing world!

4. **Management system**
   Horses which live out need the extra hair and grease to keep them comfortably warm and weatherproof, while you can trim and clip a horse which has the warmth and shelter of a stable to your heart's content, provided you make up for what you've taken off with extra rugs and a draught-free environment. However, even a hairy sort which is living out will appreciate being clean, and if it is going to wear tack or rugs, it is essential that the horse is clean underneath them to prevent rubbing.

GROOMING DO'S AND DON'TS
Grass-kept horses: Need to retain their natural protection against the elements, but poor hygiene can lead to ill health and skin conditions such as mud fever (see Section Four), so it's a matter of balancing health and practicality.

Do:
- Pick out the horse's feet daily, taking care not to dig into the sensitive frog.
- Use a stiff, long-bristled brush such as a dandy brush to remove mud and obvious dirt.
- Untangle the mane and tail with your fingers or a brush and some baby oil.
- Sponge the eyes, nostrils and dock clean.
- Apply fly repellant if necessary.

Don't:
- Remove essential grease by using the softer body brush.
- Clip, unless you are taking off a minimal amount of hair to allow the horse to work comfortably, and rug him up well to compensate.
- Remove protective hair by trimming the legs and head or pulling the mane and tail.

Stabled horses: Are denied the chance to roll, rub and mutually groom to the same extent as grass-kept horses. Dust, dead hair and bedding accumulate under rugs and because the horse is not walking around in the sun, rain and fresh air, its skin needs stimulation to keep it healthy. The advantage of grooming a stabled horse is that it is unlikely to be covered in mud and can be clipped and trimmed to make matters easier.

Do:
- Pick out feet and brush off the stabled horse before and after exercise (known as 'quartering').
- Devote at least three-quarters of an hour daily to intensive top-to-toe grooming and massage (known as 'strapping').
- Keep the horse's rugs clean inside, either by airing and brushing the lining regularly or putting an easily washable cotton summer sheet beneath a warmer rug.
- Make sure the horse is adequately compensated for being clipped by adding extra feed and rugs.

Don't:
- Use the stiff dandy brush on clipped or sensitive areas.
- Strip the rugs off a clipped horse on a cold day in order to groom it thoroughly. Instead, fold them back as you groom beneath them, then replace when you go to work on a different area.

GROOMING KIT
There are many wonderful gadgets on the market for grooming and improving your horse's appearance, but a basic grooming kit may generally be used as follows:

- Keep a *hoof pick* handy in your pocket, by the field gate, at the stable door and in your grooming kit. Used to remove stones and clean the sole of the horse's feet in a heel-to-toe direction, going down either side of the delicate frog. This should be done at least once a day, and always before and after riding.
- The soft, short-bristled *body brush* removes grease and dandruff and is idea for use on sensitive areas such as the face, and on clipped horses.
- A *metal curry comb* is drawn across the body brush to clean it after every few

strokes, and is not actually used on the horse.

- A *rubber curry comb* removes dried mud and loose hairs and is used in a circular motion for a massaging effect.
- The stiff, long bristles of the *dandy brush* are ideal for removing dried mud and dirt, but are too hard for use on clipped or sensitive horses.
- *Sponges* should be different colours – one for the eyes and nose, one for the dock and one for tack cleaning.
- The *stable rubber* is any clean cloth which can be dampened and wiped over the horse as a final polish.
- *Scissors* for trimming should be round-ended for safety.
- *Mane and tail combs* come in different shapes and sizes, and are really only needed if you intend to plait or pull your horse's mane or tail.
- A *sweat scraper* is more often used to remove excess water from the coat after a bath than actual sweat.
- A *water brush* is a slightly softer version of the dandy brush, used as a scrubber for feet and legs and to dampen the mane and tail so they lie flat.

KIT HYGIENE

There is little point getting stuck into grooming your horse thoroughly if your brushes are thick with grease and dust! Apart from wasting your efforts, it is unhealthy for the horse as they can harbour bacteria and disease.

Remove grease and dead hair from brushes before each use and wash them regularly in a mild soap solution. Rinse in clear water, shake out excess and leave to dry with bristles facing downwards. Keep clean brushes in a covered box or carrier.

Try and keep an individual set of brushes for each horse. Sharing brushes spreads disease. If your horse contracts a contagious skin condition such as ring worm (see Section Three), it is very important that its brushes are not used on any other animal and that they are disinfected with a specifically recommended product. Ordinary detergent will not kill certain bacteria and fungal spores.

BASIC GROOMING ROUTINE

1. If horse is stabled, tie up outside to keep the box as free as possible of dust and dead hair.
2. Pick out feet (also see 'Horn condition' in Section II, 8).
3. Work through the mane and tail in small sections, using your fingers, a body brush, or a dandy brush provided it doesn't pull out or split the hairs.
4. Remove rugs or fold them back if it's cold.
5. Use rubber curry comb in a circular motion over the horse's muscular areas, e.g. neck, shoulders, back, quarters, to remove dirt, lift scurf and massage the skin.
6. Follow with dandy brush over the body and legs of grass-kept horses or body brush for clipped/stabled horses, using the metal curry comb to clean the brush every few strokes.
7. Gently clean around the face, head and ears using a soft brush or damp cloth.
8. Sponge the eyes and nose. Use a separate sponge for under the tail.

GROOMING HEALTH CHECK

As you groom your way around the horse, check for:

- Heat, lumps, bumps, minor injuries, fly bites, and evidence of itching.
- Weepy eyes, runny nose.
- Hoof and shoe condition.
- Skin parasites or signs of them, such as lice, mange mites, sweet itch, ringworm, mud fever, (see Section IV).
- Bodily condition – your grooming kit is the ideal place to keep a weigh tape, which will give an indication of significant weight gain or loss before it becomes obvious to the naked eye.

SHEATH AND UDDER CLEANING

Male horses produce a dark discharge called smegma which can build up in the sheath and cause discomfort, swelling and infection if not cleaned regularly. Ideally you should take the opportunity to do this when the horse has relaxed or let down his penis to urinate. Use a sponge, warm (not hot!) water and mild medicated soap. Rinse thoroughly, dry and smear a thin layer of petroleum jelly in and around the sheath to protect the skin and soften future smegma build-up.

A mare's udder is easier to get at, but many are ticklish or sensitive in this area. Use the same procedure but take care not to get kicked.

Because these areas are often neglected, many horses are touchy about having them cleaned at first, but for the health of your horse you should persist until it becomes an accepted part of their grooming routine.

BATHING

If you really want to get all the dirt and grease off a horse, perhaps for a show, you can bathe it. However, horses take a long time to dry (especially hairy ones!) so bathing depends to a large extent on the weather. If it is cold you can wash just the tail or one particularly dirty area and towel dry.

For a proper bath, brush off all obvious mud and dirt, then soak the horse completely with water, using either a hosepipe or bucket. Use a mild shampoo designed for animal use and read the instuctions – some can be poured directly onto the horse's coat, others are better diluted in a bucket of water. Warm water is appreciated by the horse and makes a better job of removing grease. Massage the suds into the horse's coat, mane and tail using fingers or a rubber curry comb. Rinse thoroughly and use a sweat scraper to remove excess water. Avoid soaping the face and ears – sponge them instead. Keep the horse warm under a breathable sweat-rug (unless it is a very sunny day) until it is completely dry.

CLIPPING

If you intend to work your horse throughout the winter, it is usually necessary to clip off some of the heavy winter coat to keep the horse comfortable while it is working and make it easier to clean and dry off after exercise.

There are several set patterns of clip to choose from depending on how much hair you wish to take off (see below) ranging from a full clip, which removes all the hair from an animal which will be required to do hard, fast work, to a bib or belly clip which removes a minimal amount from the underside of the neck or belly. Choose the one that suits your horse's work load as well as your stable management routine.

Depending on the extent of the clip, you must compensate for lost warmth by providing extra rugs, feed and stabling, so there is little point making work for yourself by clipping off more than you have to.

WHEN TO CLIP
Unless you have a particular autumn event which you need the horse to be smartly clipped for, wait until the winter coat is established and the horse is starting to get visibly hot during exercise before clipping. Depending on your horse's hair growth rate, you will need to repeat the clip every two to four weeks. By early spring there will be a period when your horse starts to change its coat and look a bit hairy, but you should resist the urge to tidy it up with one final clip, as this can interfere with summer coat growth.

CLIPPING PROCEDURE
If you have never clipped before, watch others at work and see if it is possible for you to practise on a quiet horse which has already had the first clip and has clear lines for you to follow. Long, firm, even strokes of the clippers against the lie of the hair give the best results, and this is easier to achieve with a pair of clippers which are the right size and weight for you to hold comfortably.

If it is your horse's first time, ensure that its first experience is a good one. Give the horse a hay net and make sure you have a rug on hand to throw over the clipped areas so it doesn't get cold. Clippers heat up with use and hot blades will make the horse fidget and resent clipping, especially on sensitive areas such as around the head, so check the temperature against your own skin every few minutes. Switch the clippers off and allow them to cool down at regular intervals. Hair should fall away quickly and easily. If it does not, it may be because the tension needs adjusting or the blades need sharpening. Follow the manufacturer's instructions regarding the correct way to clean and adjust the blades. Clippers should be taken apart and cleaned thoroughly after use, serviced regularly and the blades sharpened.

If you do not wish to clip the horse yourself, there are usually plenty of people who advertise this service locally. Good clippers are expensive and it is a dirty and time-consuming job, so if you only have one or two horses to clip you may consider it worthwhile to pay someone else to do it.

You will need:
- A clean, dry horse.
- A sheltered area with power supply.
- Plenty of daylight.
- Chalk or coloured pen to mark out the clip.
- Something stable to stand on if the horse is large.
- Clippers.
- Sharp clipper blades.
- Clipper oil.
- Small brush to remove clogged hair from blades and filter.
- Long extension cable.
- Power-breaker socket plug.
- Overalls, hat, face mask and rubber-soled boots for yourself.
- Body brush, haynet, tail bandage and rugs for the horse.

TYPES OF CLIP

Hunter clip.

Trace clip.

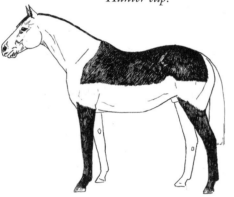

Blanket clip.

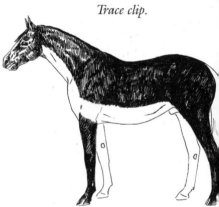

Irish clip.

Chaser (steeplechaser) clip.

Breast and gullet clip.

- An assistant to pull forward each of the horse's legs when you come to clip inside the elbows.
- Plenty of time. You will need to prepare the horse and your clipping area beforehand, stop several times throughout the clip to cool, clean and lubricate the clippers, and allow time to clean up the horse, clippers, yourself and the clipping area thoroughly afterwards.

PULLING AND TRIMMING

In addition to clipping, there are other ways you can smarten up your horse's appearance and make it easier to keep clean and dry, but bear in mind that all hair serves a purpose and it is unfair to remove it if your horse spends a lot of time outdoors. Breed societies and showing organisations have different rules about what is correct turnout, so check if you plan to show.

Areas suitable for trimming include the lower jaw (but not the antennae whiskers around the muzzle), down the tendons, fetlock and coronet, and any fluff poking outside the ear. When trimming the ears, fold them closed and use a pair of round-ended scissors to remove excess fluff, as pictured. Never remove the hair inside the ears as it is designed to keep bugs and foreign bodies out.

On the legs and along the jaw line, use a comb against the lie of the coat to lift small sections of hair away from the skin before cutting the hairs protruding between the teeth of the comb.

The mane and tail look much better if they are thinned out rather than cut with scissors, and this process is called pulling. The mane and tail hairs are brushed right through so they are tangle free. A few of the longest hairs are selected and wound round a comb, then pulled out from the roots with a sharp tug.

Pulling can take the place of plaiting if done thoroughly, or make a very thick mane and tail easier to plait.

SPECIAL OCCASIONS

Plaiting, hoof oil, coat gloss and patterned quarter marks are the finishing touches and are usually only done for shows or hunting. Beware of using coat gloss on the saddle area in a ridden class, as it make the coat very slippery. Go easy on the glossing products if your horse has sensitive skin, testing on a small area before you cover it with them.

Depending on the class entered, the breed of horse and level of competition, correct turnout may require you to plait. Plaiting is intended to show off the horse's neck and hind quarters. To be strictly correct there should be an odd number of plaits along the neck, with the one in the forelock making the total number even. Many small plaits will improve the appearance of a short, thick neck, while fewer, chunkier plaits can give the illusion of shortening a long neck.

8. SHOEING

The horse's foot is a perfectly engineered structure of tissue and bone which supports and cushions its considerable bodyweight and provides grip and protection over a variety of terrain.

In the wild, where the horse is constantly on the move and does

HOW TO PLAT A MANE

How To Plait A Mane.

Divide one section of the mane into three strands.

Plait downwards.

Use needle and thread to secure the bottom of the plait.

Fold up the plait.

Fold again.

Secure by passing the thread around the plait.

Cut off the thread underneath the plait.

Divide into three sections.

Keep the strands equal and tight.

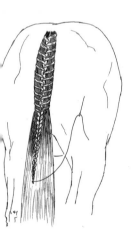

Finish the tail and continue to plait down, securing the end with thread.

Making the loop.

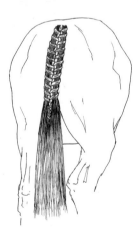

The end result.

not have the added stress of the rider's weight or regular jumping and roadwork to cope with, the feet pretty much balance themselves and wear down naturally.

However, in order to stay comfortable and fit for work, the domestic horse needs regular attention from a skilled farrier. This is one of the major and unavoidable expenses of owning a horse, especially if the animal has poorly-shaped feet or weakness in the horn.

FINDING A FARRIER

Anyone who has horses in their care will spend a great deal of time in the company of a farrier. He plays an integral part in the horse's overall fitness and performance, and it is important that he is competent and professional. Ask yourself the following questions:

1. **Is he qualified?**
    Farriers should be properly qualified and registered with their governing body. In the UK, it is illegal for any unqualified person except a vet to shoe other people's horses, although they may shoe their own.
2. **How much does he charge?**
    Be suspicious of a cheap farrier. There's more to a good service than putting on new shoes at regular intervals. Your horse's hoof condition, balance and action should be his ongoing concerns even between appointments. A good, experienced farrier may well cost more, but is generally worth the extra investment. Most farriers charge extra for travel but you may be able to share this with others at the yard.
3. **Does he understand your needs?**
    The farrier should take time to find out the type and quantity of the horse's work, assess his movement and discuss any potential problems with you.
4. **Where is he based?**
    If your farrier works from a central forge, you will have to take the horse to him which may not always be easy or convenient. Others have portable forges which travel around yards and allow the farrier to heat the shoe and fit it to the horse; some farriers still shoe 'cold' and fit a ready-made shoe as well as possible.
5. **Do you and your horse like him?**
    This should be the beginning of a long and mutually beneficial partnership.

WHEN TO SHOE

As with a human's fingernails, different horses have varying levels of horn strength and growth which influence how often they need to be trimmed or shod. A horse with good feet may only need attention every six to eight weeks; a horse in hard work or with poor feet may need the farrier's services every three or four weeks.

It may not even be necessary to shoe an animal with tough feet which only does light work, or a resting horse turned out to grass. Brood mares often go barefoot, to minimise the damage should they tread on any part of the foal sleeping at their feet. But an unbalanced foot will put stress on the leg and skeleton, resulting in poor movement, injury and unsoundness, so even if your horse does not need shoes it should still have its feet trimmed regularly.

THE BALANCED FOOT

While no horse is perfect, it is essential that the conformation of its feet is as good as possible. They must provide good support and have the shock-absorbing properties necessary for good performance and injury prevention. Having a strong and balanced foundation minimises stress further up the leg and skeleton. It is also possible to improve or correct some biomechanical faults with skilful foot balancing, changing the horse's action for the better. Equally, poor foot balancing and incompetent farriery can change it for the worse.

HORN CONDITION

The horn of the horse's hoof is living, growing tissue. Like human cuticle, its superficial horn layer, the periople, can dry out, shrink and crack, or become too moist, expand and go soft. Moisture can also enter at the 'white line' or through insensitive hoof wall cracks and splits. When this happens, the non-expanding metal shoe nailed to the foot won't fit so well any more and can come off, sometimes pulling a piece of horn with it and damaging the foot. It is therefore important for the horn to be in good condition in order for the horse to keep its shoes on.

Generally, the horn is able to regulate its own moisture content by allowing excess water to evaporate, or absorbing more water if the horn becomes dry. However, recent research refutes this ability *if* the horn is healthy. Applying a layer of hoof oil to the hoof can be detrimental to horn condition, so it should only be used occasionally, when a smart turnout is required.

The surface on which the horse is forced to stand all day also influences horn condition. Certain types of bedding such as wood shavings can be very damaging, if not kept clean and any ammonia is also damaging to the hoof.

TYPES OF SHOE

Traditionally, front shoes have a single toe clip and are quite round in shape. Back shoes have two quarter clips, and are more oval to match the natural shape of the horse's feet. They are held on by three nails on the outside branch of the shoe and two on the inside, although this can change depending on the size of the horse's foot and the weight of the shoe. A small foot requiring a light, small shoe may need only three or four nails to hold it on. The type, weight and grip of the shoe depends on the horse's feet, movement and work and you should discuss your preferences with the farrier.

REMOVING A SHOE

Although under normal circumstances you will not be the one fitting shoes onto your horse, there are occasions when it is useful to be able to take them off. If a shoe is dangerously loose or hanging off, it is likely that the protruding metal and nails will cause further damage to the horse's legs and feet, so the horse is better off without it until the farrier can come and sort things out properly.

When a horse is shod, the nails are driven up through the insensitive wall of the hoof and the protruding ends cut off and bent over into 'clenches' which lie flush against the hoof wall. When taking a shoe off, these clenches must be cut off before the shoe is prised away from the foot, to allow the nails to withdraw cleanly without damage to the hoof.

To remove a shoe you will need a coarse flat file to rasp the top off the clenches,

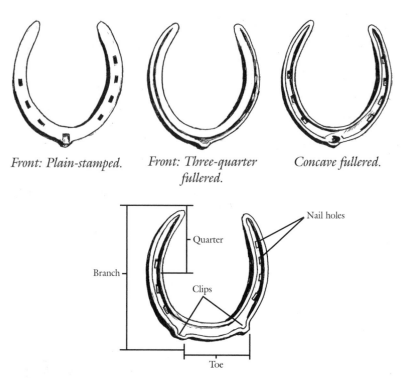

Front: Plain-stamped.   *Front: Three-quarter fullered.*   *Concave fullered.*

Hind: Showing the different parts of the show.

or a hammer and buffer to cut them off, as used by the farrier. Once the clenches have been removed, work around the shoe from heel to toe, easing it away from the hoof with pincers or a hoof pick until it comes away. Assuming you are only attempting this because the shoe is very loose already, this should not be too difficult. Count the nails to make sure there is nothing left in the horse's foot. Many horses will quickly go footsore without a protective shoe so keep them on grass or soft bedding until the farrier can come and replace the shoe.

STUDS

Extra grip can sometimes be needed to help the horse cope with different weather or ground conditions. Rather like football boots or a track athlete's spikes, studs of differing lengths and sizes can be screwed into the heel of the horse's shoe during exercise or competition. Horse shoes do not automatically come with stud holes, but it is a simple matter for a farrier to put them in at a small extra cost. There are many different types of stud, but basically, longer pointed studs should be used in hard, dry conditions; in mud and wet, large square studs give extra grip.

Studs should be removed from the shoe immediately after exercise to avoid injury resulting from the horse treading on itself (or you), and also because, like wearing

TYPES OF STUD

The stud your farrier selects depends on the state of the ground. Pointed studs are used when the ground is hard and dry; large square studs give extra grip in muddy conditions.

high heels, they have an unbalancing effect on the horse's foot, leg and overall posture. To make it easy to screw studs in and out, you need a correctly sized spanner or tap which is often provided in the stud kit. When not in use, the stud holes need to be kept clean by stuffing them with greased wads of cotton wool or by screwing in flat 'dummy' studs.

9. FEEDING

This is a complex subject to which many books have already been devoted, and your horse's health, happiness, behaviour and performance depend on you getting it right. The basic rules of feeding that always apply are:

1. Allow the horse a constant supply of clean, fresh water.
2. Feed according to the horse's type, size, temperament and workload.
3. Feed little and often. The stomach capacity of a 16hh horse is only about 2kg for example, so any extra feed will be pushed through into the gut too fast and not digested properly.
4. Feed plenty of fibre. In the wild, the horse eats for around seventeen hours a day in order to satisfy his physical and psychological need to chew. The ideal feeding programme emulates this natural system as closely as possible. The horse's stomach is small but its gut is very long, so 'trickle feeding' low-energy fibre ensures that the gut is kept working without overloading the stomach.
5. Make no sudden changes. The horse's gut contains a number of 'good' bacteria and enzymes which aid the digestion of specific feeds. They need time to build up their numbers and adapt to new feeds or else they die and release poisons which can cause colic.
6. Buy good-quality foodstuffs formulated for equines. They may be more expensive but the nutritional value will be higher so less is required, and the possibility of harmful mould and dust damaging the horse's respiratory system is reduced.
7. Keep to a routine. Horses are creatures of habit and become stressed if food is not forthcoming at regular times.

8. Leave at least two hours for digestion between food and exercise. Exercise diverts blood flow away from the gut to the heart, lungs and muscles. A full stomach will also press on the lungs and prevent maximum oxygen uptake.

9. Include succulents such as grass, carrots, apples, sugar beet or turnips in every feed. A diet of hay and cereals is very dry.

10. Feed by weight, not volume. Nuts and pellets weigh more than the same volume of coarse mix, and hay varies enormously in weight. To simplify daily feeding, obtain volume of prescribed weight of newly purchased concentrate.

BASIC DIET

The cereal grain part of your horse's ration provides a concentrated form of energy, often referred to as 'concentrates', 'shorts' or 'hard feed'. The domestic horse's diet should include some concentrates if extra energy is required for work, competition or breeding. The ration should then be topped up with fibre such as grass, chaff, hay, haylage, silage or straw.

It is important not to overfeed these high-calorie foods as they are much richer than the fibre that the horse's digestive system is designed to cope with. The system can easily be overloaded resulting in physical and psychological problems. It may be that your horse requires no extra hard feed at all, and is fittest on a low-energy diet of fibre and a multi vitamin and mineral supplement or lick. If the horse is eating more calories than it burns off, they will be converted to fat and that will place a strain on the horse's heart, lungs and tendons.

The exact ratio of hard feed to hay needed by an individual horse depends on a number of factors such as:

* The horse's size. Feed according to bodyweight (see 'How much to feed' below).
* How much extra energy your horse needs to carry out its job comfortably.
* The type of horse – like people, some put on weight more easily than others!
* Its temperament. If a horse is naturally fizzy, it may become over-excited on a high-energy diet and require a fat-based conditioning feed in order to maintain its bodyweight.
* The time of year. Horses require more energy to stay warm in winter, and grass has little nutritional value at that time of year.
* Your management routine. A horse which stands rugged up in a stable for much of the day will use less energy than one which is free to walk around, although the amount and quality of grazing must be taken into consideration when formulating a ration for the grass-kept horse.
* The rider's skill. The type of high-concentrate diet needed to provide sufficient energy for hard work and competition can make some horses excitable and hard to handle.

MIXING CONCENTRATES

Fortunately for horse owners (and horses) everywhere, the hard science of what constitutes a correct and balanced diet has largely been dealt with by feed manufacturers and their equine nutritionists. It is now a relatively simple matter to choose a nutritionally balanced hard feed designed for your horse's type, age, temperament and workload.

If you have any questions about the feed or your horse's diet, all reputable horse feed manufacturers will be happy to advise you and supply further information. Many run a telephone help-line service.

These 'compound' or 'complete' feeds come in the form of pellets, nuts or coarse mixes that look rather like muesli (for humans!). It is often thought that horses prefer the variety of a coarse mix, but unless the horse is a particularly fussy feeder, it is more likely to be the owner who thinks it looks more appetising! The advantages of feeding nuts or pellets are:

- The horse cannot pick around the bits it does not like!
- They are generally cheaper.
- They are denser so require less storage space.
- The ingredients are mixed evenly in every mouthful, ensuring a consistent diet.

For traditionalists who still wish to mix their horse's feeds from individual ingredients such as oats, barley, wheat, bran or maize (known as 'straights'), special care must be taken to analyse the nutritional value of each batch of cereal and ensure that the horse is receiving a balanced diet.

Whatever form your hard feed takes, it is always a good idea to mix it with a few handfuls of chaff to aid chewing and digestion, and to follow the basic rules of feeding.

HOW MUCH TO FEED

The most important consideration when deciding how much your horse should be fed is body weight. The weight of a total ration (hard feed and hay/roughage together) is normally 2.5 per cent of a horse's own body weight. A weigh bridge is the best way to find out your horse's exact weight. If you do not have access to one, use a weigh tape around the girth, or the formula: heart girth then squared, multiplied by the horse's length in cm divided by 8717 (as in diagram, page 94).

Multiply your horse's bodyweight by 0.025 to find out its total daily ration in kilograms. Then decide how much of this total daily requirement should be hay and how much should be hard feed. As a general guide:

- Maintenance (no work): 100% roughage, no concentrates.
- Light work (hacking three or four times a week and the occasional show): 80% roughage, 20% concentrates.
- Hard work (eventing, cross country or endurance): 50% roughage, 50% concentrates.

NOTE: The roughage level in the horse's diet should never fall below 50%.

If the horse is out at grass, it can be hard to calculate how much it is eating. Assume that most of the horse's feed requirements are being met if it is out full-time on good grazing through the spring and summer. At this time, grass has a high nutritional value and only horses in hard work will require additional feed. In winter, additional hay will certainly be required, plus hard feed if the horse is working or losing weight.

STORING FEED

Hard feed keeps best in a metal or plastic bin, in a cool, dry, well-ventilated feed store. It should be kept out of direct sunlight and covered to protect it from vermin and dust. Mice may also chew into storage sacks and vacuum-packed forage. As well as making a mess and eating expensive feed, mice pose a health hazard to your horse

MEASUREMENTS FOR CALCULATING BODY WEIGHT IN KGS.

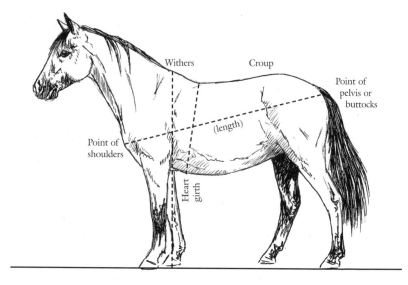

$$\frac{\text{heart-girth}^2 \times \text{length}}{8717}$$

through contamination, so care should be taken to keep your feed vermin-free.

Hay needs protection from damp and the weather. For good ventilation it should be stacked in an open-sided barn with small gaps between the bales, on raised pallets if possible to protect the bottom layer from moulding.

10. TRANSPORT

Although it may initially seem like an unnecessary luxury, there is no doubt that having your own transport can be a big help. Not only will you achieve more with your horse by getting out and about to shows, lessons and anything else that interests you, but you can also transport it to a vet or farrier in an emergency, or home in case of an accident. It's true that there are plenty of specialist horse transporters about if you are really stuck, but they offer a professional and expensive service more suited to the jet-set lifestyle of an international competition horse. They are generally only used by ordinary horse owners as a last resort or when it is necessary to transport the horse a considerable distance, for example when moving house.

TYPES OF VEHICLE

There are basically two types of vehicle suitable for transporting horses by road: horsebox and trailer. Which one you choose depends on how much money you wish to spend, how many horses you need to transport at any one time and how far and how often you intend to travel.

Generally, a horsebox provides a more comfortable, stable ride for the horse than a trailer, and is easier for the driver to manoeuvre. You can also fit a larger number of horses inside, and tack, storage and preparation space is less of a problem when you go to shows. If you travel long distances, or are frequently away overnight, then a horsebox with a living area is convenient and will save money on accommodation. With a horsebox, you can often check on your horses in transit and make sure that everything is in order without having to stop. However, it will obviously cost a great deal more to buy, run and maintain, and needs frequent use to keep the engine in good working order.

A trailer is cheaper to buy, run and maintain than a horsebox and takes up less space in the yard. It is a good choice if you only wish to transport one or two horses a relatively short distance from time to time, but you will need a suitable vehicle to tow it with. You will also need space for all your gear in the car.

Vehicle safety checklist:
- Rubber mats secured to the floor and possibly halfway up the walls are ideal for deadening road noise, providing grip and protecting the horse's legs. If there is none, put a layer of the horse's normal bedding down.
- Clean the vehicle out immediately after use, and lift mats or bedding to allow the floor to dry thoroughly and prevent floorboards rotting.
- Check the ramp and floorboards before loading, and ensure the electrics are working before setting off.
- Beware of removing partitions to allow the horse more space unless he particularly requires it. More space allows more movement, and a restless horse will destabilise the vehicle.
- The horse must be tied short enough to prevent it turning round in the box or getting a leg over the rope.
- Always tie the horse to breakable twine when travelling, not directly to the tie ring.
- When travelling a single horse in a double trailer, it should go on the side behind the driver, not nearest the kerb, to avoid affecting the balance and handling of the trailer around corners; this is also the correct position for the heavier horse of two.
- Consider investing in a special horsebox recovery service, and check what exactly it will cover in case of accident or breakdown, e.g. will it pay for alternative stabling or transport to get you and the horse home?

TRAVELLING TIPS
1. Familiarise a young or new horse with the vehicle at home.
2. Be patient and allow plenty of time to load.
3. Make sure the interior of the vehicle is welcoming and the ramp is both stable and not too steep.
4. If you are competing, travel with someone who is capable of loading the horse and driving the vehicle in case you have a fall.
5. Drive slowly and carefully, practising several times without a horse while you are learning. Horses have no way of anticipating changes of speed or direction and the stress of trying to remain balanced in transit can take a lot out of them.
6. Aim to arrive at your destination with plenty of time to spare, to give the horse time to recover and to ensure that you are not tempted to drive too fast because of time restrictions.
7. Always travel with a supply of the horse's regular food and water.

8. A hay net is a good idea provided that the horse is drinking regularly – hay without water can cause gut blockage and colic.
9. Dehydration is the biggest danger when travelling, so offer water at regular intervals and ensure the vehicle is well ventilated.
10. If it is a very long journey and there is a safe place to unload en route, do so. Walk the horse around for half an hour, check that it is a comfortable temperature and encourage it to have a pick of grass, drink, stale and pass droppings. Muck out the lorry or trailer and add fresh hay and bedding before reloading.

11. HORSEMASTERSHIP

The practice of managing a horse on a daily basis requires:
1. Learning.
2. Planning.
3. Doing.
4. Assessing that all is well.
5. Recognising that all is not well.
6. Considering the results or benefits of the 'doing'.
7. Learning more.
8. Replanning.
9. Doing better.

It implies, requires, a continuing perception around a daily inspection and other, one-off, concentrated inspections of the horse:
(a) In its stable.
(b) In-hand when led out.
(c) Ridden (driven).
(d) At grass – part-time or turned away 'at rest'.

'All well' implies that it is a willing, able, capable and an at-ease animal.
'All not well', implies quickly appraising it as an unwilling, not able, incapable, diseased animal which requires closer inspection of some or all of its systems, structurally and functionally.
  Patently an essential knowledge of a healthy animal's structure and functioning is required as a basic skill. This knowledge should encompass:
* What it should be fed.
* How it eats and excretes (the digestive system).
* The patterns of breathing.
* Breathing and heart rates and associated abdominal excursions (the respiratory system).
* How it stands, lies down and gets up.
* How it moves in the various gaits.
* What these gaits are, the discipline requirements of them (the locomotor system).
* Fitness and its assessment.

- How it responds to the rider's aids.
- Tack and its fitting.
- Shoeing and hoof-trimming.

In addition, this knowledge is all set against the background of:
- Stable construction and management.
- Set-up and management of the yard and the grazing.
- Transport.
- Legislation relevant to the horse and horse use.

HEALTH CHECKS

The horsemaster is primarily concerned with recognising changes towards dis-order, in particular to dis-ease in the three designated systems (respiratory, digestive and locomotor), which are important as those most likely to be overstressed – they are evolution-related systems. The physiology of the horse aims at homeostasis for a reasonably steady state of functioning, which naturally changes to meet requirements of 'working' additional to just 'living', but which returns to resting normal soon after these extra demands cease. In other words, the horse lives as economically as it can, the vital parameters being:

- The resting heart rate, the pulse, has a basic count per minute, around 40.
- The resting respiratory rate likewise, 10-15 breaths per minute.
- At strenuous work both will accelerate, e.g. the pulse to 200 beats per minute in flat racing, the breathing to 150.

The basic activity involves an expenditure of energy for muscle contraction and other biochemical processes. Energy comes from the horse's feed which is converted, on average, to 25% work output, 75% heat.

When this heat brings the horse's core temperature to that required, at rest, to keep it warm and to maintain a temperature environment for enzymatic activity, the remainder must be dissipated. The amount and the physiological methods for this heat loss come under one feature of the autonomic nerve control, the thermoregulatory system. A horse has a diurnal normal temperature around 1°F higher in the evening than the morning's 100.5°F.

These three vital parameters, of heart rate, respiratory rate and temperature, can be 'taken' by the horsemaster. With sports horses it is advisable to record their average levels over a period of 3-4 days at the same time and relative to other activity, preferably at morning rest, to obtain a recorded base reading. This can then be compared with other selected 'takings' as required. For example:

- The 'elevation with exercise' and, more importantly, the speed at which that returns to 'resting normal' during the post-exercise 'recovery towards resting rate' period. With increasing fitness the rate's returns will be quicker.
- The elevations associated with the greater tissue activity resulting from:
   — inflammation and consequential 'fever',
   — associated pain,
   — associated interference with system functioning,
   such as with broncho-pneumonia.
      In such a dis-eased state the rates, to some extent, equate with the severity and eventually with the recovery (or worsening).

The return to 'resting normal' in a dis-eased state is variable.

In a dis-eased state the various other clinical changes induced become clues, disordered signs, of structure and functioning, which point to 'something being wrong'. They can indicate:

- What tissue (system) might be affected.
- What pathologic process might be involved.
- In some cases, what the actual disease is. This becomes easier with experience, and by building up background knowledge.

Paradoxically no horsemaster is anxious to gain this knowledge from his own horse(s)' experiences. They will be well-advised to ask, listen and to read in order to enhance their background knowledge.

As is detailed elsewhere in this book, observation in its widest sense of 'perception' is necessary at all times. However, knowing what to 'look for', whether right or 'wrong', is but part of horsemastership. An understanding of what is required to improve and then maintain those practices, comes from the teachings of others, such as:

- The more experienced (and qualified) instructor.
- The experts in the various related trades and crafts, e.g.
  — the farrier
  — the saddler
  — the nutrionist from a feed manufacturer
- Grassland managers in:
  — soil
  — drainage
  — seed varieties
  — weed control
  — fencing
- The veterinary surgeon to discuss an annual programme for:
  — dental care
  — worm control
  — skin parasites
  — vaccination and other disease controls
  And to oversee the application of those others listed above.

A veterinary surgeon's advice regarding first aid equipment and practice which will complement his later management of wounds and other injuries is certainly more helpful than a cupboard full of an Aladdin's cave of potions, lotions and dressings. Wound care has been much simplified in recent years.

FOR THE ACTIVE HORSE

Horsemastership becomes more exacting when the horse has higher athletic involvement. Of course any horse requires careful daily attention. A delay or a mistake regarding any changes in condition does impose welfare factors. In a competitive horse a year's programme can be ruined as well.

In such horses, evidence of changes in a horse's 'condition score', if not actual weighings become most important; the fit of the saddle in relation to such condition changes is often associated with deterioration in stride length, sometimes unilaterally, as well as with frank pressure galls and sores which must be 'caught' early and appropriately managed. An instructor's observation regarding possible bit evasions and a farrier's comments concerning subtle changes in shoe wear are indicators which must not be ignored. The possible associated locomotor imbalances can lead to more serious disorders.

It pays to have such competition horses daily trotted up in-hand on the hard, and dressage horses, if not all disciplines, in circles as well as straight lines. The morning after a strong workout, especially if there has been a marked hardening of the going on the last outing or training session, are important occasions for a more critical assessment.

'Look and see', 'listen and hear', 'touch and feel' are the guide words for all-over assessment.

FOR THE HORSE AT GRASS

The horse at rest requires more than a passing look at it in a field. Early signs of low-grade, often progressive disorders can easily be missed even on a daily inspection if not done diligently, but if the horse is seen to be:

- Not grazing! When did it do so last, to your knowledge? Is it really off its food? Look again later. Don't wait for a general disease picture to develop or an obvious loss of condition: offer some dry feed as a test for appetite. Look for other clues.

- Not moving! Is it just chance that you see it dozing now, or does it not want to move, perhaps can't? Check it out now, then again later in the day. Test action in-hand on the hard if deemed necessary. Pick the feet out regularly as a routine.

- Accelerated respirations! Could it just have finished a free run exercise? Let it 'cool down'. Is the weather hot and humid? What are its companions like under these similar conditions? Check its nose and eyes for a discharge, move it and listen for a cough. Get help to take its temperature if still concerned.

And inspect all round for minor injuries which could 'go bad' if neglected now.

Beware agitation from flies. Consult your veterinary surgeon for suggested repellants; possibly have the horse(s) yarded in the shade during the day. Sweat-itch subjects do need extra care in the late afternoon, until dark.

12. FINDING A SERVICE

Most of the local services you will need on a regular basis, such as feed merchants, vets, saddlers, farriers, instructors and riding schools, will be listed in your local telephone directory. Others may be found advertising at equestrian retailers, in the equestrian press or local newspapers, or simply by word of mouth at large yards or through other horse owners. Some key national organisations and useful addresses are listed on the following page.

UK
Association of British Riding Schools
Queens Chambers, 38-40 Queen Street, Penzance, TR18 4BH
British Equestrian Federation
British Equestrian Centre, Stoneleigh Park, Kenilworth, Warks, CV8 2LR
British Equine Veterinary Association
5 Finlay Street, London, SW6 6HE
British Horse Society
British Equestrian Centre, Stoneleigh Deer Park, Kenilworth, Warwks, CV8 2XZ

USA
American Horse Council
1700 K Street NW, Suite 300, Washington DC 20006
American Horse Shows Association
220 E 42nd Street, 4th Floor, New York, NY 10017
US Pony Clubs Inc
The Kentucky Horse Park, 4071 Iron Works Pike, Lexington, KY 40511
National Show Horse Registry
11700 Commonwealth Drive, Suite 200, Louisville, KY 40299

SECTION IV

HEALTH AND SICKNESS

All present-day species of animals have an innate power of self-survival against disease. Such can be defined as the state of being no longer at ease with its immediate environment – being unwell and, as a result, unwilling and/or unable to live normally.

In the domesticated animal, a horse for example, this abnormality, having something wrong with it makes it, temporarily at least, uneconomical for its owner. Here is, of course, the important aspect of welfare for the animal which is the responsibility that man takes on when he exerts his dominion over it.

It requires man to so husband the horse that he can, firstly, correctly observe when all is not well and, secondly, quickly take damage limitation steps of:

(i)   First Aid.
(ii) Nursing.
(iii) Subsequent management.

This person must have some degree of skill. Treatment, which aims at inducing recovery or a cure is, sooner or later, direct or indirect, the responsibility of a veterinary surgeon. Prevention of dis-ease is obviously a skill. It relates, in the case of a horse, to:

(a) General husbandry, at rest or in work, in field or in stable.
•   Feeding

101

- Fittening
- Exercising and using
- Hoof care
- Correct tack
- Considerate transporting

(all subjects covered in Sections III and V).

(b) Specific husbandry.
- Artificial immunisation (vaccination).
- Strategic worm control.
- Awareness of injury risks and contagious disease probabilities in using the horse.

(c) 'Skill' covers:
- Recognition that all is well.
- Awareness of the signs of all is not well; these are 'clues' of dis-ease or injury.
- What to do when dis-ease develops.

(d) All these worthy and essential attributes come with
- Learning
- Understanding
- Practice – under more experienced, professional guidance,

so that the horse can be perceived (with all one's senses) as a 'whole' and, more importantly, nursed as a whole animal. Sickness will affect a range of body systems; injury can affect areas other than the primary site.

Get to know your horse, its foibles, its idiosyncracies, its individuality. Try to understand changes in these, for the better as well as the worse. Try to relate them to coincidental happenings. Records are important, whether routine dates or one-off features which could become important in the future. Above all, be aware that the horse is not as tough as you might like to think.
- Perceive it thoroughly after strenuous work.
- Manage it according to weather conditions, especially regarding the risks of chilling by wet and cold grazing and post-exercise turning out or transporting when over-heated or tired.

The background skills of prevention can be learnt: use your veterinary surgeon; use people you know to be more skilled than yourself.

DEVELOPMENTAL CONDITIONS

Those conditions which a horse is born with or to which it is hereditably susceptible is a matter for breeding policies, albeit in a limited extent. They are in the foal. Obvious conditions are often lethal or economically unviable. Others may become a liability, a susceptibility to other disorders. The former are self-eliminating, the latter a matter for action, as and when, and how, they arise and present themselves.

INFLAMMATORY DIS-EASE

This is where nature plays such an important part in survival. Had inflammatory response to a variety of physical and biological traumas, macro and microscopic not been an essential part of evolution and inheritance, the individual and the species would not have survived.

Nature's aim was to limit the damage and to effect a cure, a recovery sufficient to permit that animal to remain a member of the herd, to benefit from safety in numbers and leadership, to be able to eat and to reproduce. If not successful, death or predatory extermination occurred. Success was not intended to restore full physical fitness. The economics of domestication and athletic use, nurture, demanded better success – a full recovery. Man had to learn how to assist nature.

There are two aspects associated with physical trauma or injuries:

(a) How much to interfere with nature, e.g. by masking pain too quickly, and other of the cardinal signs, especially swelling.
(b) How to improve the healing process not only in time but also in quality. Individual tissues have inherent time factors which, so far in medical research, cannot be improved without risking quality. This is most important in recovery from tendinitis, tendon strain, especially that of the fore limb flexor units; where physical trauma was associated with an open wound there was the added fact of bacterial contamination, a micro trauma.

In such cases man can successfully intervene to minimise this with:
(i) Correct first aid with emphasis on antisepsis by
• Lavage with and without antiseptics.
• Drainage.
• Professionally advised medical antisepsis with appropriate drugs. The fewer the bacteria, the less the natural need for inflammatory responses. Antibiotics and chemotherapy in this situation only reduce germ numbers; they have no healing properties per se.

(ii) Subsequent management particularly to prevent reinfection.
Mammals have evolved along with associated parasites and have inherited the capability to develop antiparasite defences in their tissues and circulating in their blood – immunity in various forms and degree.

The dis-ease table lists these primary and secondary invaders. Immunity is most successful against viruses and bacteria. It is stimulated by the presence of the germ and usually follows recovery from clinical evidence of the particular disease, e.g. Influenza virus or Strangles bacterium. This is called natural active immunisation.

An artificial immunisation can be stimulated by inoculating a non-lethal factor of a disease germ, two or more times, into a susceptible animal: i.e. by vaccination. For example:
• Influenza.
• Tetanus – against the toxin produced by a particular bacterium, *clostridium tetani*.

Viruses are relatively new in terms of present-day medicine. Some, such as influenza, develop 'drifting' strains against which new vaccines must be developed.

Viruses do not lend themselves to direct medical treatment; any secondary opportunist bacterial invasion does, but the correct type of antibiotic or chemotherapeutic drug must be used.

Nursing, special management of the patient, is an extension of horsemastership. What is called constitutional immunity is a vague concept implying a general resistance to infectious disease. It may be inherited; horses for example, are not susceptible to Foot and Mouth viral infection. In more mundane terms it is also a reflection of good management which includes

- Nutrition
- Hygiene
- Fitness
- Awareness of disease germ sources,

as well as judicious use of vaccination. It must be stressed that for routine purposes only influenza virus and tetanus toxin lend themselves to this.

Some bacteria and protozoa as causes of disease can be kept under control by tactical medication. This is a veterinary matter.

Parasites, both ecto, i.e. of the body surface of skin and of hair, and endo, e.g. worms of the surfaces of the inner system tracts, do require management. These are just above or just below microscopic size.

A knowledge of their life-cycles is required. For example:

- Lice can only survive *on* a *horse*.
- They are active in the winter.
- Their eggs are resistant to applications.
- The adults and the larvae are not.
- A generation requires a minimum of one week.
- Treatment is three applications of a suitable ectoparasiticide at ten-day intervals.

The more important parasites are the endos, the helminth worms; their control is discussed elsewhere in the book.

Horsemastership therefore is very much a matter of dis-ease prevention:

- Minimising the risk of injury by using a horse fit for its job, in as stress-free a 'climate' as possible.
- Reducing infection
  — topically – at the site e.g. in wounds and in 'mud fever'.
  — systematically in non-viral infections.
  — immunisation against systemic disorders.
  — strategic and tactical medication.
- Maintaining the nutritional status.

THE METABOLIC DISORDERS

Metabolic disorders can develop from inherited susceptibility, others from mistakes in management within nutrition, e.g. an imbalance in the amount and the ratio of the minerals calcium and phosphorus. Several are associated with man attempting to get more athletic performance out of a horse – a production overstress. Rhabdomyolysis is one example. Laminitis is frequently associated with permitting, even forcing, a pony to consume too starch-rich a diet, with consequent entero-toxaemia and subsequent endotoxic dis-ease of the blood vessels, which constriction becomes clinical within the hoof capsule.

Horses have no innate power of defence against these metabolic disorders. They may survive them if the underlying overstresses are removed by management corrections. All are basically 'man-made' in the first place.

NEOPLASTIC DIS-EASE

There are various explanations for neoplastic dis-eases; some can be 'prevented', e.g. the formation of sarcoids in incorrectly managed healing wounds. In general there is little to stop them coming and, in the horse, little to 'cure' them. Surgery in its several forms has to be resorted to where feasible. Some sarcoids respond to a specific topical application (see your veterinary surgeon).

Sooner or later neoplasia become lethal in themselves or such as to make the horse unusable.

DEGENERATIVE DIS-EASE

Simply, this is the result of living and working. In horses degenerative dis-eases occur in the units of locomotion and particularly in the joints, especially those of the limbs. The spine is also susceptible but not so obviously.

Inherited and acquired deviations from normal limb formation predispose the animal to either a sub-acute joint trauma, or a persistent overstress on one or more joints in a limb as a column of support, or a gradual subclinical weakening of the structures which degenerate or wear out.

The animal has no way to prevent this. It can, however, in the later stages invoke chronic inflammatory response to produce an osteoarthritis which slows it down – which theoretically should reduce the overstress, but too late. In some cases, as in spavin, osteoarthritis of the hock's small aliculations, the joint ankyloses to 'lock up'.

More general, multisystemic degenerations come with advancing years. (See The Older Horse Section IV, 8.) Basically these relate to exhaustion or deterioration of the hormonal and enzymatic functionings; structural degeneration often follows.

1. UNDERSTANDING HEALTH

This part should not be seen as a comprehensive treatise of all that can go wrong with a horse. It is written on the understanding that readers will have a basic knowledge of mammalian structure and functioning, as well as an appreciation of their normal signs of living and 'working'. Conversely, that they will be aware of clues of abnormality suggestive of disorders which are reducing the ability to live and to work freely and successfully. Their personal experience of 'not feeling so good' can be a useful gauge, for example, as judged by:

* Inappetence.
* Digestive pain.
* Excretory disorders.
* Being fevered.
* Coughing, sneezing and/or being 'short of breath'.
* Having to limp when walking.
* Muscular soreness and stiffness.
* Even a wound.

These are all signs they could notice in an ill horse – if they looked for them. Signs, not symptoms; only man can tell what he thinks he is experiencing, particularly when there is no outward evidence; the horse can 'talk' only by the exhibition of physical clues over which he has no control. Such signs can vary from acute and marked to subtle and indistinct.

ROUTINE INSPECTIONS

Horsemastership is perceiving, assessing and recognising. Routine daily and special inspections are basic to employing the essential knowledge whereby they can say:

(a) Everything looks normal, all is well – my horse is 'at-ease'.

(b) There is something wrong, an abnormality – my horse is 'dis-eased' somewhere, and sufficiently to show and to attract attention.

The word 'dis-ease' is better suited to general use; it does not suggest what is basically wrong but rather where and what signs are perceivable. A horsemaster's skills need not be in clinical diagnostic detail. Such are required for accurate assessment, and need much experience and training to acquire the necessary background knowledge, both practical and theoretical.

The aim of basic recognition of 'OK', or the quick awareness of something wrong, is essential to expedite the horse being taken out of work, the application of first aid and early management to decide whether the horsemaster can confidently cope or if professional (or at least more experienced) help is advisable for assessment, diagnosis and/or treatment.

The routine health inspection occasions are part of:
- Stable management opportunities.
- Pre-work inspection at the halt and at in-hand walk and trot. During training. These are all useful to 'perceive' that something is wrong.

The 'one-off' occasions are effected after:
- Listening to the rider's comments gained through the 'seat of his/her breeches' and other senses.
- A particular upgrading of training, or an event which might have occasioned an occupational trauma or over-stress.

Routine, daily inspection of horses at grass must never be forgotten. Many a good horse is ruined by a missed injury or by hoof infections following neglect of regular appropriate trimming and the failure to see the horse move on a daily basis in this resting phase of being 'turned away'.

The verb 'to perceive' was deliberately used: it implies the use of all one's senses backed up by common sense:
- To look and to see.
- To listen and to hear.
- To touch, to feel
  — contour changes reflecting skin and underskin changes
  — consistency likewise
  — warmth or heat (as judged by the back of one's hand)
  — to induce clearer signs of pain by digitally increasing pressure on suspected traumatised tissue and to compare suspected abnormalities on one leg with the contralateral one, or 'from memory', or knowledge of what should be.

- To smell.
- To taste (this is one where particular use of common sense is wise).
- Kinaesthesia, an additional 'feeling' sense of movement and alterations therein by hand, 'seat' and other aids and responses to these.

Such inspection is for reasonably sudden changes – things that were not there yesterday but are present today! It will be remembered that conformation does not change and that condition changes slowly. In some acute illnesses involving fever, inappetence and diarrhoea, condition can show dramatic changes over a few days, popularly described with such phrases as "really tucked up" (when the abdomen appears to have been pulled up) and "the flesh just melted off it", where the fat has been burned up; but there are usually other earlier signs of the causal illness.

Perception also implies, and common sense dictates, that the horsemaster should look at the whole horse, and more specifically at other areas which could be involved or even be the less obvious primary seat of the clinical condition that is more apparent elsewhere. (This whole-body appraisal has a different meaning from the word 'holistic' current in some complementary medicine disciplines, where it implies treating the whole horse and not just directing the therapy at one part or one particular cause of the disorder.)

The need for a wider view does suggest the skills of a more experienced horsemaster. A common mistake will serve to explain.

EXAMPLE 1

The signs

A horse is discovered lame at morning trot up after the previous day's cross country exercise.

Inspection shows a distinct linear swelling on the inside, the medial aspect, of the cannon area of the lame leg. There is, on palpation, an associated, more diffuse but not marked, swelling towards and over the fetlock.

The 'spot' diagnosis and treatment

The horseman's constant fear of a 'leg', the colloquial term for a strained tendon, a serious trauma, which he knows invariably occurs in the mid shaft of the cannon, tends to lead to 'spot' (i.e. not fully considered) diagnosis of this disorder.

The logical decision as to treatment in the first instance for such a trauma is:

- Rest.
- Cold hose at 2-hour intervals and bandage between times.

The considered diagnosis

However, a tendinitis – and it is usually the superficial digital flexor tendon that is injured – will produce a swelling all round the posterior aspects of the cannon *not* a one-sided linear distension.

A more careful, less anxiety-driven inspection would have shown that the swelling was a soft, depressible tubular lesion, in fact an enlargement of the single vein that drains the distal limb. Its distension in the lame leg indicates an increase in blood flow to a distal area as part of an inflammatory process. More blood going – accommodated in an increased arterial flow – requires room for a return flow – in a dilated vein.

Palpation of the sides of the distal fetlock region would reveal a more throbbing arterial pulse than usual and greater than that of the other leg. This demands – as should have been done originally on noticing any lameness – an examination of the hoof capsule for:

(a) Increased heat, in comparison with the other foreleg,
- Around the wall.
- Along the coronary band.
- Over the heel bulbs.

(b) Inducible increased focal pain, by tapping with a light hammer.
- First the nail head, then the sole – especially at the toe and along inside the shoe web line.
- Under the shoe web.
- In the groove at the side of the frog and especially in the buttress area.
- In the sole horn.

Then searching for an embedded or wedged stone, or a nail similarly embedded.

Failure to do this as a routine could, in this instance, have unnecessarily prolonged the horse's pain, and seriously delayed correct management, with the risk of sepsis (pus) in the hoof and spreading to more vital areas in that region.

EXAMPLE 2

If a horse is lame and there is swelling around a fetlock joint, it could be a sprain, but stop to consider what else might it be. Ask yourself, where and what did it do yesterday?

For example, if it had hunted, did it jump 'through' hedges? Search for a wound; clip the hair off all round. Search for an embedded thorn – usually in the front of the joint. The first aid or early management varies accordingly.

Could it be some other penetrating object, *and*, more seriously, could it have penetrated over a vital area, possibly into the joint capsule or the related tendon sheaths? If this is even suspected, veterinary help is essential. (See First Aid.)

ABC OF HORSEMASTERSHIP

It has been the authors' long-held view and practice in training all levels of horsemasters that reeling off an alphabetical list of diseases, with signs, diagnosis and treatments is a waste of everybody's efforts. Management of equine disorders has been approached from the eye level of the handler who should be trained to practise *perceiving* the Appearance, Behaviour, Condition of the horse on a daily basis or on special occasions as required. The acronym 'A B C' is a tag; the actual states of Appearance, Behaviour and Condition are not definitive nor always applicable to sudden disorders, but they do suggest a routine approach, a 'one, two, three' of horsemastership. They are more useful than trying to relate a name of a disease to a state of dis-ease. Most traumas do not produce a specific dis-ease per se, e.g. a rash, an abrasion, a swelling. Sometimes the underlying condition is a specific disorder, e.g. tendinitis. Lameness is a sign; the diseased state is the cause. In others, the secondary condition is a particular disorder, such as a 'ringworm'-infected girth rash.

DAILY CHECKS

Some routine tasks can provide important evidence as to the state of a horse's health. For example:

Sponging out the mouth: This is an opportunity to detect sores on the bar or at a commissure of the lips. More so if the horse:

- Took a strong hold on yesterday's rider.
- Was evasive.
- Showed blood as well as saliva on the bit.

Grooming: This – and looking and feeling at the same time – is an opportunity to suspect, even confirm:

- Saddle pressure sore.
- Girth rash especially in a 'soft not fit' horse.
- A swollen posterior cannon indicative of some trauma – not which or what, but certainly a warning for a more careful check for lameness at the advisable daily in-hand walk and trot before ridden exercise.

Mucking out: This is a time to check quantity, colour, and consistency changes in the faeces and relate these findings to:

- How well did the horse eat up during the night?
- Were there signs on its clothing of excessive rolling, suggesting colic?

It is a question of having a little but progressive learning over a period – not a little imperfectly understood knowledge that gives a false impression of ability.

COMMON PROBLEMS

Common things (disorders) are common. Common traumas in the wild horse are in those parts of the body which evolved to make it a more efficient 'escaper' (athlete) and in those parts exposed to contact blows or injuries.

Common illnesses are in those systems which evolved to ensure the usually successful requirements of a nomadic grazer's existence but not necessarily to cope with the sins of omission and commission associated with domestication and the related athleticism, such as:

- Feeding errors and digestive disorders such as colic and diarrhoea.
- Infections of a primary nature.
- The stress of road transport with immediately following exertion in close contact with other, unknown and possibly contagiously 'diseased' horses.
- Closed over-stress traumas, the occupational hazards resulting in tendon and suspensory ligament strain.
- Open traumas of wounds from sharp objects, in work and at rest.
- Closed bruising traumas of the hoof capsule and elsewhere up the limbs.

These should always be in the forefront of the horsemaster's mind, encouraging efforts in prevention, for example by proper feeding, immunisation and training, and applying first aid and early management following quick recognition when they do occur.

External traumas are mainly inflicted on the abaxial areas (the limbs) and less frequently elsewhere. These may have been witnessed; or post-injury bruise swelling or even open wounds are obvious signs in addition to the all-important *pain plus loss of use* shown as lameness. This may be mild, even subtle and/or clinical only during or after the extra stress of subsequent work.

Internal traumas, such as strains of tendons or sprains of ligaments usually show as swollen relevant areas and evince variable degrees of lameness. In low-grade suspensory ligament strain, or desmitis especially, the usually mild, associated swelling can be missed visually. It could have been 'felt' on careful routine palpation such as should be carried out later in the day or on the day after any exerting work. The recent work history of the horse should always be seen as a pointer to possible injury; a particularly close perception of all susceptible areas should be carried out. By doing this a horsemaster avoids the risk of exposing the potentially serious strains such as in the suspensory ligament to the adverse effect of inadvisable fast work during the next workout. Desmitis lameness subsides quickly to be subclinical at the walk and the trot, only to become clinical if the horse is exposed to the faster asymmetric gaits.

Disorders, as distinct from traumatic disease, are usually medical in type, and are therefore thoracico-abdominal and/or neurologic in location. The signs in the early stages even of what later becomes acute and serious are not always readily perceivable.

Infections invariably reach the end of their incubation period with a fever, the recognition of which can be missed unless, as in elite athletic circles, the use of the thermometer is a twice daily routine. To confuse matters, the other clinical signs in influenza viral disorder may appear only after that fever has subsided whereas Herpes' fever continues.

Premonitory signs vary with the system involved and with the cause. Virus inflammation of the respiratory system is often ushered in with:

- Inappetence.
- Dejection and fever.
- Reluctance to move freely.

This is particularly the case if the lower airways are involved. These are quickly followed by:

- Coughing.
- Increased respiratory rate.
- Nasal discharge.

These last three can appear on their own. If for no other reason than determining the possibility of a contagious cause, such signs should be investigated professionally.

In digestive disorders fever is not so common. Irrespective of the abdominal type involved there is invariably:

- Inappetence.
- Discomfort.
- Change in the frequency of defecation, the amount and the consistency, usually reduced and firmer but occasionally, and then often more serious, as a diarrhoea.

Thereafter the area of the bowel affected and the relevant morbidity can produce the syndrome of colic, for which a collection of signs that may be indicative are:

- Pawing the ground.
- Lifting a hindleg towards the abdomen.

- Looking at the flank.
- Patchy sweating.

These signs should be sufficient to justify veterinary help but they may pass off quickly. No colic case is better until all signs have disappeared, faecal output is normal and appetite, advisably restricted to limited grazing and/or hay, has returned with the horse in an alert mode.

The generally ill horse has a very expression-variable head appearance:
- Dull eye with lack of interest in the environment.
- Tense muzzle.
- Pulled back commissure of the lips.
- Headache-suggestive position of the ears.

And in colic cases:
- An overall tenseness.
- Dropped upper eyelid.
- Sometimes an irregular dipping of the muzzle into water and then blowing frothy bubbles.
- Other signs of abdominal discomfort (as above).

Except in what are called 'hyperacute' cases, which fulminate very quickly such as the enterotoxaemias, there is usually time for recognition of 'something wrong' and a considered decision to seek veterinary help. Obviously, the hyperacute cases must be seen by a veterinary surgeon as soon as possible. Acute and serious colics certainly require professional help, and also those which go on for more than one hour or deteriorate in that time.

A horse rarely ever salivates nor does its muzzle become dry and hot as in the cow and the dog. The exception is in cases of 'choke' where saliva escapes as an overspill, mainly down the nostrils. Painful mouth sores which stimulate tongue and chewing activities will reflexly stimulate salivation; although most is swallowed, some may 'drool'.

VETERINARY EXAMINATION
Veterinary examination of all cases except straightforward lameness and skin diseases will involve recording:
- Pulse: average 25-30 beats per minute.
- Temperature: average 37.4 °C but rises by 0.5 ° at night (a diurnal rhythm).
- Respiratory rate: average 8-15 breaths per minute.

All of these are well within a good horsemaster's skill. (In colic there is the imperative need for a professional auditory assessment of gut movement and rectal assessment at least at the second, preferably at the first, veterinary examination to complement the above.)
The veterinary surgeon can use:
- The stethoscope
- The endoscope   =
- The ultrasonagraph   x

during practice in the 'field', and support these findings when required by:

- Radiography   x
- Arthroscopy   = x
- Scintigraphy   x
- Thermography   x

in the clinic. The imaging techniques identified 'x' are not inexpensive. The two marked '=' permit actual visualisation of deeper tissues in the U and LRT (upper and lower respiratory tract) and of joint cavities, as well as being alternative, less drastic routes for some surgical interventions. Along with various laboratory tests on blood and other fluids, they are grouped as ancillary aids, not as direct means 'on their own' for diagnosis.

TYPES OF DIS-EASE

DEVELOPMENTAL DIS-EASE
Developmental dis-ease can establish permanent weaknesses and lead to degenerative disorders of welfare and economic importance. Visible and palpable lesions of the orthopaedic types (DOD), if not overcome in the skeletal formative years, will be obvious in the adult animal, home-bred or purchased, when brought into work. Superimposed work-induced or accidental trauma will be a 'new' stress or even an over-stress on these. The latter is more likely to become clinical through work's wear and tear than in a 'normal' horse. Such superimposed trauma is again a 'new' condition.

INFLAMMATORY DIS-EASE
Inflammatory dis-ease, if not always the most worrying, is certainly frequent. Associated with it are the allergic responses and sensitivities, features of inflammation which tend to remain potentially active and so detrimental at intervals at least.

Inflammatory dis-ease, or even 'disease' is an equivocal term. It is the clinical evidence of nature's response to some traumatic assault. Whilst trauma suggests a wounding or an injurious blow to the surface of the body with variable depths of damage that has to be seen as a macroscopic assault, the assault of micro-organisms and parasites which cause morbid changes in body tissues both surface and internal are micro, usually multiple, contiguous lesions.

If it was not for the inherited ability of living tissue to respond in this defensive manner and thereafter with healing or repairing effect, that life would have succumbed, in part or in whole, long ago.

Micro Trauma Inflammation
Infectious inflammation is also a state not a disease as such. In practical terms the type, degree and duration of this active defence can often be descriptive of the morbidity and of the counter defence action against a micro-organism invasion; activity which clinical picture not only points to the system, organ or tissue under attack, but may also point to which 'attacker', germ or parasite. It leads to a specific diagnosis sooner or later with a 'name' which can be informative to the veterinary

surgeon and to the horsemaster. As the disease is brought under control, naturally and with medical help, the signs decrease and may disappear or they may in some cases become chronic.

The consequences of chronicity can be:

- A periodic return or flare-up, a recrudescence as in some Equine Herpes infections, from a sub-clinical lesion or lesions.
- A secondary functional and/or structural effect such as abortion in the mare, weakness in a unit of locomotion from neurologic complications or a secondary myositis.
- A carrier state or shedder of certain germs such as the stallion post-viral arteritis infection.
- A chronic, fibrosing tissue replacement such as a skin scar or reduced functional areas in the lung.

Further 'consequences' are:

- A variable duration of immunity to the effects of a subsequent specific re-infection when clinical signs are either ideally absent or much less severe.

  Such re-infection unaccompanied by clinical signs (the re-infection is not obvious, even non-morbid) can, however, be 'stressful' in itself causing susceptibility to other opportunist infection, reduced metabolic abilities and/or poor performance.
- A degree of sensitivity, an incomplete immunity. Re-infection here is likely to cause an allergic reaction, either in the original site or elsewhere, usually in epithelial tissues such as skin, respiratory tract and digestive tract.

Inflammation, when stimulated by invading germs, seeks to minimise tissue damage and incidentally reduce severity and duration of disease, by attacking the germs by:

- Defensive blood or tissue cells ("killer" blood cells).
- Scavenging cells from the blood and tissue cells.
- Antibody-carrying blood serum (humoral immune agents); the serum also lavages and cleanses the area.

Macro Trauma Inflammation

Inflammation following macro-traumas aims to control bleeding and then to begin cleansing and repairing the damaged area. When secondary (bacterial) infection has occurred, as in an open wound, the response is greater and includes the sequence of events described below.

It requires, varying with the severity in a more restricted, particular area, a directed increase in blood flow by the reflex dilation of the related arteries, thus increasing blood-flow volume and a greater serum exudation, along with the necessary healing blood cells and other elements. The blood does not flow faster through the site but if the heart is stimulated reflexly in response to the inflammatory degree and the associated pain, there will be a faster pulse rate overall with the increased volume in the affected area. In the limbs, the more readily physically distended blood-flow return veins will, in some areas such as the medial cannon, be visibly and palpably bigger.

This increase in blood volume produces a clinical picture – the signs of inflammation and, as emphasised, the signs of a disease state. The picture has the cardinal inflammatory signs of:

- *Swelling* – caused by blood volume increase, serum exudate and tissue fluid 'escape'.
- *Heat* – caused by blood volume increase, tissue-increased metabolic heat, and fever in systemic disease.
- *Discoloration* from the increased flow of (red) blood – rarely visible in the pigmented and the hair-covered skin, but recognisable in the white of eye, gums and bulbs of heels, and the back of some pasterns.
- *Pain* and related muscle spasm to limit movement.
- *Loss of functioning* caused by the painful affected area and 'stiffness' as around joints and/or swollen tissues.
- *Oedema,* which increases retention of protein-loaded serum now requiring increased lymph flow; and local and dependent swelling with increased loss of functioning from the hydrostatic stiffening.

Within the terms of the three specific systems selected for this book, these would show in the horse, for example, as respectively:

- Failure of the gut to reclaim water, i.e. diarrhoea
- Lameness
- Respiratory embarrassment

Discharge in such situations as:

- Open skin wounds.
- Systems with exit through skin orifices, e.g. the nostrils (respiratory tract viral infection) or the vulva (from a uterine bacterial infection).

The 'waste' material from the inflammatory activity will appear as an outflow of variably purulent mucus, e.g. the snotty nose syndrome in young horses with Herpes infection.

In bacterial infection, primary or secondary, and especially if it is pus-productive, the discharge will be thicker and more copious. The later, more chronic stage of this, is described as 'catarrh'.

METABOLIC DIS-EASE

Metabolic or functional biochemical upsets are not confined to elite athletes – those under hard work output and peak levels of stress – but are also important disorders of all horses, as both acute and chronic conditions. (See The Locomotor system)

NEOPLASTIC DIS-EASE

Neoplastic disease, whilst sometimes important in certain types, is usually slowly progressive, appearing first as indeterminate 'lumps or bumps' on or in the skin; some are malignant and invasive; others are only of nuisance or cosmetic importance, liable to insect and tack irritation, with possible secondary maggot or germ inflammation.

EFFECTS OF EVOLUTION AND OF DOMESTICATION

For several reasons man required his horses to live in: it was cleaner, less expensive than keeping them warm outdoors, he could maintain condition better, and he knew where they were when wanted. As a result he dramatically changed the horse's feeding habits, resulting in:

- Quicker ingestion and mastication, so less eating time per feed.
- Less use of mastication, leading to less correct wear of the teeth (see later) and less output of saliva.
- More likelihood of rapid changes in types of food.
- More restrictive grazing and that often not 'correct', with less herbal selection and more chances of worm infestation.
- Greater danger from mouldy food.

So too with its respiratory system, resulting in varying exposure to 'foreign' viruses – with greater concentration of aerosol spread and poorer ventilation – and to mistakes in grass conservation, with increase in mould spores into the lungs.

In addition, locomotion and man's ambitions for his horse's athleticism and competitiveness, ridden or driven, usually well in excess of the natural requirements for survival, led also to the possible overstressing of the abaxial and the axial skeletons and their functioning. The increased demands of metabolising the extra levels of absorbed, more nutritive, digesta with positive feedback, had sometimes a bad effect on appetite and indirectly on digestion.

The stresses of domestication, more important in some horses than in others, were built up by the need for stabling with long periods of inactivity and short periods of often intense work, and so led to other worries, compensated for by stereotypical behaviourism during times of boredom.

2. THE RESPIRATORY SYSTEM

The respiratory system has three major functions.
(a) Getting atmospheric air in, and used, oxygen-depleted, air out.
(b) This expiration is a secondary means of losing excess body heat – a thermo-regulation.

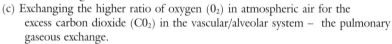

(c) Exchanging the higher ratio of oxygen (O_2) in atmospheric air for the excess carbon dioxide (CO_2) in the vascular/alveolar system – the pulmonary gaseous exchange.

A fourth function is phonation. A fifth is reflex sniffing of atmospheric 'suspicious' molecules for identification by the olfactory nerve endings.

The equine system, designed for fast and prolonged activity in the wild state has an extensive exchange mucosal surface, some four times bigger than the bovine. It has two anatomically and functionally divided areas:
(a) The upper respiratory tract (URT) or airway – outwith the chest cavity.
(b) The lower respiratory tract (LRT) or part airway, part exchange surface – within the chest cavity.

The entire length of the joint airways are lined with epithelial mucous membrane. In the gaseous exchange areas of the distal tubules and of the alveoli this is separated from the pulmonary capillary wall by a nominal intercellular space. The respiratory tract's alveolar blind ends are but one cell thick, as are the capillary walls. In some cases these fuse into one communal layer.

The general plan is basically similar to that of most mammals but there are some specific differences which evolved for equine survival. These differences, still in use, are now exposed to problems associated with domestication, and stresses of exerting activity often greater than nature required, in terms of speed, distance and carrying a rider and tack.

These differences are as follows.

- The horse cannot inspire through its mouth. In extremes of oxygen demand, as in acute pneumonitis and heat over-stress, attempts at panting (oral inspiration) are made with some success but with much physical distress.

    This restriction is no doubt an evolutionary design associated with the stride/respiration synchronisation and the need to maintain or secure the cuff around the larynx which is rarely released in fast work except for occasional excess saliva swallowing. (First aiders will be happy to know that respiratory failure requiring mouth to mouth resuscitation is not only rarely required but is also impracticable!)

- The respiratory rate at rest in mild environmental conditions is around 10 to 12 breaths per minute. This will increase to well over 100 at times of maximal

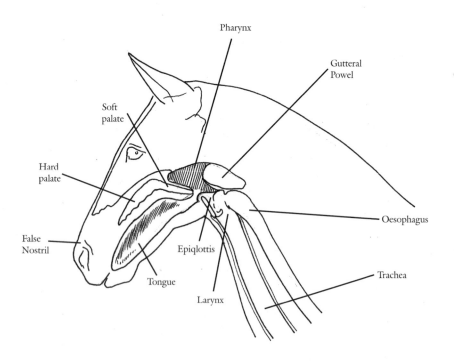

The respiratory system.

aerobic requirements, when 13 times the amount of oxygen per unit of time is required above the resting quantity.

- The breathing is mainly diaphragmatic: the excursion, limited at rest, is measurable by watching the flank from behind and to the side of the animal.

  Inspiration is a backward, outward and downward movement with a short 'hold'. Expiration is a reverse movement, immediately followed by inspiration. Both, from the outside, are noiseless.

  Any increase in demand will speed up the rate and cancel the hold phase of the resting rate, and will increase the range of movement. The increase in demand automatically responds to 'fear' – it instinctively induces 'more' oxygen to be ready for fight and flight – and to the need to meet the increasing muscular exercise and its aerobic functioning.

The respiration rate quickly returns to resting normal, although after hard exercise this is prolonged to 30 minutes in two steps which in much part is due to the demand for repaying the oxygen debt of regenerating muscle-cell glycogen and assisting in heat loss.

- The false nostrils are automatically held dilated during inspiration to maximise inflow volume.

Faster breathing produces increasing expiratory noise often augmented by a

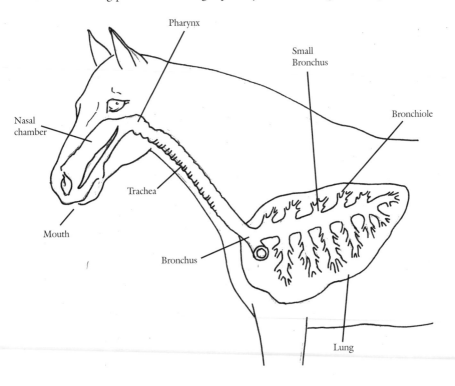

The respiratory system (simplified).

117

vibrational noise of the dilated 'false' nostrils; this is colloquially known as 'high blowing'.

Severe exertion will produce inspiratory noise. Inflammatory thickening of the URT will also induce inspiratory noise, often spoken of as 'thick of the wind'.

In the asymmetric gaits a full respiratory cycle parallels a full limb stride. Expiration begins with footfall of the leading hind limb and ends with the leading foreleg. It occupies the overall sequential stance and stride phases. Inspiration takes place during suspension. In cold weather the expired air visibly condenses at the nostrils: these 'puffs' coincide with the start of lift-off into suspension from the leading foreleg.

- The horse is one of the few mammalian species to have specific enlargements in the Eustachian tubes which run left and right from the pharynx to the middle ear. This is the guttural pouch, thought to be an additional air pressure amending structure. Whatever its function or purpose – this is not yet fully understood – it has the perhaps important disadvantage of collecting inhaled bacteria and mould spores which colonise therein to form pus and a diphtheritic membrane respectively. The latter can ulcerate through the wall to damage the underlying cranial nerve with consequent paralysis of the throat, and the cranial artery with fatal haemorrhaging.

- The tonsils are not congregated as in dog and man but are dispersed over the mucosal wall of the pharynx. The significance of this is still debated, as is the persistent, chronic-like state of tonsillitis often seen in young horses.

- The several cranial and facial sinuses are well developed in the horse: they are diverticuli of the URT. The maxillary sinuses can become infected; a particular type is from upper molar apical root inflammation in numbers 3, 4, 5 and 6 whose roots project into the maxillary sinus where they are covered by a very thin bony partition. This readily breaks down under pressure from inflammatory fluid collecting over the roots. Their infection then spreads into the associated sinus. The subsequent purulent sinusitis is variably detrimental.

- The pharynx or throat: a communal passage for air and ingesta, solid and liquid.

- The larynx: the single entry to the trachea (windpipe). During respiration it is held in a cuff of the muscle-walled pharyngeal roof and sides and of the cupped soft palate forming the floor and lower sides. This is reflexly released for swallowing. The larynx, a series of paired cartilages, is mobile cranially where the aperture, the glottis, can be altered to accommodate more or less airflow as required. The glottis can be shut off during swallowing by the coming together of the paired most anterior cartilages, which also carry the vocal cords, and by the upward movement of the epiglottis to add to this temporary sealing off. It is permanently patent distal to the glottis.

- The trachea: also held permanently patent by a series of horizontal incomplete cartilaginous rings. The airway mucous membrane and its wall bridges over the gaps; elsewhere it lines the cartilage; the membrane passively is responsive to air-flow pressures at the gaps. It has no muscular component.

RELATED SKELETAL ANATOMY

The bony skull protects the nasal passages and the sinuses. The pharynx and the larynx are partly between the jaw bones and also under the skull/anterior neck bones. The trachea is sheltered by the dorsal cervical vertebrae but is exposed ventrally, as is the ventral throat, the weak link resulting in predators 'taking it by the throat'.

The LRT (the lungs) are protected within the bony thorax. This airway begins as a single bronchus which soon diverges into two bronchi, one to each main lung. These are separated by the mediastinum, a double thin facial layer which is continuous with the thoracic pleura. It surrounds the heart and major blood vessels, nerves and the thoracic gullet. It is lacy in texture cranially in front of the pericardial outer covering of the heart. These several small holes makes the horse likely to be lethally affected from collapsed lungs even if only one side of the chest is perforated by external trauma. The air which enters the collapsed negative-pressured side crosses over and onto the intact side lung with compressive collapsing effect.

Each lung is divided into lobes and within each lobe the bronchi continue to branch, as in all mammals, till they become microscopic airways leading to clusters of alveoli. Here gaseous exchange occurs. The bronchi, down to the bronchioles but short of the terminal tubes, have circular muscular walls which are under the control of the autonomic nervous system to regulate their diameter and so the flow rate and volume of air in a respiration. The main bronchus and the larger bronchi have incomplete cartilaginous rings to prevent collapse but not so as to prevent diameter changes.

Both airways' mucous membrane secretes a defensive germ and particulate-material-trapping mucus. The mucosal cells have cilia which automatically waft trapped material to the pharynx where it is swallowed. The cranial URT wafts backwards to the throat.

NEUROLOGIC CONTROL

The upper respiratory tract where it is alterable in terms of diameter or function is under the control of reflex neuromuscular systems. It cannot be voluntarily manipulated. The lower tract diameter is likewise under autonomic nerve system control.

The changes in overall volume of the lungs on inspiration and expiration is a passive feature associated with the tissue's elastic response to automatic muscularly effected expansion and contraction of the 'sealed' thoracic cavity.

As far as is known the horse cannot 'hold its breath'. Even if it could, the rapid build up of CO_2 would soon trigger a reflex counter-inspiration as in humans. The glottis can also be stimulated to close if irritated by particulate foreign material. Such is usually followed by a reflex, defensive cough. This forced expiration is not one which can be voluntarily effected; the horse has no nervous or attention-seeking polite coughing ability.

DISEASES OF THE RESPIRATORY SYSTEM (ILLNESS)

Developmental and traumatic dis-eases are not relevant to this text.

INFLAMMATORY

The adult horse is prone to viral infection of the system in its upper respiratory tract – down to the trachea; and in its lower respiratory tract – the lungs (and the pleura). Both can be affected but the upper is the more common.

The characteristic inflammatory signs are:
* A cough: not always present, and when present on its own suggestive of a low-grade virus infection or a primary bacterial one.

- Increased respiratory rate.
- A nasal (sometimes also an ocular) discharge especially when secondary bacterial infection develops.
- A fever, which can last only 3-4 days to subside between the start of the active infection and the onset of the clinical signs – the incubation period.
- Variable inappetence.
- Loss of athletic performance.
- Occasional damage to heart muscle especially if fast exercise is persisted with by the trainer/rider.

The main viral infections are as follows.

Equine influenza, which is now endemic

It has a tendency to mutate to new strains which, once developed abroad, if introduced to this country act as epidemic infections. The absence of a specific resistance to these 'foreign' strains can cause local to national outbreaks. There is an efficient vaccine which the drug manufacturers do their best to keep up to date with new strain antigens. (An intranasal droplet vaccine is undergoing field trials.) Its use is mandatory in competitive disciplines.

Equine Herpes Virus 1 and 4 (one cause of 'snotty nose' of young horses)

It is endemic and widespread and has the properties of persistence both patent and latent, recrudescing especially during extra stress such as mixing of young horses, or transit. The infection has strong contagiousness, and short immunity especially when artificially induced as with vaccination.

Type 1 can, with minimal respiratory signs, directly or recrudescently invade the uterus and cause abortion. 'Storms' of these can develop; for this disorder alone vaccination in studs is advisable.

By hypersensitivity reaction it can damage the CNS (brain and cord) to cause from a paresis to a paralysis and subsequent recumbency. This, per se, is not contagious but small apparent 'group' outbreaks do occur in a stud which point to the primary viral infection of the respiratory tract.

The availability of an improved type of vaccine has proved particularly useful in Racing and Elite Athletic yards where physical and functional overstresses are more likely. It will not prevent infection but any subsequent clinical disease is often much less active in terms of severity of effect. Persistent subclinical disease especially in young horses is shortened with apparent beneficial effect in at least minimising one cause of the Poor Performance syndrome. In adult event and dressage horses the risk of a recrudescence triggered by physical and travel overstress as well as by re-infection is reduced or modified. It is particularly efficient in preventing abortion if the protocol is correctly followed. It may also reduce the risk of paralysis. Its use is not mandatory.

This infection is often associated, in URT inflammation, with submandibular gland enlargement suggestive of Strangles, but the Herpes 'gland' rarely if ever suppurates and any nasal discharge is a later and much less profuse clinical sign.

Equine viral arteritis (Pink Eye)

Of limited endemic presence, mainly in studs, this is a venereal contagion as well as a respiratory aerosol spread. The respiratory disease except in foals is mild. The abortion rate is high. Stallions can remain symptomless shedders via the semen for several years, even life. There is a vaccine, but the one permitted in the UK is not fully efficient, although it might minimise the risk of abortion if not the respiratory disorder.

The 'Cold' virus

Some three other viruses, colloquially called 'The Cold' virus, are endemic, mild, and usually URT-invaders with fever, cough and nasal discharge.

One type, Rhinovirus 1, can be very active in yards of young racehorses in their first year of training – mixing and related over-stress is a precipitating trigger factor.

ALLERGIES
See page 168

STRANGLES

Is not a true respiratory disease, but because it is a mucosal infection of the naso-pharyngeal region with marked purulent inflammation, it is often erroneously grouped with URT viral disease.

The bacterium involved is *Streptococcus equi*. Its isolation from throat swabs or pus samples is confirmatory of the usually easily recognised clinical disorder. Signs are:

- Marked fever.
- Excessive ocular and nasal discharge.
- Limited coughing.
- Difficult breathing (the strangles name!) partly from the throat swelling, occasionally from secondary broncho-pneumonic complications.
- Inappetence – associated with 'sore throat' swallowing difficulties and with inability to smell and to taste food.
- Secondary 'inhaled' gangrenous broncho-pneumonia.

These last three being, the results of naso-pharyngeal inflammatory swelling, can be fatal, especially in the young.

Strangles is:

- Very contagious to the non-immune horse.
- Highly immunogenic and self-curative.
- The germ is sensitive to penicillin but most outbreaks are left to 'run their course' untreated except for nursing.
- Liable to spread to internal organs from which 'ruptured' or released further infection will cause pleurisy or peritonitis which is invariably fatal. Colloquially called "Bastard Strangles".
- The glandular abscesses may need heat ripening and lancing.
- There is, as yet, no vaccine *in the UK.*
- A small percentage of convalescent cases are subject to an immune mediated, usually fatal, blood cell disorder called Purphor haemorrhagica.

Viruses are not susceptible to any practicably usable antimicrobial drugs; secondary bacterial invasions are. In general there are antibacterial, antifungal and antiparasitic drugs all used in respiratory disorders. Their usefulness relates to the diagnostic confirmation of the germ involved. When antibiotics are used it may be necessary to determine the sensitivity of the drug for a particular germ especially a bacterial type.

Not all bacteria are susceptible to all antibiotics and the sensitivity is further related to aerobic bacteria, micro aerophyllic bacteria and anaerobic bacteria. In addition, not all sensitive germs can be reached by the antibiotic; the level of success may relate to tissue penetrability, route of administration, presence of pus and/or organic or inorganic matter, and unsatisfactory dosage. There is also the risk of adverse reactions caused by the antibiotic itself, or if it is given in conjunction with other therapies.

HELMINTH PARASITIC DISEASE OF THE RESPIRATORY SYSTEM

The respiratory system is parasited either by:
(a) An adult worm in the airways or
(b) A migrating, larval stage, en route back to the digestive system via the lungs.
Either way, the initial entry is via the digestive system, and from grazed, larval-contaminated pasture or some other locality from which a deposited egg can be ingested, as in the case of the large white worm.

Ascarids (Parascaris equorum) – the large white roundworm of the foal

Essentially a bowel worm but its larvae can cause respiratory signs. The adult, in extremely small numbers, lives on in the adult gut from which it passes out its large numbers of eggs.

These are highly resistant to climatic and weather changes except in dry, sandy soils and can survive in bedding, incorrectly made dung clamps etc. It becomes 'hooked' onto the adult (mare's) perineum and from there onto her udder as a risk to the new-born suckler. It would seem that the adult worm becomes a prolific egg layer when the mare is heavily pregnant. Certainly, unless she is correctly wormed during the last month of her pregnancy, her foal will become infested by her and the immediate environment.

The larva, which hatches out in the foal, penetrates the gut wall to migrate through the liver, usually without any clinical signs, and there enters the veins to journey to the heart. Its presence is subclinical. From there they reach the pulmonary circulation to the lung alveoli from which they escape into the airway and up the trachea to the throat, where they are swallowed back to the small intestine. Various aberrant other 'dead end' routes can occur.

Over the first few months of the foal's life large numbers of young and mature adult worms collect in the small intestines. A common burden is up to 800 nine-inch long worms.

The journey, gut-to-gut, is about 10 days or longer, but another 8-9 weeks is required for them to become mature egg-laying adults. At some stage further migration is prohibited. At around one year old the weanling throws off the static infestation: the worms disappear but the environment has been heavily egg-infested meantime. Both these events are the result of a developed specific immunity.
Signs: Before expulsion they can irritate the bowel, and ulcerate it, and live off the foal's or yearling's ingesta and gut wall tissues, causing:
- Loss of condition, pot-belly and staring coat.
- An anaemic and easily exhausted foal host.
- Colic from obstruction, sometimes with intestinal rupture and fatal peritonitis.

An infested foal may show
- Elevated temperature
- Slight cough
- Clear mucoid nasal discharge

as the larvae migrate into and up the airway.

Management: Before and after foaling, the mare's perineum and udder should be kept shampooed to wash off any eggs. The stables must be kept clean, together with the nearby environments, by consistent removal of dung pats. Mother and foal should be turned out onto clean pastures as soon as possible.

The foal should enter the stud worming programme around 6 weeks, well before a heavy adult worm burden develops. Stud control of all endoparasites is a vital part of management.

Dictyocaulus arnefieldi – Lungworm

This species of lungworm infests equidae only. It is similar to that of cattle and sheep in its life cycle but there is no cross infestation. It is comparatively rare in horses but its persistent, irritating, associated cough has to be differentially diagnosed from this sign caused by infections and allergies.

The horse is not an original host: it maintains a resistance to the worm, inasmuch as the adult worm survives only a limited period before being expelled, and only about 10% of infested horses pass live larvae back onto the grazing.

A donkey is a natural host inasmuch as:
- An infestation can be persistent.
- It does not react to the worm's migration and adult existence: it has a subclinical condition – *no* cough.
- Viable larvae (the eggs hatch en route up the trachea) *are* excreted onto the grazing.

Life cycle

(i) Viable larvae are ingested.

(ii) They penetrate the small intestinal wall's lymphatic system and go through the mesenteric lymph glands (where they stimulate an immunity in the horse. This feature limits adult worm duration in the bronchi and possibly prevents re-infestation).

(iii) From these glands they enter the blood stream and eventually the lung capillaries, through which they break into the airways. They mature in the bronchi.

(iv) Subsequent eggs and therefore larvae are exhaled into the throat and then swallowed.

(v) Larvae, viable or not, are excreted.

Signs: The horse develops a variable mucosal surface inflammatory reaction to the invading larvae as well as to the adults in the upper airways. A cough is induced which persists for several weeks.

Treatment: A suitable anthelminthic such as Eqvalan can be used.

Management: Do not mix-graze horses with donkeys. The donkey should be isolated until two faecal samples at a month's interval are negative for larvae. Infested donkeys can be successfully treated but the isolation protocol is still essential.

DEGENERATIVE DISORDERS OF THE RESPIRATORY SYSTEM
'Whistling'

The horse is specifically subject to a degeneration of the left side nerve to the larynx. This nerve travels down the neck just above the jugular groove, enters the chest in which it turns round a major artery from the adjacent heart to ascend the neck to the larynx. The right side nerve is much shorter and has no bend. As the recurrent nerve degenerates, the motivation which opens and closes the glottis on the left side at the front of the larynx deteriorates.

A paresis or weakness is followed by a paralysis. The inability of the left side to respond to the demand for more air flow interferes with inspiration especially in fast work. The deficit in oxygen interferes with performance. The coincidental adventitious noise on inspiration gives the condition its colloquial name, a 'whistler'.

'Roaring'

The cranial larynx or glottis is held in a cuff formed by the caudal pharynx and the curved soft palate during respiration as already described. Upon swallowing, this grip is relaxed, the glottis is closed and the bolus of food or water is directed into the gullet or oesophagus which opens out of the laryngo-pharynx dorso-distally.

For several reasons such as

- Viral myositis
- Bacterial and viral neuritis
- Disorders of the autonomic nervous system
- Physiological overstress possibly engendered by laryngeal paresis as described above
- Possible genetic weaknesses in anatomical structure and functioning

the horse is subject to a weakened soft-palate muscular effort, the grip is lost and the palate is sucked up in the inspired air-flow to flutter noisily in front of the glottis. The displacement gives the name to the disorder, which is accompanied by a snoring sound or intermittent *roaring* with an associated air-intake impedance. The horse world calls it '*swallowing its tongue*' mainly because it frequently develops in the horse 'taking a strong hold' on the bit. Technically it is known as upward displacement of the soft palate (UDSP). There are several other colloquial terms.

3. THE DIGESTIVE SYSTEM

This system evolved dramatically, if slowly, to cope with grazing changes in the selection, prehension, mastication and eventual fermentative digestion of the coarse fibrous grasses of the 'new' pastures.

Whilst domestication didn't have to remove the various species of Equus from the natural, indigenous grazings, man's need for bigger, stronger, faster animals required nutrient addition to the potential energy value of the 2.5% body weight per day which was about its maximum in cellulose-rich fibrous herbage. The remainder had to come from more concentrated, more soluble rich feedstuffs as found in cereals. The fibrous food, moreover, had to be reduced to make room for this.

In nutrition there was greater opportunity for sins of omission and of commission whereby nurture was often detrimental to nature. It was easy to break away from the rules of feeding which were meant to simulate nature as far as man could. Here was the need to encourage and allow for prolonged periods of feeding and coincidental mastication and salivation, resulting in the steady 'trickle' flow into the stomach and the rapid passage to the small intestine for the much longer period of microbial digestion. The digestion could readily become indigestion.

FOOD AND FEEDING EFFECTS

The strains or subspecies of fermentative organisms are most effective when established in a ratio to best act on the current type of cellulose containing long fibre (incidentally this is masticated into small pieces approximately 1 to 5 mm long). A horse at grass has the ideal consistent intake of more or less steady feedstuff. It must be remembered that the sap-to-fibre ratio of grazing will vary with the herbage growing rates as induced by moisture and temperature. The lush growth in warm rain following a cold dry period is the most markedly different grazing. (See Laminitis.)

Management changes must be made gradually, for example:

(i) Grass to hay.
(ii) Hay to grass.
(iii) The introduction of concentrates to either.
(iv) A change in the basic concentrate constituents.

This should be accomplished over a period of 7-10 days. This permits the establishment of a bacterial flora suited to the 'new' ration. (The sudden addition of

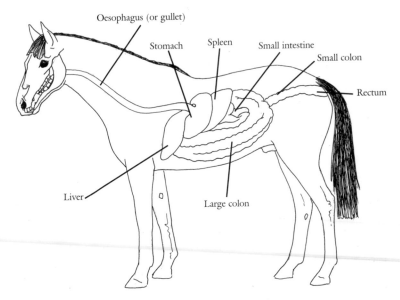

The digestive system (Simplified).

feed-sized quantities of bran, as in a mash, to replace the existing feed, is ill-advised.)

A mixed diet of grain (cereal) and hay is never as thoroughly fermented as an all hay ration. There is a compromise in the addition of the starch diet, some of which 'escapes' into the large intestine with the fermentation production of different ratios of the three volatile fatty acids. This can have a variably detrimental effect on the subsequent liver metabolism and a relatively lower energy availability. In addition an excess of such soluble carbohydrates (starch) will lead to a lactic (metabolic) acidosis.

The bacteria, when they die, are the source of the water-soluble B vitamins. A horse cannot synthesise all the amino acids it requires if the original protein was only from cereals and hay. Some additional protein of higher 'biological value' is necessary, i.e. one containing the essential amino acids such as lysine, especially as required for:

- Growing horses.
- Lactating mares.
- Elite athletes.

DIS-EASES OF THE DIGESTIVE SYSTEM

DEVELOPMENTAL

Cleft Palate: usually discovered soon after suckling begins, by the return of milk down through the nostrils. Surgical repair is possible but not always successful. Hare Lip, as in man, is a rare complication.

Oesophageal disorders such as congenital structural narrowing and dilatation have been recorded but fortunately are rare.

INFLAMMATORY
Traumatic

May be caused by injuries to the jaws and to the teeth from kicks and from bites (see Dental Disorders). Also, wire, hook, nail and other sharp objects being mouthed by the inquisitive animal can cause tongue and lip lacerations; the former heal well, the latter may require surgical repair.

The remainder of the system is well-protected but occasionally the throat is injured by bites when the respiratory system is coincidentally also involved. The anal sphincter can be injured by aggressive attack as well as by human perversion and from self-inflicted damage from the rubbing invoked by a skin itch.

Infection: Secondary

The above mentioned wounds are all exposed to secondary bacterial infection which enhances the initial inflammatory response to the extent that prehension, ingestion, mastication and deglutition – eating – is made more difficult than with the original trauma. Fungal infection of wounds is rare.

Viral Infections

These are not a serious problem in the adult horse's digestive system.

Infection: Primary

Strangles is the main and the most serious oro-pharyngeal infection (see Respiratory system). Abscess formation in the head and throat worsen the eating and the swallowing discomfort of the primary mucosal infection.

Bacterial infections

Other bacterial infections are some Clostridial species. The toxin of Cl. botulinum, which is liberated onto contaminated food before ingestion is lethal in effect: throat paralysis is an early sign of infection. Its possible association with Grass Sickness is again under investigation as is the toxin produced in the gut lumen by other saprophytic Clostridia en route through the bowel as a soil/food contaminant; they can gain a colonising hold in the stomach and the intestine of foals and in the large gut of adults when primary disorders are present such as ulceration of the mucosae or disturbance of the microflora with an associated enteritis. They then become pathogenic there with toxin absorption. The germ itself can penetrate to the vascular system; if blood is 'leaked' into traumatised body tissue as with a muscle tear or heavy bruising it will multiply in this tissue and liberate its toxin to cause further, often lethal, toxaemia.

Salmonellae germs

These are widely distributed in nature and so are coincidental 'travellers' through the gut tract. Salmonellosis, the name for the inflammatory stage of their presence, can develop when there is a fall in the horse's natural overall immune status as from:

- Over-stress.
- Transit stress.
- Heat exhaustion.
- Intercurrent disease.
- Acute upset to the gut bacterial flora from feeding mistakes.
- Post surgery of a major nature.
- Serious injury, with shock.

Thereafter, the enhanced virulence in this active salmonella can be contagious to in–contact healthy horses. It is basically incurable and so is often lethal.

Toxins from mouldy feed

Can cause enteritis with or without diarrhoea on absorption, to produce a lethal hepatitis.

Starch overloading

This and its association with gut micro-organisms from lush grass (soluble fructose of its hemicellulose) or from gorging excessive quantities of concentrates, results in increase in lactic acid bacteria. This in turn leads to a fall in gut pH, causing general indigestion and upset to normal microflora and/or to a rise in E coli pathogens which can cause endotoxaemia with, for example, subsequent laminitis.

It is in the subclinical stages of this complex that the use of Probiotics is often helpful. (The need for probiotic therapy can be determined by an analysis of a faecal sample. It is essential that any corrections in diet are made before this supplementation.) By replenishing the gut with normal, essential micro-organisms, stability can be regained with a return to normal cellulitic digestion (and correct absorption of nutrients) and better metabolism (improved performance).

Poor Performance Syndrome

The above indigestions *without* the acute clinical signs of
* Diarrhoea
* Obvious illness
* Marked loss of appetite or altered feed selection

can be *one* of the possible causes of Poor Performance Syndrome.

Mouth ulcers

In the later summer ulcers inside the lips and on the gums are a transient, sometimes irritant disorder caused by Bot Fly larvae penetrating the oral mucosae in migration to the gullet and then to the stomach.

Parasitic Infestations

Their presence in, on and in the wall of the digestive system is variably associated with disorders of digestion and of absorption affecting the availability of nutrients. Their larval migration stages have more serious consequences. These have been described on page 122, Helminths.

Metabolic Disorders

These are not often recognised as having digestive consequences. Imbalances in (mineral) electrolytes and disorders of their absorption can influence their presence in internal tissues such as muscle (see Rhabdomyolysis Locomotor System) and bone (low-grade osteoarthritis).

Neoplastic

Melanomata do grow on the peritoneum and on the serous coat of the abdominal organs. Even when present in large numbers they are not, per se, serious. They can become points of entrapment for the mobility of the lower small intestine and the small colon. If they are pedunculated, i.e. on a long stock or pedicle, they can fall across to strangulate bowel and/or the mesenteric blood vessels. In all such cases surgery is necessary for the associated colic.

Lymphosarcoma is more common in the more mature horse. They develop at many sites either as lymph gland enlargements with pressure effect, or as enlargements in the gut wall to interfere with absorption and nerve supply in and from the gut wall.

ALLERGIES

These can arise in this system but will frequently show as facial swellings, difficulty in swallowing as well as with mild enteric dysfunction such as diarrhoea. Their presence is difficult to confirm. They may be direct food allergies or idiosyncrasies or actual allergic side-effects exhibited on the digestive mucosae.

GRASS SICKNESS

This is a non-contagious, but presumably infectious, usually fatal disease of all equidae. It was first reported in Scotland in 1909. It is primarily and mainly a disease of Great Britain, especially in East Scotland, though it has been recorded in Europe.

Related disorders are:
* 'Mal Seco' in Argentina and Paraguay.

- Equine motor neuron disease in the USA and Europe.
- Dysautonomy of Hares in Great Britain.
- 'Mucoid enteropathy' of rabbits, worldwide.

It affects mainly 2-7 year old horses of either sex, usually under five years old. There is little or no sex discrimination. Well-conditioned animals are more susceptible.

Epidemiology indicates:

- Cases in animals that have been moved to new pastures within the previous 8 weeks.
- Possibly in longer-domiciled animals moved from one field to another in the last 4 weeks.
- It usually follows a period of cool dry weather of more than 10 days, especially if a morning ground frost occurs. This weather factor possibly affects grass growth and its microclimatic effect on the micro fauna and flora, the suspected organisms.
- It is less likely to occur if susceptible stock are housed for part of the 24 hours and fed hay with or without concentrates, but not if fed concentrates alone.
- Cases are more likely on land previously grazed by affected equidae.
- Recent research indicates a link between cases known to have been intensively wormed, but not to the drugs used themselves. The explanation is still being debated.
- Early in the century the toxin of Clostridium botulinum was the prime suspect but artificial infection could not be established. Factor X perhaps was missing! Its possible role is being re-investigated at present, on whether the toxin is ingested or liberated in the gut from the parent germ. Either way it is argued as being significant.
- For many years fungal toxins have been considered important but their artificial administration did not cause the disease; again there must be an unknown factor. It is still the germ that is most likely to be incriminated.

Whatever the pathogen, its pathogenic effect is to cause morbid destruction of the gut's specific myenteric nervous system and subsequent disease of the main autonomic system, hence the name Dysautonomy, which is the basis for the rapidly increasing paresis and eventual paralysis of the gut peristalsis, an 'ileus'.

The subsequent signs occur in three categories of speed of onset and of severity.

Acute clinical signs are:
- An acute colic syndrome
  — sweating.
  — enlargement of the abdomen from
  — gastric fluid retention.
  — small intestinal distension.
  — colonic impaction (these three as diagnosed by veterinary rectal examination).
  — absence of gut sounds.
- Inability to swallow
  — drooling of saliva
  — regurgitation of food from the throat down the nose
- Trembling.

- Pulse above 60 per minute.
- Obviously very ill and in pain.
- Dies (or is euthanased) within two days.

Sub-acute signs:
As for the acute, but less obvious, less serious and slower to evolve.
- The nasal discharge is often marked following the persistent discharge of the regurgitated food.
- The trembling is less marked but continues intermittently over the shoulder and neck region.
- The pulse varies above and below 60.
- The illness is not so serious-looking.
- The loss of condition is more noticeable.
- The rectal examinations are similar except that the colic inpaction is slightly less marked.
- The patient tends to play with the water in its bucket, and is seen to persistently lie down – peacefully.
- The horse does eat, but mastication is much slower and some of it is spilt out.
- Death or euthanasia within seven days.

Chronic signs are:
- Severe loss of weight: very tucked up and eventually 'skeletal'.
- Patchy sweating
- Dry of eye
- Mucoid nasal discharge, gumming the nostrils.
- Slow mastication.
- Oral mucosae reddish and dry.
- Trembles less.
- Stands with all four feet 'together'.
- Mucus-coated, dry faecal pellets. Colic impaction is less common as judged per rectum.

Recovery is possible with intensive nursing, including specific therapies, and hand-feeding. If the horse survives more than five weeks it should convalesce successfully over several months.

DISORDERS OF THE DIGESTIVE TRACT

CHOKE
An obstruction in the oesophagus as it turns upwards and inwards at the base of the neck, to enter the chest cavity section of the digestive tract. The cause of choking varies but is often:
- Hay and/or straw which has been offered without a slow introduction as when changing from grass to dry feed, or to the tired horse after work, with respirations still accelerated and salivary flow depleted from sweating – when mastication is not efficient or sufficient and bolus formation is not complete. It may also cause choking when fed in a trailer or horse box from a high hay net to a tied up horse still under adrenaline excitement as well as with exciting noises

all around, or to the travel-exhausted horse.
- Dry concentrate feed under similar conditions as above or improperly soaked sugar-beet pulp – especially to a greedy feeder.
- Unaccustomed succulents and corn cobs which are too quickly swallowed and so act as a bridging cross-oesophageal blockage.
- Any horse with dental disorders which interfere with mastication or pharyngeal inflammation which reflexly interferes with passage through oesophagus.
- Foreign body ingestion, such as twigs, brambles, bark, wood chips, even bits of wire, which stop the onward movement of the bolus.

Signs: A sudden acute change in behaviour whilst eating.
- Marked reaction to the oesophageal distension with stimulation of its serous coat sensory nerves from distension and subsequent distal spasm – a 'choking' arching of the neck and of the head on the neck in quick and repetitive bursts. Simulates a person 'trying' to vomit.
- Regurgitation of some of the offending or held up food from its cranial surface and much of the saliva build-up on top, either through the nostrils or spluttering out of the mouth, as well as any ingesta and saliva therein but not yet swallowed.
- An anxious expression.
- Occasionally a frantic pawing of the ground.
- Rarely, if ever, any attempt to lie down to roll.
- Patchy sweating of the neck, top muscles which often go into spasm.

There is a risk of inhalation of regurgitated material which, when it passes over the glottis rostrally, stimulates explosive coughing and subsequent reflexly induced quick inhalation.

Treatment: None by the horsemaster. Send for veterinary surgeon.
- Do not drench.
- Do not attempt to pass a stomach tube.
- Take away all feed, hay, water and straw bedding.
- Lead out for gentle walking for 3-5 minutes at 10-15 minute intervals. Choke may self-relieve but don't stop the veterinary surgeon from coming.

If still choking and the distension at the base of the neck on the left side can be seen and felt, gentle inward and cranial-ward massage can be tried. Do not be vigorous. (Beware marked reaction by the horse.)

The veterinary surgeon will administer smooth muscle-relaxing drugs. Only if the choke persists despite two such treatments will he consider probing with a stomach tube and possibly the careful administration of liquid paraffin through the tube. When the choke is relieved he will almost certainly advise:
- Immediate antibiotic cover against broncho-pneumonia.
- On correcting the diet and/or the feeding management.
- That the teeth be examined and treated as required.

It is not lethally serious as with laryngo-tracheal obstruction.

COLIC
The collective name for pain emanating from the abdomen and, by inference, from the 'hollow' digestive tract. The pain is produced by:

- Organ distension and consequent stretching of the serous (outer) coat with sensory excess stimulation. This is acute when from excess gas production, and less acute when from the build-up of impacted ingesta.
- Interference to the blood supply with pain associated with lack of oxygen – a cramp-like anoxic pain – from varying levels of thrombosis, i.e. intravascular obstruction in part or in whole, or physical obstruction, i.e. 'outside' or peritoneal pressure obstruction, associated with bowel displacement.

The acuteness and so too the relative pain – from mild discomfort to intermittent severe pain to continuous with intense pain – varies with the causes and the areas affected. The accompanying behaviour varies from occasional crouch and foot stamping to recumbency, violent rolling and intense sweating.

Some mild cases pass off, others may go unnoticed, others progress to shock and collapse with fatal outcome.

The severe attacks, especially if continuous, usually require surgical intervention. Such a decision is made by the veterinary surgeon on the basis of:
- The apparent severity.
- The pulse rate from above 50 and rising and staying at around 80-100.
- The findings of a rectal examination. This should be done as a routine; and certainly if a repeat or follow-up examination becomes necessary, or in all attacks of more than one hour's duration, it is essential. The findings, of course, are the decisive clues. It is almost as accurate as an exploratory laparotomy, an opening-up which, of course, is part of surgical interference.

A decision to operate and get the horse 'on the table' must be made no later than eight hours, preferably sooner, from the onset. When shock develops, success becomes unlikely.

Surgical correction is not always the final solution. It only, but significantly, cures the end result, but the primary cause often remains. Naturally suitable advice regarding this is offered – sometimes in vain.

Anatomical sites of colic

The Stomach: Relatively small, reasonably resistant to displacement, but liable to gaseous distension. Eructation (belching out of gas) is impossible unless fatal rupture occurs.

This means the stomach is susceptible to the ill effects of consuming:
- An excess of grain.
- Fermenting grain.
- Excess lush grass.
- Lawn mowings, especially if from a stacked heated heap (even more dangerous if from 'treated' gardens).

Treatment is by stomach tubing to siphon off and/or flush through with appropriate therapies. Surgery is usually impracticable because of physical difficulties in reaching the stomach.

The Small Intestine: A long tube-like organ having three distinct parts: (a) *the fixed duodenum* into which flows bile (the horse has no gall bladder) and pancreatic juices;

(b) *the jejunum*, some 20 meters in length, the site of starch and protein digestion. It lies attached to a large mesentery which gives it and the next part (c) *the ileum*, some 6 meters long, freedom to be displaced.

When disordered there is:
- Marked gaseous distension.
- Liability to 'twist' or volvulus.
- Entrapment by tumours or in openings in the mesentery, natural or unnatural.
- Enteritis especially with marked thickening of the ileal wall.

Normal passage of ingesta is fast, no more than six hours. Pain elsewhere in the abdomen or from disorders of the autonomic myenteric nerve system (as in Grass Sickness) can cause a marked small intestinal slowing of peristalsis to a full paralysis which is called 'ileus'.

The Large Intestine: Inclusive of the caecum, the triple-folded large colon, the small colon and the rectum. It has a total length of eight meters but a relatively much greater capacity, related to its diameter, than the small intestine. It is in this vat-like intestine that microbial fermentation of the cellulose-rich long fibre takes place, to:
- Liberate the volatile fatty acids, the metabolisable precursors of glucose.
- Leave the indigestible lignin which, with used micro-organisms and with water, is the bulk of the faeces. It is said that more than half the dry weight of the faeces is the micro-organism residue.
- Produce the B vitamins.

The caecum: A large blind-ended sac which leads from the ileo-caecal valve and also onwards from an adjacent caeco-colonic valve.

The large colon: Has four regions of varying diameter, the changes taking place quickly at the flexures or bends. Such are the common sites of impaction usually of ingested, poorly masticated straw or coarse hay as:
- When taken off grass suddenly and stabled on straw and/or offered hay.
- Having the concentrate feed suddenly withdrawn.
- Molar teeth mal-effect on mastication.
- Parasitic effect on the myenteric nerve supply to cause reduced peristalsis or partial 'ileus' of this area.

It is the disorders of the digestive micro-organisms which are the forerunners of colic-producing morbidities in the large intestinal complex.

ASSOCIATED DISORDERS

The morbid disorders, which can affect the large intestine, are excess gas production, especially in the caecum, and also deficient blood supply from:

- Thrombo-embolic obstruction of the arteries following the large redworm *Strongylus vulgaris*, larval damage to the main stem artery. (This has become much less common with the advent of the use of the specific larvicidal Ivermectins (Eqvalan) anthelminthic).
- Displacement with pressure entrapment. The obstruction permits the accumulation of gas and of digesta, adding to the vascular problem's pain and loss of function.

- Interference with the combined peristaltic and churning movements on the ingesta from autonomic nerve damage, usually from small redworm larval invasion of the mucosal layer of the gut; another cause of 'ileus' or cessation of peristalsis.

This may result in:
- Torsion.
- Intussusception or telescoping with vascular obstruction. The presence of heavy tapeworm infestation around the ileo-caecal valve is also suspected as a possible cause (see Endoparasitism).
- Impaction proximal to a large colon flexure, especially the pelvic one.

The degree of pain and so of the signs of colic relates to the type and to the sites, as has been emphasised. The vascular disorders produce the worst scenario, justifying the descriptive name of an 'acute abdomen' and, more scientifically, 'Ischaemic bowel disease'.

Colic signs can also arise from the intermittent, and usually temporary:
- Spasm of a length of the gut (spasmodic colic) of neurogenic origin either from larval pressure or from psychoneurotic influences, as in the excitement or worry of transit and competition and/or of a new environment.
  It can be followed by impaction. Incidentally horses do not become constipated as such. The nearest to this is retained meconium or foetal faeces of foals and from the more persistent and prolonged 'ileus'.
- 'Ileus' from a variety of causes, along with the lesser states of spasm or cramp.
- Sub-lethal thrombo-embolic obstruction of the blood supply.
These all lead to even more ischaemia.

These changes in peristalsis or mobility can also precipitate:
- Intussusception.
- Torsion or volvulus.
- Displacement with strangulation.
- Hernias.

All, one way or another, are associated with reduced vital arterial capillary perfusion of tissues with shock, fall in blood pressure and death, unless surgery is carried out, and even then the risk is at least 25% mortality.

Enteritis: inflammation of the intestinal mucosae usually secondary to a primary over-stress disorder such as in Transit Stress, and the resultant morbid effects of opportunist bacteria, e.g. Salmonellae. Endotoxaemia is a likely sequel.

Larval mucosal damage is the most common primary cause. The associated loss of condition is the result of:
- Reduced available digestive areas.
- Reduced ingesta absorption areas.
- Loss of protein through the devitalised gut into the lumen and lost via the faeces.
- Interruption of electrolyte movement between gut-wall capillaries and bowel fluid, and possible subsequent entero-toxaemia.

- Failure to reabsorb body water.
- Diarrhoea with loss of water (dehydration especially in foals).

The veterinary surgeon will classify colic into:
(a) Spasmodic.
(b) Tympanitic.
(c) Ischaemic.
(d) Obstructive.
(e) Neurogenic.

The interplay of morbidity and the resultant signs have been suggested throughout this sub-chapter.

Feeding mistakes, management discrepancies in feeding and in the control of parasites and failures to recognise stressful situations are the main causes.

The wild and the feral (one which has escaped back to the wild) horse was liable to internal parasitism but its nomadic grazing habits and low levels of horse per hectare were inherited defences to dangerous levels.

It can be argued that digestive disorders are mainly man-made. A very common example of this is the failure of the horsemaster to recognise the potential danger of turning out in-work horses especially, and leaving them out in cold wet conditions to consume chilling wet, especially lush grass, as is common in British springs and 'delayed' summers. A break at grass is one thing, unnecessary exposure to risk is another.

4. TEETH

The teeth in *Equus caballus* are a significant example of the marked changes in structure and in functioning required, as 'today's horse' developed from the Eohipps or Hyracotherium of 60 million years ago.

Equus, a single-toed, cursorial, *grazing*, horse evolved to successfully survive:
- In the openness of the extensive grass lands post the Ice Ages.
- On relatively but variably (climate and season-related) coarse-stemmed herbage, but also programmed to crop close to the ground with its incisor teeth and so obtain a proportion of young, more nutritious grass.
- Able to outdistance predators.
- In the comparative safety of herd or group numbers.

Long-fibre herbage, its stem, leaf and its flower and seed case, owed its structural shape and strength to a high-percentage content of the compound carbohydrates, cellulose and lignin. It is these fibrous constituents which require maximum mastication to lacerate and fragment them in order to:
- Release the sap which contains a variable but relatively small amount of soluble starch, protein, oil and minor nutrients (minerals, trace elements and vitamins or their precursors). These are susceptible to chemical and to biological (enzymatic) hydrolytic digestion in the stomach and in the small intestine.
- Break up the hemicellulose, a compound carbohydrate intermediate between the solubles and the cellulose. It itself is partially soluble and so likewise open to simple digestion.

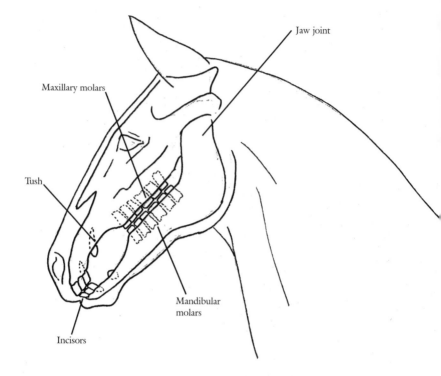

Dentition (Simplified).

Hemicellulose becomes a significant component of herbage when that is immature and growing quickly, and especially so in young, lush 'improved' pasture grasses of modern farming. Its nutrients are absorbed through the small intestines. Some, along with those in the true solubles, is carried through to the large intestine as a nutrient contribution to essential microbial multiplication there. In improved pastures for a short 'growing' time a larger amount may leak through so as to lethally overload the micro-organism with the release of endotoxins. Their subsequent circulation has a morbid effect on blood-vessel muscular walls. Hemicellulose is but one contributor to this 'disease'. Laminitis is the classical example of the effect of endotoxaemia.)

- Grind down the residual fibrous material separating the essential nutritional cellulose from the indigestible lignin. The latter acts as bulk for the constant stimulation of gut peristalsis to keep the digesta slowly passing through but with time for the absorption of the volatile fatty acids extracted from the cellulose by microbial fermentation; the natural precursors of 'energy', and the water content and electrolytes, a reclamation.
- Produce suitably textured ingesta as a substrate for all the above activities.

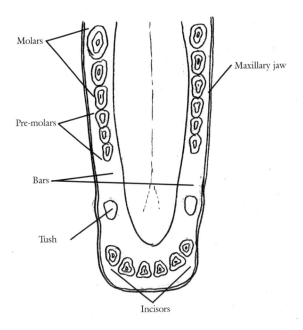

Molars

Maxillary jaw

Pre-molars

Bars

Tush

Incisors

The lower jaw (Simplified).

The horse has one opportunity for dealing with its fodder by mastication and that is when it is just ingested (unlike the cow which regurgitates for a secondary 'chewing of the cud'). The horse must make a thorough job of this 'one bite at the cherry'. Its molars and associated soft tissues must be in good working order. To this end it requires:

- Four arcades or batteries of cheek teeth ('molars' from the Latin 'to grind'). There are 24 permanent molars.
- Each arcade to form a continuous table surface.
- Ideally no interdental spaces.

This is necessary to maintain an ongoing mastication continuous with ingestion, which can take up to 18 hours in periods throughout the 24. The action is that of a lateral-with-rotary-sweeps movement of the mandibles over the stationary maxillae, molars to molars. Along the horizontal arcades the two table surfaces occlude at an angle of about 10°-15°. The strong pressure exerted table-to-table eases off towards the edges, the outer or buccal aspect of the maxillae and the inner or lingual aspect of the mandibles markedly reducing the wear pressure on the two resilient enamel pillars or cusps projecting on the respective lateral walls. The exposed tops therefore experience only part abrasion so that tips are left to project by 0.5mm or so from both upper and lower arcades.

The tips are colloquially known as points. It should be appreciated that they are normal consequences of natural mastication of all foodstuffs; their incidental function may be to guide cross movement and limit the excursions of the tables.

Unless further disorders develop, the points, per se, are relatively small in keeping with molar tables' general attrition and are usually non-traumatic; but they are potential sources of soft-tissue injury, cheek and tongue respectively, causing painful excoriation or an 'uncomfortable mouth' especially for bitting; later, when bigger, they can interfere with the full range of masticatory movement and so have a disordered effect on mastication as well as on acceptance of the bit, with consequent evasion.

The main cause of serious attrition wear is not a reflection of the hardness or otherwise of the ingested foodstuffs but of the ubiquitous presence of a hard mineral, silica, in fresh grazing *and* in conserved rations. It is, therefore, 'available' to stable fed horses as well as to those roaming free. This is nature using a non-nutrient to maintain necessary (dental) structure in association with the self-sharpening ability of the molar tables' enamel surface pattern.

The physically softer seeds harvested for domesticated feeding as cereals, do not require as much mastication as does the fibrous long-stem fodder either as grass or hay. Especially if fed separately or with only a little hay as chop or chaff, this concentrate feed requires a molar range much reduced laterally; once ground down the physical stimulus for automatically induced mastication ceases. Consequently the rotary action tends to leave the molar edges even less abraded so that the points become relatively longer and also more intrusive of the occlusal table; a serried, sharp edge is left to become an active defect with a more likely traumatic potential. Moreover the table itself tends to be gouged rather than filed across, into shallow hollows to form a vaulted surface which is progressively less effective as a grindstone. They also predispose to torque forces on the other arcades which then:

- Open the interdental spaces with food-trapping effect, fermentation of that causing gingivitis which leads to periodontal disease, then cavities and possibly apical infection.
- Alter the arcades' apposition, leading to further changes in wear patterns, e.g. the formation of hooks.

The equine molar has to:
(i) Grow, up to 7 years of age, from its apices or roots.
(ii) Erupt and keep erupting to replace the crown loss from attrition (by 2-3 mm per year on average).
(iii) Retain post-growth 'hold' within the bony alveolus despite diminishing length of unerupted crown at least until the late 20s. (The total apical and reserve crown length is some 80-90 mm.) These abilities explain the equine's possible age being greater than the bovine's.

The actual dynamics of mastication include (a) the pestle-like action of the tongue to keep the ingesta moving back to between the arcades; and (b) the reflexly stimulated flow of parotid saliva which:
- Softens the masticated fibre.
- Binds the ultimate food bolus for swallowing.
- Adds buffers against the eventual gastric acidity.
- Lubricates deglutition (swallowing).

There is also (c) the powerful action of the jaw (mandible) muscles so positioned as to exert maximum leverage well rostral to the temporo-mandibular joint. (Note the size of the vertical rami of the mandibles.)

Oral activity demanded large cheek teeth well set into their maxillary rostrums and into the horizontal mandibular rami to form four rectangular boxes occupying most of the anterior skull. To offset this bulk the oral cavity for the tongue and the ingesta was kept relatively narrow but elongated. There is a constant throughput of ingesta at any one time by trickle feeding to minimise bulk volume yet leave sufficient time and area for the necessary mastication.

The high face, broad between the eyes for maximum all round visual acuity, lies between and above the lateral walls of the maxillary cheek teeth to leave room for capacious nasal passages: important for respiratory volume flow, a high oxygen input, for 'flight' muscle metabolism and in other forms of athleticism.

The diastema or space between the tush teeth (if present, or the incisors if not) and the lower first premolar is called the bar of the mouth. On it will set the bit.

Ideally the rostral vertical aspect of the top and the bottom first premolars should erupt so as to have them sloping caudally to allow the bit to rise up or down their anterior free surface with minimal resistance. In some horses this has to be manually sculpted.

TYPES OF TEETH
Incisors
There are 6 in each jaw, forming close fitting arcades. They appear as deciduous, temporary or foal teeth, at or soon after birth. The permanents replace them and themselves come into full wear by 5½-6 years of age. The temporaries are smaller, pearly white and shell-like. The permanents are greyish-brown, bigger, and stronger-looking. They are identified, in both sets, left and right sides as:

- Centrals.
- Laterals.
- Corners.

The tables are abraded with wear, which alters their shape and the design of this occlusal surface.

The permanents grow until about 6 years old. From the time of eruption through the gum their attrition is compensated for by continuing eruption of more reserve crown which adds more than is required. Hence 'long in the tooth'. Unlike the molars this replacement is not so well maintained and the old horse eventually wears the incisors down even to the gum level. Their roots remain well secured so loss is a very late occurrence.

The main function of the incisors is to cut the herbage. Secondly they are aggressive weapons for attack and for defence. Thirdly they are self-grooming equipment and for mutual grooming.

Ageing: In general the tables of the incisors progressing from the centrals outwards have a great species similarity in appearance up to 5 years old. Even here there can be significant differences, but nevertheless they remain reasonably good markers for age and are used thus as (legally speaking) 'assessments' of age. An acceptable 'birth certificate' is one identified against a foal's markings soon after its declared birthday.

One is advised never to look a 'gift horse in the mouth'. Not all horses are gifts and, in the absence of certifiable records, an oral inspection backed by an appraisal of the whole horse's condition can help a trained inspector to a reasonable assessment. Reference to the dental formula will show that a 'full mouth', i.e. when all the incisors in the arcades are in full wear or apposition when occluded, occurs with (a) temporary or deciduous teeth at 2 years and with (b) permanent teeth at 6 years old, perhaps later.

Unless a distinction is made as to the pearly white, smallish teeth of a 2-year-old and the brownish yellow, vertically grooved, larger teeth of a 6-year-old and an assessment of immaturity or not (some 2-year-olds if well done can be deceptive in this respect), then 'ageing' is going to be awry.

The inspection (always look at both sides) is not just for age but considers possible disorders.

(i) First, the profile, to show:

- Angle of occlusion. 180° at 6 years, pincer-like, gradually reducing year by year until the old (over 15 years) incisors meet at around 100°, and getting much longer. Some breeds such as Arabs have plier-like teeth characteristically for picking (dates) rather than for cutting (grass).
- Fullness of wear or occlusion of the corner teeth.
- The presence of a caudal hook on the upper corners, said to show at 7 years and possibly (again) at 11 years, and Galvaynes groove which remains on the corner teeth from 10 years on, diminishing downward from 20-30 years old.
- Parrot mouth and other abnormalities.
- The presence of tushes, eruption between 4-6 years old (males only as a rule), with excessive tartar and over-sharp edges in the older horse.

(ii) Second, face on to show:

- Closed jaw to estimate size and the presence of any wear marks on the labial occlusal edge from gnawing wood (usually both 'sets'), or crib-biting (usually just the uppers).
- Broken, chipped or missing teeth.
- Unerupted incisors – impacted, or displaced with interdental spaces and the risk of gingivitis.

(iii) Third, the appearance of the tables, the plan or outline altering with the years from

- Narrow, ovoid and relatively horizontally long
- More roundish broadening front to back
- Triangular with rounded corners, point towards tongue

to

- Rounded broadening from back to front.

Ageing becomes more difficult after full mouth at 6 years. Until then the centre of the incisor table will be occupied by a cup or infundibulum which in a 5-year-old's corner tooth goes right to the posterior edge. In this there is an inner ring of concentric dentine enamel called the 'mark'. As the teeth abrade – further on in the centrals, then the lateral and finally the corners – the mark moves nearer the lingual edge and eventually becomes a dot at, on average, 6, 7 or 8 years before disappearing. At 8 years the tip of the pulp cavity, now all dentine, is revealed. It is an elongated horizontal line which increases in diameter through 9 and 10 years and moves centrally, leaving a dot in the centre of the now triangular table. It is called the 'star' and begins to fade at 12, 13 and 14 years.

Tushes or Canines

Mares rarely have these; the male animal does and uses them as weapons. (Compare the boar and the elephant, the original definition of 'tushes' being 'teeth which protruded from the mouth'.) The maxillary tushes are further caudal from the incisors than the more rostral mandibulars. As they grow (permanents only) from very long caudally directed roots, they erupt between 4-6 years and eventually by 10 years become pointed with vertical edges. They have no masticatory use. Their isolation makes them a site for tartar deposition. The resultant gingivitis is irritating and encourages the horse to explore them with its tongue, sometimes with traumatic effect – one cause of an uncomfortable bitted mouth.

Molars (from the Latin *mola* 'millstone')

In practice these are spoken of as 4 arcades each of 6 molar or cheek teeth. Academically there can be 7 if the first and rudimentary 1st premolar is present.

Known as the Wolf tooth, the first premolar is variable, small and peg-like and variably rooted. When present it usually lies close up against the first cheek tooth; it can be more rostral and even laterally placed. These premolars are present soon after birth but have no deciduous elements nor any masticatory function. There are rarely 4 present, only occasionally in the mandible where the rostral position is common, and not always paired in the maxilla. The numbering of the molar arcades should technically begin with this 1st premolar but it is simpler to record them as a Wolf tooth.

This leaves 6 cheek (grinding) teeth. The first three, or premolars, are originally deciduous being replaced with permanents. The last three, as true molars, are permanents only. The roots of cheek teeth 3, 4, 5, 6, 7 protrude upwards into the maxillary sinuses where they are covered by a thin film of bone.

Molar teeth have no gum-line neck: the erupted length is described as the crown; that still below the gum line is known as the reserve crown, ending at apices which surround the roots and the active area of the pulp within its cavity. A continuous eruption is, in the average, normal horse, assured by the extent of this reserve crown even though it finishes growing around 7 years old, to see the animal remains 'toothed' well into its thirties. By this time the bony hold on a molar is by means of the remaining apices.

Molars fall out in old age but in no particular order and not in appositioned pairs. The resultant gaps are hindrances to satisfactory mastication, hence the essential need for geriatric dental care.

The molars, unlike the incisors, maintain a steady above-gum size of about 2 cm throughout life. Their occlusal surface attrition is a reflection of the high pressures involved in mastication and an indication of the functional demand of fibre maceration.

CONSTITUENTS OF TEETH

Four materials, of varying embryological origin go to make up the hard structures of all teeth and especially of the molars.

Pulp

Pulp is the softest, relatively speaking, as its name implies. It consists of vascular and neural tissue in a spongy connective tissue matrix and occupies the apical cavity, the 'pulp cavity'. It penetrates deeply along the length of the tooth; its tip is well into the reserve crown (see incisor teeth occlusal surface patterns). Only in severe traumas and/or infections is the cavity penetrated.

Apical injury does occur from excessive reverse pressure on them during eruption and the growth years especially. In the mandibles this shows by the development of bumps along the base of the horizontal rami.

Pulp dies off to become an inert area replaced by dentine at around 6 years old in both the incisors and the molars.

Dentine

A yellowish white, hard material which makes up the bulk of any one tooth. It is not a 'dead' tissue but has some powers of regeneration rather similar to hoof-wall horn.

Enamel

Harder even than bone, this shiny, blue-white, highly mineralised, brittle but resilient material lies between the vertical columns of dentine. On the lingual and buccal walls of the molars it stands out like buttresses to form columnar cusps, the tops of which form the ultimate points. Within the tooth it surfaces at the table in a convoluted pattern, different in maxillary from that of the mandibles. The two patterns at occlusion and subsequent mastication effectively perform the necessary grinding 'blades'; they are also self-sharpening.

The depressions between these 'proud' edges are called infundibula. These overlie the dentine columns which are protected by the covering of cement.

Cement

A bone-like, but less hard than enamel, material which covers the roots as in other animals and so lies next to the bony alveolar spaces. Specifically in the horse it, as described above, fills the infundibula. It stains black with the incessantly squeezed-out vegetable juices but is impervious to them (see molar caps below).

DENTAL 'JARGON'

Anatomically the dental plan is described (much simplified here but sufficient for practical communications) as the juxtaposition of the molar and incisor surfaces of the erupted crowns. 'Jargon' is as follows.

- Tooth wall or table edge next to the tongue is *lingual*.
- Tooth wall or table edge next to the lips is *labial*.
- Tooth wall or table edge next to the cheeks is *buccal*.
- The masticatory surface (molar) or table, is the *occlused surface*.
- The cutting surface (incisor) is the *occlusal surface* or 'table'.
- The space, however tight, between the teeth is *interdental*.
- Where gum length is visible it is called a *diastema* and where it forms the area of bit contact, the *bar*.
- The angle formed by the anterior wall of the first premolar and the adjacent gum is known as the *bit seat* with special reference to the *mandible*.

A SPECIAL EFFECT OF DOMESTICATION

The significant difference between a grazing horse and a stabled one is in its eating patterns. Grazing necessitates a head (and neck) down position. In most stables, man has invariably and for various reasons, usually his own convenience but also for putative welfare considerations, imposed a head-up position: for manger height and even higher hay net and rack.

In nature a horse grazes, ingests, masticates and swallows in a more or less continuous action for variable durations and intervals up to 18 hours out of the 24. Only the fear of danger, real or imagined, and the onset of muscle fatigue engendered by this action will interrupt it. Satiation by the consumption of the arbitrary 2½% dry-matter feed per day will also determine when it stops to rest generally or to self-exercise.

In domestication, even with ad lib hay supplies, most horses will interrupt feeding to investigate what is going on outside. Since its food is there for the eating and there is no necessity to walk about for it, the stabled horse will have longer rest periods and inactivity with boredom. (See Stereotypes.)

A ration of cereals will always be consumed more quickly than one of long fibre, nutrient value per nutrient value. The cereal is not only concentrated nutrients but also requires much less masticatory processing. As has been described, the reduced mastication involves not only a time factor but also a reduction in lateral sweep distance with the risk of the molar vaulting.

Most importantly the head-down position is said to be accompanied by a horizontal displacement of the incisors whereby the mandibular incisor tables come to lie several millimetres rostral to the maxillary arcade.

It is assumed that this visualisable incisor change is accompanied by a similar displacement of the molar arcades into what must be a more ideal and better functional occlusive masticatory position. Conversely, when the horse is not eating and has its head up, the molar arcades will return to 'table to table' apposition and, logically, the most comfortable position for overall locomotion – fortuitously, also to give a comfortable bitted mouth. To see this is practically impossible, certainly in the moving animal.

In head up eating position the same rostral displacement has not been seen to occur. By implication therefore, mastication must be compromised in this situation, at least to some extent. Molar table attrition must, for the same reason, be altered; malocclusal action and effect with associated table wear changes, result in the formation of enlarged points, rostral and caudal hooks and enlarged interdental spaces from torque pressures – much more common in stable-fed horses than in grazing animals.

This is now known to be a functionally induced disorder, not related to the type of food as has been previously thought.

5. THE LOCOMOTOR SYSTEM

Reference has been made to the structural and functioning aspects of this system in the horse which distinguish it from other herbivorous mammals. These developed specifically to improve its survival chances against fast galloping predators over short distances.

In these first few minutes the 'big cats' or the wolf – depending on the indigenous geographical terrains – were faster than the horse, and even more so if an elderly, lame or ill horse was picked out or a youngster got left behind. Hence the need for agility and strength to attempt fighting the predator 'off its back': twisting, turning, rearing, bucking and if possible striking with forelegs, kicking with the hind and even biting, although these three aggressive actions were usually employed in horse-to-horse combat.

If and when free from attack the horse's speed over the next few, up to about four, minutes, utilising anaerobic (sprint) muscular activity, could often outrun the tired aggressor. Thereafter the herd would continue aerobically for longer periods to outdistance the predator which soon gave up the now unequal chase. A more exact use of this instinctive behaviour was:

(a) Fright – a quick awareness of danger to the herd or group.
(b) Flight – in two phases, to escape as a gregarious unit.
(c) Fight – only by the unlucky individual 'caught' before flight could be effected.

The domesticated horse 'resting' at grass would practise these alone or in groups of grazing animals. The mare with foal at foot would make bursts of speed slowing to a canter to encourage the foal to respond to the need for the mental and muscular exercising or 'training' necessary. Young horses would mimic defensive fight and flight with each other which, in the male, was also directed to stallion behaviour.

The horse in work would be trained to go the distance likely to be involved in any discipline in terms of speed and relevant agility by going for a shorter distance but at a faster speed, and going for longer but at a slower speed. They would also practise power work as in jumping. This is not so much for aerobic but for anaerobic work – more a repetitive 'doing' to get 'its eye in' and to increase agility as well as strength.

If the horse was put to work for which it had not been 'fully' trained or if exposed to inelegant or unbalanced strides during the work, a limb could be overstressed by this sudden excessive effort on an absolutely or on a relatively fatigued musculature. The end result could be a strain or a sprain in one or more of the components of a unit of locomotion whose basic resilience had been overstretched.

A unit of locomotion is the lever system involved to work around or to 'hold' on a fulcrum or pivot, and so either

(a) Support a limb in the stance phase of a stride, or
(b) Stabilise the spinal column and the associated trunk over the flight phase as well as the stance to complete a stride's protraction, retraction and footfall – the biomechanics of locomotion.

The levers worked around the articulations or joints to execute a series of movements called extension, flexion and 'hold' or fixation.

In every stride the foot is the ultimate fulcrum, although, technically, biological fulcrums do obey the laws of the three mechanical lever systems. A kick, for instance, doesn't use the hoof as a fulcrum but as a 'weight' at the end of the 'power' when it makes contact with the target.

THE FOOT AND THE DISTAL LIMB: STRUCTURES AND FUNCTIONING

THE TENDONS AND LIGAMENTS

The muscles of the distal limb, fore or hind, come no lower or more distal than points proximal to the carpus or 'knee' and the tarsus or 'hock'. From there the respective extensor and flexor tendons continue distally to attach to the skeleton of the limb to effect movements on the knee and hock and, more distally, on the fetlock, pastern and hoof. These three units of locomotion are synchronised in movement.

Evolution resulted in a single-toed limb formed by the one hand or foot bone (fore or hind) called the canon. This is partly bordered by residual hand or foot bone II and IV, known as the splint bones. These have no distal articulation and end some inches above the next joint which is the fetlock equivalent to the human knuckle. The finger or toe of the horse is a single digit much enlarged to form the pastern. The third phalanx is encased in the horny capsule – a hoof. From the diagram (page 145) these main bones and three ancillary bones, the paired proximal sesamoid bones and the distal sesamoid or navicular (shaped like a simple boat's hull) bone are seen. Tendons transmit the contractile pull or 'force' of muscles onto distal bone(s) and so cause either flexion or extension.

An important feature is the stretch imposed on a relaxing muscle by its opposite number pulling the joint(s), back into extension or vice versa.

Foot fall and the related ground force reaction to the down thrust of the body's mass is summated into stress (weight is mass multiplied by speed) which increases from stance through walk gait to gallop.

When unencumbered by a rider, more than 50% of a horse's weight is on the forelegs. A rider will increase this except in advanced dressage movements. Moreover, the leading foreleg carries, if only momentarily, the full load at support and lift-off in the asymmetric gaits and when jumping. The trailing foreleg takes a different force but one which exerts a particular stress. The superficial flexor tendon is the one most likely to be overstressed. Apart from the tendons, the suspensory ligament, originally a muscle tendon unit in its own right, is liable to overstress,

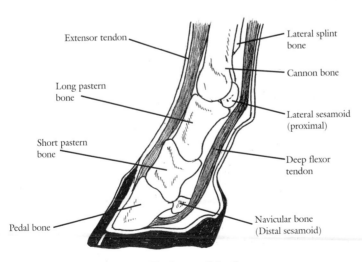

Extensor tendon

Long pastern bone

Short pastern bone

Pedal bone

Lateral splint bone

Cannon bone

Lateral sesamoid (proximal)

Deep flexor tendon

Navicular bone (Distal sesamoid)

The bones of the foot.

especially in a branch or at its origin just below the knee. Overstresses of the sesamoidean ligaments are less common. The check ligaments of both superficial and, more likely, of the deep flexor are also sites of overstress (especially in inelegant strides). As a weight-bearing limb 'lets down' – a form of concussive stress dissipation – the deep flexor tendon passing very close (in contact) under the navicular bone exerts considerable compression force on that bone (see Navicular Disease). The hindlegs 'work' differently and are not so likely to be overloaded; slips will adversely affect the suspensory and 'curb' ligaments.

As a limiting factor to overstretch of muscles involved in both forehand and hindquarter dynamics, the equine musculature is widely supported by ligamentous tissue paralleling the muscle bundles. Some of these ligaments have, over evolutionary time, lost their muscle content and remain as joint limiting factors on their own. The best example is the stifle/hock locking mechanism whereby movement of one or other of these joints must be accompanied by a similar movement in the other. This, with the temporary fixing of the patellar ligaments over a knuckle on the medio-distal aspect of the femur, plays a significant role in the stability of the hind leg in propulsion and at rest. In the latter the hind legs can alternately lock, with but minimum muscle effort to remain weight-bearing almost passively, whilst the other leg rests to permit muscles to 'recharge' their energy supplies.

Special ligaments are integral parts of joints where, as the outer layer of the joint capsule, they give support to and also limit the range of the joint's excursion. They are also present in many joints as accessory limiting, directing and supporting factors.

The sesamoidean ligaments of the the palmor (or plantor) aspects of the distal fetlock and the pastern area are good examples of these special ligaments where they are part of the suspensory apparatus. They occur also where extra support for joint stability is required, usually on the surface not covered by muscle tendon – for example, the lateral and the medial ligaments of the stifle (of human skiing injuries to the knee). In well-muscled areas such as the shoulder and the hip, such external ligaments are not found.

Although not part of the distal limb the ligaments of the spine are essential supporting factors in that area.

The colloquial 'foot', i.e. the horny hoof capsule or 'hoof' and its contained bone, ligament, tendon, vascular and neural supply, is also exposed to considerable stresses especially on weight-bearing and particularly during locomotion. This stress changes with

- Physiological resting weight of the horse, its mass
- Dynamic weight (mass x acceleration)
- Yield of the ground surface

and the variations further imposed at

- Landing
- Support and
- Lift-off.

The downward thrust of weight is ultimately focused on the pedal bone, the 3rd phalange.

It is attached all round its vertical surface to the inside of the horny wall by interlocking vascular laminae or leaves. The stress is transmitted across this 'corium' or quick onto the outer avascular horny wall whose vertical tubules 'take the strain' which ends at their ground or bearing surface. Here the inner wall joins that of the sole to form the 'white line'. The sole horn interlocks with the pedal bone's solar corium.

The flow of blood is vital not only to nourish the coriums but also to remove the venous blood. Its volume also acts as a hydraulic cushion or shock absorber.

The flow is shut off momentarily on dynamic weight-bearing and presumably reduced at static weight-bearing by the operation of an arterio-venous shunt mechanism. The posterior third of the wall is relatively flexible, partly as a concussion reducer, but its recoil plays a part in venous blood return, as does the frog, the lateral side bones and the flexible bulbs of the heel.

The art and the science of farriery is discussed – to a limited extent – later.

The sole horn is not required to be weight-bearing, certainly in the shod horse. Arguably neither is the frog, which acts as a support at 'let down'. When this pressure is relieved at lift-off, the frog's return works as a type of piston-pressure, again involved in blood flow.

Horn is a keratinised form of special skin which grows down from its 'quick' or corium situated in the coronary band around the top of the hoof from heel bulb back to the opposite heel bulb.

The distal fulcrum, colloquially the foot, is that part of the whole system which is in contact with the ground. It is exposed therefore to several stresses of:

- Concussion.
- Compression.
- Stretch or flaring of the wall.
- Friction.
- (As well as abrasive or penetrating wounds).

The abaxial tissues above the foot, the stay and suspensory apparatus of ligaments and tendons, especially in the distal limbs, are also exposed to the overstresses of:

- (Concussion – progressively dampened proximally.)
- Compression.
- Stretch.
- Torque – of bone.

All of which are internal closed traumas – strains, sprains and micro and macro bone fractures.

Through external traumas (blows) onto the skin, the resultant bruise can penetrate to the:

- Subcutaneum.
- Tendons.
- Ligaments.
- Bone.
- Synovium.
- Cartilage.

Such blows can so weaken these tissues that they become more susceptible to overstresses. The trauma may penetrate the skin and further through the tissues mentioned above. The result is an infected wound. This is most serious when a vital unit is entered – the synovial cavity of a joint, tendon sheath or bursa.

The consequences of this intrasynovial sepsis are:

- Inflammation of the secretory lining of the synovial capsule, a synovitis which becomes swollen, ineffective in producing a healthy synovia, and painful.
- Inflammation of the outer ligamentous layer, which becomes swollen and less supportive.
- Degeneration of the cartilage, with loss of integrity and reduced shock absorption and joint mobility.
- Erosion, and eventually erosion of the underlying bone with severe pain.
- The involvement of synovial sheath leads to suppuration and fibrosing adhesions, periosteal reaction and osteo-arthritis.

At some point in the acute stage there is a risk of septicaemia.

The consequent reduction in joint and/or tendon mobility affects the related muscular functioning with resultant atrophy. Such wasting is also common to the muscles involved in sterile inflammatory loss of use.

MUSCLES

Muscles can only contract and thereby shorten to exert a force, or relax – and thereby become able to be lengthened by being 'stretched' to the original length by the contracting force of an opposing muscle. This is exhibited during flexion and extension of the related joint(s). This 'take and give' is done elegantly, rhythmically and without jerk. If the movement does not conform to these it is called a 3rd order acceleration which causes friction in all the components of the joint and especially the joint surfaces themselves, with resultant overheating and possible tissue damage.

The correct dynamics should involve a period of zero movement in the joint, not a sudden reverse action. It is this incorrect effect which can also result in overstretching and resultant spasm of muscle, if not an actual tear. In some situations it can result in strain of the associated tendons.

The control necessary is neurologic based on proprioceptive sensory nerve input from (a) muscle stretch nerve endings, (b) tendon stretch nerve endings and (c) joint capsule sensory nerves including balance, which all refer subconscious information to the lower centres of the brain. Extremes of information implying serious disorder will be 'put through' to the conscious brain in the form of painful sensation. Normally the proprioception supplies negative feedback – 'all is well, carry on as before' – or positive feedback – 'something is wrong, slow down or stop until this is assessed and corrected'.

CARTILAGE

This glistening white, smooth tissue covers the articular ends of bones to form the friction-reducing feature of a joint. It has no direct blood supply and therefore is not capable of inflamatory repair. Its vitality and integrity is maintained by the pressure-driven flow of synovial fluid into its spaces when the joint bears weight and more especially when that is induced by dynamic weight bearing. The synovia exudes back out when the pressure is off. It has no nerve supply. Cartilages are also found as an integral part of certain tendons, for example that of the anterior surface of the deep flexor tendon as it passes over the bursa separating it from the navicular bone. Regeneration is possible and can be therapeutically assisted.

THE JOINT CAPSULE

Both the synovial layer and the fibrous layer act as a supporting cuff to a joint. The synovial layer contains the lubricating synovial fluid and is further supported in itself by the articular ligaments and the annular ligaments.

There is a rich vascular supply to all the tissues in a unit of locomotion with the exception of the cartilage and of the mucosal layer of the synovium. This inner absence explains why an intra-articular infection does not immediately produce an inflammatory response, as mentioned earlier. All such infections sooner or later penetrate the synovium secretory layer and much later the cartilage to reach sensitive and therefore vascular areas which respond in a normal fashion.

FARRIERY

Hoof horn is a specialised form of epidermis or skin. As such it is continuously growing. Unlike most areas of the body surface the horn is exposed to pressures from:
- The downward push of gravity which reflects the static weight, the mass multiplied by the
- Acceleration of the body, as a force of gravity, the active weight.
- An equal and opposite upward thrust of the ground reaction force, which can vary from hard to yielding, as one or more limbs make contact with it and adopt a stance phase on it both at rest and in motion.

Such combined forces can alter the growth lines of the hoof wall even in the shod animal. In the limb with correct conformation the forces do not divert the hoof wall growth provided there is regular paring and balanced trimming of the wall, usually at four-weekly intervals.

A delay in trimming will result in normal growth being:
- Directed outwards at the toe and anterior quarters.
- Directed inwards and under at the heels.
- Unilateral-sided flaring or rolling under at any point.

As a result, horn can be respectively prized off sensitive tissues or compressed on to them, with disturbance of the critical vascular flow within the capsule, leading to disorders of hoof functioning and structure, as well as creating breaks in the white line protective continuity.

If, as is often the case, the conformation of the limb as a column of support and especially the hoof capsule itself results in unequal distribution of the forces on ground contact, there will be a redirection of the forces with ill-effect all the time, again more so with overgrown feet.

It cannot be over-emphasised that good farrier attention is necessary and that the farrier must be given time to study each horse, with veterinary input if necessary, and that the owner is prepared for the additional costs involved. This will pay dividends in the long run.

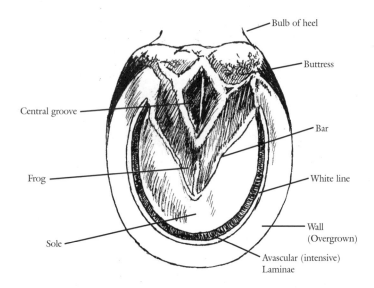

Bulb of heel

Buttress

Central groove

Bar

Frog

White line

Sole

Wall
(Overgrown)

Avascular (intensive)
Laminae

The surface of the hoof.

A farrier should see a 'new' horse walk out in-hand:
(i) Before the old shoes are removed, perhaps also at the trot.
(ii) Possibly immediately afterwards.
(iii) After trimming of the horn to the limb's conformation as a 'column of support'.
(iv) After re-shoeing.
Acquired hoof pastern malconformation takes time to correct, during which time some impediment to blood flow is likely. This can be improved by tactical veterinary-prescribed medication, provided competition rules regarding non-normal nutrients (NNN) are not likely to be contravened. Farrier co-operation is required. In some cases electron microscopic examination of hoof parings (obtained when the farrier reduces the wall) is necessary to establish nutritional causes of horn weakness.

Veterinary advice should be sought for the correct treatment of concurrent hoof horn disease or when that develops on its own. It is important to differentiate between the two main deficits in the wall at the white line, i.e. the junction with the sole:
(a) In the external horn layer with loss of structure. This is biotin-responsive.
(b) In the middle horn layer with loose horn squamas which become susceptible to bacterial infection and need supportive antibacterial therapy. This is calcium-responsive.

Other aspects of conformation have been discussed in Section I. Whilst all are not direct problems for the farrier, any which produce an unbalanced action horse will alter the forces imposed, especially on forelegs as compared to hindlegs and, more importantly, one limb as compared to the contralateral one. Wall growth can be consequently distorted unilaterally.

Deviations may be as follows.

- *Hoof and distal limb deviations* from the acceptable normal, as seen from in front and from behind, and the associated flight patterns will weaken the symmetry of hoof placement and the security of stance and of take-off. The counter-balancing involved can cause over-stress on the medial and the lateral aspect of the tissues around the distal joints as well as the risk of interferences.

- *Deviations from the square profile* and ratios of measurements with them, which give the impressions said to be required for balance and self-carriage. Variations must cause counter-balancing over-stresses. The units of locomotion both axial and abaxial can develop in compensation but the basic weakness remains.

COMMON DISORDERS

Of all the traumas hazarding a horse the most common are strains, a sterile over-stressing from the effect of jerk, whiplash and/or snatch by the related muscle or from a failure of that muscle to support tendons and ligaments as a joint is 'let down', in shock-reducing effect, as the result of a very inelegant step or from fatigue. Tendons and, in particular, flexor tendons are more liable to such trauma than an extensor tendon or an articular ligament, but the risk still applies to them.

The tendon most usually affected is the superficial flexor tendon of the foreleg in the mid-cannon region. The deep flexor tendon, when over-stressed, experiences strain more distally in the region of the back of the short pastern bone, the navicular bone and at its insertion into the pedal bone.

The Accessory Check Ligaments (ACL) of these two tendons can also be overstressed: the proximal ACL between its origin at the back of the distal radius and its insertion on to the superficial flexor tendon at the level of the back of the knee; the distal check ligament at its origin from the fascia at the lower border of the knee and the top of the cannon.

The suspensory ligament can be overstressed:

- At its origin close to the distal (deep flexor tendon) check ligament.
- In the shaft at mid-cannon level.
- In one or other of its branches (rarely do both suffer together except in severe sprain of the fetlock joint) in the fetlock region.

Muscles are subject to micro strains and only occasionally to severe macro strains or tears. These usually occur in the propulsive muscles of the quarters and of the shoulder region of the foreleg. The abaxial postural muscles are less readily over-stressed. Their check ligaments and tendons are much more susceptible.

As can be appreciated, the risk of over-stress increases with speed, and duration of work and associated possible muscle fatigue – both related to the state of fitness of the horse. It also increases with 'the going': hard, unyielding going can set up jarring, vibratory stresses which in time can so weaken the structures that they more readily give to ordinary work levels; soft holding going permits forward slipping of the limb and overstretch of the flexor tendons and causes difficulty in lift-off, exerting an excessive pull on the tendon as its muscle contracts against the holding ground.

A common morbidity of a muscle is a spasm, a fixed contraction which aims to minimise the movement of an injured joint or tendon and thus protect these tissues from further overstress. The spasm is usually restricted to a relatively small area, or 'knot', close to the muscle's origin; similar spasms can occur without clinical tendon strain. This is most common in muscles in the proximal limb regions and in the neck amd croup areas. Unless the related trauma of a strain of a tendon or a sprain of a joint is quickly resolved and so allows the muscle to relax, with the help of a massage if necessary, a continuing spasm will quickly result in atrophy of the whole muscle.

The dorsal muscles of the 'back' (the epaxial muscles of the spine) are in fact a sequential series of small muscles working in unison from the pelvis to the skull but mainly to more cranial areas of the back and to the neck, to stabilise, make rigid, the back into what is in fact extension or dorsal flexion. Severe strains, resulting in a variety of muscle tears and resultant spasm, do occur, from falls, severe twists and other inelegant movements.

The majority of these injuries usually show as marked disturbances to freedom of movement as well as signs of the sterile inflammation with heat, swelling and inducible manual pressure pain. Minor injuries from such lesions may appear as unilateral, sometimes bilateral, more localised disturbances in action and in balancing during locomotion. In some cases the tearing of the ligaments and of muscles through their tendinous insertion will cause damage to the underlying bone with resultant periostitis and space occupying new bone formation. Nerve entrapment may follow either from the chronic fibrosing and/or osteitis but also from the consequential oedema around the vertebrae, particularly in the area of foramina.

Less obvious trauma can result from the use of an ill-fitting saddle (see page 197). Disorders such as galls, sores and abrasions will cause minor pain and often considerable discomfort until the damage resolves, usually quickly, and the wrong pressure areas are reduced. In other cases particularly from the points and the saddle bars pressing down or into underlying muscles, spasm of these muscles can follow. The same will result from saddle panel pressure on the fascia and epaxial muscles close to midline. Such pressures primarily cause occlusion to the flow of blood through capillaries both into and out of the capillary bed with resultant escape of serum and the stimulation of pain sensory nerve endings. If the pressure is maintained for more than two hours then more serious thrombosis can occur with longer lasting effects such as skin ulceration and muscle spasm.

In a substantial number of cases the associated persistent pain and the altered proprioceptor messages, even distant to the lesion, will markedly affect the way the horse goes; its balance of movement is upset. From the effect of an ill-fitting saddle a spasm can be persistently invoked.

The balanced symmetric movement of a horse can be disordered anywhere along the 'coil of activity'. The rhythmic flexion and extension of all the joints of both the axial and the abaxial skeleton and the carefully timed phases of 'hold' can be thrown out of cadence.

The 'coil of activity' is as follows.

(i)   The neck and shoulder girdle part-propulsive, part-postural.
(ii) The 'back' region together with
(iii) The linkage of the loins – the axial group.
(iv) The propulsive quarters and their associated thigh muscles.
(v)   The ventral abdominal muscles.
(vi) The auxiliary effects of the hind limb postural muscles which through the

reciprocal apparatus of stifle and hock establish a firm lever system for the above propulsive effort.

(vii) The postural muscles of the foreleg for stability during landing, foot fall and lift-off.

Whilst anatomically distinct, these movements are functionally dependent on a unified synchronised whole.

Some possible factors which can upset this balanced rhythm are:

- A forefoot low-grade lameness which weakens foot support and inflicts further unbalancing by overloading the contralateral limb.
- An arthritis of one hock (a spavin) with a similar contralateral unbalancing.
- One or more degenerative joint disease complexes in the thoracico-lumbar region with unilateral weakness and contralateral complementary rebalancing and associated muscle hypertrophy.
- A neck lesion's pain upsetting head and neck carriage reflected along the spine to the quarters whereby propulsive effort can be asymmetric and unbalanced.
- More indirectly but none the less still important are the evasions to the bit engendered by disordered molar teeth and subsequently induced mouth pain and/or irritation of the wolf teeth – the 'uncomfortable mouth'.
- Finally, an unbalanced rider throwing weight to one side and requiring axial rebalancing and abaxial asymmetric effort.

All these will have an effect and will show in a variety of ways, often seemingly converse, such as:

- Stiff neck leading to foreleg lameness.
- Bit evasion on one side producing cranial unilateral neck spasm.
- Saddle or loin muscle stiffness upsetting the necessary rigidity of the dynamic spine.
- Quarter weakness on one side and subsequent three-track action.
- Hindleg lameness with unilaterally reduced propulsive power.

More serious consequences from the above can be seen in the eventual development of navicular disease and/or spavin, with or without associated conformation faults.

It is essential that, when a rider complains of his horse 'not going well, being wrong of its back', the veterinary surgeon sees the horse as a whole organism which is unbalanced somewhere, perhaps even in the back.

Paradoxically it is the peripheral effects from pain located in the

- Fore feet
- Hocks
- Mouth
- Neck
- Quarter areas

which can induce torque stresses which become yet another cause of the 'bad back syndrome'. Lameness is not always a simple focused disorder.

There are, of course, dis-eases of the locomotor system which, although they are overt lamenesses, do not necessarily involve prolonged overall imbalance; though the horse is too lame to be worked, the condition is of short duration with minimal contralateral overloading. These might include disorders of and/or within the hoof capsule, such as open traumas, penetrating nails, sharp flints, etc; causing an initial wound which if not discovered and correctly managed will lead to purulent infection of the sensitive tissues of the hoof capsule laminae, of the corium of the sole and possibly of vital areas of the unit of the coffin joint. Colloquially and collectively these are known as 'pus in the foot'. Paradoxically they are most frequent in horses turned away to grass where the initial opening wound is not seen, or is not looked for, such as with flaring of an untrimmed wall forcing open the white line. This trauma is rarely serious enough in itself to provoke open lameness but the subsequent purulent infection is certain to do so.

Horsemastership entails:

- Knowing what ground conditions will predispose, e.g. soft, to allow wall overgrowth, subsequent dry surface to effect leverage and distal wall splitting into the 'white line'.
- Maintaining a close observation of weather/ground changes.
- More effective farrier attention to trim or to rasp down at regular intervals.
- More exact inspection of the resting horse's action by seeing it trot freely for at least several strides even on the grass. If suspicion arises, then confirmation will require in-hand exercise on a harder surface as well as a more detailed inspection of the hoof.

The more important the horse and the closer the training starts for its future competitive programme, the more critically such lesions must be looked for. This may even mean all such horses being caught up and trotted on the hard each day, particularly if the grazing ground is soft and so more likely to produce hoof wall deficit but masked by the soft going. Such time-consuming action will, of course, allow a better all-round inspection for other possible defects.

Traumas do, of course, occur in the working horse such as a pricked foot caused by a misdriven farrier's nail or a 'rogue' nail or stone picked up during work; or when a horse is overdue for shoeing when the shoe will prise the overgrowing wall off its solar attachment and the shoe heel will be pulled forward off the buttress and onto 'the seat of corn'. The bruised solar horn may produce a sterile inflammatory pain. If not, or if not appreciated as a lameness by the horsemaster, the damaged horn will 'die' and liquefy; the resultant fluid will be pressurised upwards eventually to invade the more sensitive corium of the heel bulb to cause marked lameness.

FOOT DISEASE
There are two specific diseases of the foot.

NAVICULAR DISEASE
Navicular disease (ND) is slow in onset, invariably progressive and usually present in both forefeet with one worse and therefore more obviously lame than the other. It is most common in light horses including Thoroughbreds and Thoroughbred crosses.

First signs:
- Pointing of the toe at the stance.
- 'Going on the toe' with a shortened stride: this action improves with work but returns when next worked after a period of rest, and eventually fails to warm up to become less lame or not lame.

Later signs:
- Clinical involvement of the contralateral limb.
- An alternate easing of both limb heels at the stance.
- A shuffling, pothery gait possibly at the walk, certainly at the trot.
- A reluctance to jump – to avoid landing on sore feet.

ND is considered to be a genetically linked dis-order in as much as there is a predisposition to weakness of the hoof's supportive structure, especially at the heels, or more exactly at the posterior third of the hoof. Such horses are more prone to acquire:
- A broken back pastern hoof axis.
- A collapse of the buttresses.

This may be following excessive work on consistently firm going, more likely to happen in 4-year-olds and upwards; farrier-acquired wrong trimming can leave the horse with long toes, short underrun heels and/or 'broken' bars.

The developing morbidity is the result of over-compression of the navicular bone by the deep flexor tendon whereby there develops:
(i) An erosion of the dorsal cartilage-covered surface of the tendon in apposition to the bone. This is accompanied by a hyperaemia of the area.
(ii) Changes in the mid section of the bone following obstruction to the venous return blood flow.
(iii) Further bony changes leading to osteoporosis and cavitation or ulceration of the bone.

There are several other disorders of this posterior third of the hoof's components which present with similar and therefore confusing clinical signs, to which the overall description Navicular Syndrome can be given. These require careful differential diagnosis including selective nerve blocking and radiography. In the final analysis true ND depends upon the clinical signs of:
- An on-going suggestive typical lameness.
- Specific radiographic findings of osteoporosis and bone ulceration supported by
- Special-technique anaesthesia of the synovial bursa between the tendon and the bore, through which synovium the specific nerve to the navicular bone and the closely related structures – the podotrochlea – run.

There is no cure for the true disease. Ameliorating, short-term treatment does work in association with appropriate rebalancing of the forefeet, corrective shoeing and expansion of the blood flow, by both physical and chemotherapeutic means supported by analgesia.

LAMINITIS
An acute disorder of the sensitive laminae, usually in the fore and invariably bilaterally, of the hoof wall, made dynamically more serious down and across the toe region. It is more likely in ponies and cobs than in 'light' horses. The heavily pregnant older mare is susceptible to a physically induced form of hindfoot laminitis.

The suffix 'itis' implies inflammation. It is primarily a vascular disorder induced by a marked decrease in the flow of blood to and from the foot following a constriction in the walls of the blood vessels under the influence of pathological toxins. Such toxaemia begins with a marked increase in E-coli strains of bacteria in the:

- Digestive system.
- Womb in which a placenta has been retained for more than 6 hours postpartum.
- Other sites of bacterial proliferation, e.g. abscesses as in Strangles.
- Hormonal influences which result in over-production of steroids as in Cushing's disease of the old equine.

The most common is the digestive form where

(i) the pony consumes a sudden excessive quantity of lush grass rich in soluble carbohydrates as well as proteins and oils or of concentrates rich in starch and,

(ii) the stomach/small intestine fails to cope and the excess spills into the large colon and into the caecum with

- lethal effect on the fermentative micro-organisms and
- morbid effect on the mucosal cells lining the gut;
- an increase in the number of pathogenic E. coli strains;

(iii) there is a rapid production of endotoxins from these two traumatised sources, as well as from the E. coli; this is followed by their absorption into the blood circulation to produce an endotoxaemia and a vaso-constriction.

The effect of this is most serious in the blood vessels confined within an unyielding hoof capsule. There is:

- Pain.
- Lameness even to the extent of the pony being 'rooted to the spot'.
- Distension of the vein on the inside of the cannon.
- A 'bounding' pulse on both sides at the back of the fetlock.

In severe cases, the laminar connections at the toe are so damaged that the animal's bodyweight tears the pedal corium away from the wall laminae. Within three days if no successful treatment is given the pedal bone itself will rotate down at the toe on to the sole or 'sink' from an all-round laminar separation (this is more common in cobs). Treatment must be urgently sought, and administered by a veterinary surgeon.

First-aid is effected by the application of a 4ins rolled-up open-weave bandage strapped on the hoof along the line of the frog from just short of the point of the frog to the heels; this will give the expedient essential support to the frog and thence to the pedal bone.

Cures are possible. The heavy pony is obviously more susceptible to laminar breakdown in terms of kg per sq cm of laminar surface.

Laminitis is a disease of ponies on improved grasses which are not indigenous to them, especially when the grass is at its most lush, as in the spring and to a lesser extent in the autumn. It is also most likely when a warm wet spell follows a dry cold one. Although a reflection of the amount of consumable grazing which is available within a small grazing area, as is the case with improved pastures, the end result is more a matter of how lush, i.e. young and rapidly growing, the grass is and therefore its percentage of enzymatically digestible solubles.

Any horse or pony which is grazing such pastures, which has broken into a food store, or which is inadvertently given an overweight of starch concentrates, should be seen as a potential case and veterinary assistance called for at once. Quick removal from the source of the overfeeding, and lavaging what has been eaten through the stomach and small intestine by means of stomach tube administered fluid, can prevent the development of the rapid rise in endotoxins.

METABOLIC DIS-EASE CAUSING LAMENESS

RHABDOMYOLYSIS

Set Fast or Azoturia are older 'names' for this condition. It is a not uncommon metabolic disorder of 'light' or riding horses such as the:

- Race horse.
- Trotter.
- Hunter.
- Eventer.
- Showjumper.
- Long distance horse.

(Approximately in that order of incidence.)

These are all susceptible to an as yet imperfectly understood range of myopathies (muscle disorders). Its occurrence is usually associated with athletic demands on muscle functioning but not always so; it, unusually, can occur in postural muscles strongly engaged in balancing against the movement in transport. The usual muscles involved are those with predominant cell types:

Type 2 (HO) fibres – especially when they have been trained into their increased oxidative capability.

Type 1 – slow twitch as in the postural muscles mentioned above but also in some forms of athleticism such as hunting and endurance riding.

It is said to be an autumn/winter disease but this is not absolute: it is related to the overall environmental atmosphere and inhaled cold atmosphere.

Some of the older theories now seem to be wrong, but basically there is a difficulty for the horse to metabolise muscle glycogen, the by-products of which build up in such a manner as to cramp the affected muscles. This results in a rapidly increasing stiffening of the loin and the quarter groups, with a marked shortening of the hindleg's stride.

Affected animals should have transport home brought to them and thereafter should be taken to the nearest stables until the hyperacute phase passes, usually in 2-4 days. A return to work must begin very slowly and the related feeding is very much a matter for discussion with the attending veterinary surgeon. In many cases the aim is to reduce sugars as a source of energy and to eventually, as required, augment the diet with vegetable oils as a source of such energy.

Rhabdomyolysis can be lethal inasmuch as severe cases or incorrectly initially managed cases may 'go down' because of the degree and the extent of the myopathy. Few get up and those that do never become athletic. Some severe cases, if not veterinary-managed as to muscle breakdown by-products, can develop kidney obstruction with severe, even fatal, consequences. ER can in rare cases cause a heart muscle complication and heart-failure death will happen quickly and early in the disease.

Confirmation of the disease and monitoring of its recovery depends on clinical signs, and the levels in a blood sample of the two enzymes released from the affected muscles: creatinine kinase (CK) and aspartate aminotransferase (AST). In a significant number of cases in Great Britain, at least, there is an associated imbalance of the electrolytes in the intercellular and the intracellular muscle fluids, which is not due to a true dietary deficiency of:

- Calcium.
- Phosphorus.
- Magnesium.
- Sodium.
- Potassium.
- Chloride.

The imbalances and the causes thereof remain incompletely understood.

The use of excessive molasses and other high soluble sugars in routine feeding of horses should always be avoided and particularly in horses which have already suffered from this condition. Once affected, a horse is liable to relapse even with all appropriate prophylaxes having been tried. It would seem to be a matter of skilled fittening and training as far as the eventer, hunter, showjumper and endurance horse is concerned; and whilst not restricting free grazing and rest periods during work, access to lush pastures must be avoided. Exercising on the lunge certainly in the early convalescent period is strongly not advised.

DISORDERS OF THE LOCOMOTOR SYSTEM: THE SIGNS
In general, disorders of the locomotor system present a variety of clues.

Changes in stance:
- Easing of the weight of one forefoot persistently, or intermittently alternate easing of both forefeet.
- 'Pointing' – when the lame leg is held forward resting on the toe.
- Taking the whole bodyweight further on to the hindlegs.
- Taking the whole bodyweight further forward on to the forelegs.
- One leg continuously off weightbearing: a 'dangling' limb.

Changes in locomotion, when free moving:
- Won't lie down.
- Can't get up from the lying position or does so with difficulty.
- A weakness in moving.
- Sways on moving; this and the above weakness is often more apparent in the hind action.
- Bizarre (peculiar) ataxic steps.
- Can't or is reluctant to turn on the fore or on the hind limbs.
- Swings an outside hindleg wide on such turning.
- Goes on three tracks.
- Goes short striding with a shuffly gait with or without knuckling of one or other fore or hind limb.
- Goes lame.

When under control, in-hand or ridden, such dynamic changes are often more obvious from 3ins down

- At the walk or
- At the trot.
- On a circle to the left or to the right.
- On hard and on soft going.

6. PREVENTION OF DIS-EASE

Many of the disorders which affect the horse are related to its athletic use. The traumas inflicted upon its distal limbs and especially its hoofs have been mentioned earlier, and emphasis has been put on the internal traumas, i.e. the subcutaneous connective tissues of bone, joint, ligament and tendon (and the more proximal muscles) as the result of overstress to produce fracture, sprain and strain (as well as spasm and tear).

These risks cannot be eliminated but they can be minimised. Fitness for the work and considerate, skilled riding are the two essentials. Well-shod balanced hooves, correctly fitting tack, especially the saddle, and a constant appreciation of the 'going' by the rider are important considerations.

The severity, the long-term effects, the potential complications and the ultimate healing are all reflections of

- Early recognition of the trauma
- Efficient first aid
- Good management
- Sensible rehabilitation

on the part of the horsemaster, with veterinary help. These skills have been discussed, in part at least, earlier.

An important feature of open wounds is secondary infection. This is usually by bacteria which are either

- Commensals existing on the horse's hair and skin, and to a lesser extent.
- Saprophytes living in the soil and therefore in the environment in grazing, hay and straw.

Whilst streptococci are the commonest commensals in the oro/nasal pharynx, those of the skin and soil are frequently Gram-negative species. The former are susceptible to penicillin and its derivatives; the latter usually require broader spectrum antibodies. Wounds are usually infected with aerobic species which thrive in the presence of oxygen and with anaerobes which survive in oxygen-deficient areas such as bruised wounds and puncture wounds.

Whilst both types of wound benefit from being opened up to be exposed to the air and made free to drain, the closed types will almost certainly require specific antibiotics. When vital areas are penetrated the immediate treatment is saline or equivalent lavage to flush out the infection.

Subsequent treatment especially of limb injuries aims to minimise skin and subcutaneous infection and thus permit restricted granulation in filling without the formation of 'proud flesh'. It is here that veterinary input is important; it will also advise on the correct wound covering for maintaining

- Temperature.
- Moisture.
- Aeration.
- Protection.
- Support.

Fractures are reparable but much dependent upon site, type and, if an open wound, the degree of secondary infection. It is a specialist decision.

The so-called 'closed traumas' are also requiring of veterinary examination and advice. This may well involve the use of ancillary diagnostic tools such as

- Ultrasonography.
- Thermography.
- Scintigraphy.

The information thereby gained helps to decide which of the further treatment modes are relevant:

- Ultrasound therapy.
- Laser therapy.
- H wave and other electric applications.

The imbalances in locomotion from directly related muscle spasm and atrophy and indirect compensatory hypetrophy may well cause functioning spinal complications requiring

- Acupuncture
- Chiropractics
- Osteopathy

as complementary adjuncts.

Owners who believe in herbalism often use this on the understanding that, at the worst, it will do no harm. Such an attitude may be dangerously misleading; recent work points to a 'deeper' effect than just mere cellular medication. It would appear that homeopathy has its effect at sub-atomic level. So too does Radionics and all electronic modes. There is a vital effect on body fluid and tissue energy wavelengths, so much so that exponents now talk of these being Biodynamic Resonance Modulators.

It should be appreciated that this 'energy' is not the same as metabolic energy, which is the biochemical factors released when glucose is converted. 25% of this 'fuels' muscle contraction; 75% is 'lost' as heat, some of which maintains an animal's 'core' temperature, while the remainder has to be dissipated by convection, radiation and evaporation under the thermo-regulatory system.

INFECTION

SYSTEMIC SECONDARY INFECTIONS
There are bacteria and fungi which survive in the equine upper respiratory tract, but when given the right opportunity, namely:

- A fall in non-specific immune substances.
- A decline in the physical defences of the respiratory tract

— the trapping mucus.
— the cilia of the respiratory escalator.
- Mucosal inflammation.

From the initial morbidity induced by a viral invader, these germs, can now invade to colonise on the respiratory mucosal surfaces and penetrate further into
- Other pulmonary tissues and
- The lymphatic system – systemic disease
- Auxiliary respiratory areas
  — sinuses and
  — guttural pouches – localised disease

to create a secondary inflammation, a complication. They are susceptible to specifically selected antibiotics and chemotheropeutics under veterinary supervision.

PRIMARY INFECTIONS

Adult horses are invariably affected by viruses and most of these, on a day to day basis, are invaders of the respiratory system, with the exception of:
- Strangles due to the bacterium Streptococcus equi
- Skin invaders causing mud fever and rain scald
- Some airway infections as apparently primary invaders
- Some bowel disorders as apparently primary invaders

which are all bacterial or fungal in type.

Viruses, as yet, are not susceptible to antibiotics. They are usually primary invaders but some minor ones can secondarily infect. Their control is a matter for the animal's immune system. Hence the severity will relate to
- The young
- The old
- The malnourished
- The intercurrently otherwise dis-eased animal

and to the standard of horsemastership/nursing.

Active artificial immunity as well as the natural exposure-engendered type are both important. It is said that viruses are dedicated pathogens (causers of disease) but they are not programmed to kill.

Anti-disease serum to give passive artificial immunity is rarely used nowadays. It is all produced in horses and therefore carries an autoimmune risk.

The exception is antitetanus serum which is invariably converted to active immunity by vaccination with the toxoid, thereby eliminating the need for more serum sometime in the future.

A special (expensive) type of serum is available for foals exposed to or recently affected with neonatal disease.

Isolation of carriers or conversely of susceptible animals does play a part in special circumstances in immediate tactical control measures.

Foals are not so susceptible certainly to the viruses of the adult. This is presumed, in fact is known, to be because the dam's colostrum carries specific humoral antibodies, artificially or naturally stimulated, which protect the foal for the first two months of its life.

As with humans, the horse, and most commonly the horse which 'works away from home' on a day-to-day basis, is exposed to viral infection from other horses. (Viruses are species-specific.) The route of infection is by aerosol droplet-carried exhaled viral particles being inhaled. Two viral diseases are venereal but one of these can also be aerosoled.

It should be appreciated that as yet no immunity whether artificial or natural can prevent a virus entering a system tract (respiratory or digestive) and colonising on the mucosal surface. Immunity as a rule either
- Limits the invasion to the lymphoid tissues or
- Minimises its effect so that the pathogenicity is either
  — tissue minimal with mild signs of illness.
  — sub-clinical.

Both can cause a reduction in performance and are often heralded by a transient fever (invariably missed except in elite management).

ARTIFICIAL IMMUNITY

This is effected by a programme of intramuscular injections (vaccination) of the specific germ so attenuated as to be

- Highly antigenic
- Negatively pathogenic

so that the vaccinated horse is resistant to pathogenic invasion of its particular systematic tissues. This requires

(i) Dose one, the sensitising dose.
(ii) Dose two, approximately one month later, the first immunising shot.
(iii) Dose three, six months later.

Thereafter according to manufacturers' instructions, but usually annually.

There is present research and development of an intranasal insufflation route for Influenza immunisation.

The viruses which are so managed in equine practice are:
- *Influenza* and its current (drifted) strains. The vaccination is mandatory under most competition rules especially Racing. An identifiable veterinary-signed document must accompany the vaccination.
- *Herpes 1 and 4.* Strain 1 can lead to abortion and occasionally to a vascular disease allergy in the central nervous system resulting in paresis to paralysis. (There is no contagion from the neurological complication.)
- *Equine viral arteritis* which can also cause abortion.
- *Infectious equine anaemia.*

The last two are not officially endemic in Great Britain. The 'arteritis' can get in via an infected stallion which in its early infected days may become a respiratory carrier before settling into an infected semen-shedder. The 'anaemia' is basically spread by insect vectors.

The Herpes strain 1 is peculiar, and worryingly so because it
(a) Has only a short artificial immunity: 4-6 months.
(b) Can remain a carrier in the absence of clinical signs.
(c) Can recrudesce infection (contagion) from its lymphoid tissues following periods of stress such as

- Transit.
- Competition.
- Intercurrent disease.

It is very much endemic. It differs from Influenza in that the latter gets rid of infection soon after clinical signs subside.

TETANUS

A neuropathy following the invasion of a wound by Clostridium tetani whose multiplication produces the pathogenic toxin.

A vaccine is made in the laboratory from this toxin; it is called a toxoid. It is antigenic but non-pathogenic, and it is inoculated three times as for Influenza and usually with this viral vaccine. After four doses repeats are at five-yearly intervals.

On certain studs where wounds are known to become contaminated with other forms of clostridia, to produce necrotising/gangrenous lesions, there are specific vaccines.

PROPHYLACTIC WORMING PROGRAMME FOR THE CONTROL OF ENDOPARASITISM

Endoparasitism is the state of being affected by infestation with worms in their larval stages as well as by adult worms. Until recent years the most lethal parasite disease of horses was caused by the larvae of the large red worm, *Strongylus vulgaris*. No drug could get at it within its migratory and thrombus-forming stages in the main artery to the intestines. The use of Ivermectin (Eqvalan) did kill these, and the associated vascular abdominal crises have all but disappeared in equine practice. In its place, the larvae of several strains of small red worms, the *Cyathostomes*, have become a worrying form, especially those third-stage larvae ingested in late summer or autumn which have an ability to 'hibernate' in their normal encysted state in the mucosa of the large intestine. They are then said to be inhibited. The build up per se can cause gut absorption deficit but their sudden release into the lumen to become adult occurs en masse with disastrous effect from January to March.

The classical signs are:
- Protein loss through the damaged gut wall.
- Loss of condition.
- Shock.
- Death in a significant number of cases.

In years at studs when the return into the gut lumen occurs later into early spring there is often a protracted diarrhoea.

Whilst most 'wormers' will eliminate adults only, one (and some under present trial which might require fewer doses) gets at the encysted larvae, and that requires five full daily doses (Panacur Equine Guard). Strategically this is done in October and again in February when, inexplicably, a single dose of 'Moxidectin', a relation of Eqalan, is effective.

It must be emphasised that an overall policy of worm control, whether for one or a hundred horses and especially if maturing horses are involved, must be planned by your veterinary surgeon to:

(a) Maximise efficiency: selection of drug; minimise risk of developing drug resistant worm strains.
(b) Maximise economy of total drug use.

The reduction in number of doses used can only safely be practised in line with faecal egg counts, which if below 100 are said to be safe – and safer still if regular faecal pat-lifting is carried out. All horses in any one environment must be dosed together. New intakes, other than in the late summer, should receive a chosen drug and be housed for three days. If brought in during late summer or early winter, they must have an appropriate five-day course and be housed for three days until adults are also expelled. If in early winter the single dose of moxidectin with isolation may be used.

The strategic plan will aim to avoid dosing horses in full work. If this is unavoidable, especially in youngsters, amendments can be made so that the horse can be 'let down' for three days before and three days after worming with a rest from hard work during that time. (The same applies to vaccinations, but boosters can be brought forward even if they are not allowed to be delayed.)

'Worming' aims at:
(i) Minimising the number of adults parasiting and affecting the gut wall from the gut lumen.
(ii) Thereby minimising the number of eggs passed in the faeces to contaminate the pasture and so reducing the risk of massive larval hatching and eventual ingestion.
(iii) Thus minimising the risk of larval damage during this internal migration.

Despite many years of attempted worm control by drugs and for pasture hygiene regarding infestive larval numbers, horses continue to be parasitised. Complete eradication and so cessation of ongoing stimulation of the immune system could be very counterproductive if 'clean' animals thereafter met 'unclean' pastures.

Worms have no 'wish' to kill the host they parasitise, for obvious reasons. The host 'tolerates' a certain degree of parasitism, i.e. preferably without associated illness, and it gives protection. What advantage the host obtains is not clear; perhaps it is a duty of care! The relationship is partly symbiotic but can often become pathologic up to and including a lethal level, especially with the larvae of some species.

All modern 'wormers' will kill off adult worms. Their ability to kill immature stages, as well as the duration of the effectiveness as a residual gut lumen drug, there to catch 'emerging' adults, varies. Since most adult bowel worms have a life span of about one month, a 'clean' gut with no eggs being passed and therefore no fresh pasture contamination, has a duration beyond one month dependent on the particular wormer used. Thus, in order of low duration to high, 5 weeks to 10 weeks approximately, we recognise Panacur, Strongid and then Eqvalan, to use the better-known trade names. This gap is known as the 'egg return time' (ERT).

'WORMERS'
There are three main chemical groups currently available for the control of equine endoparasites.

The following list is selective for explanatory information. It gives the main chemical, generic names, the subgeneric names followed by the trade title and the manufacturer/distributor. It demonstrates the need to read the small print when the horsemaster is deciding on a change for tactical reasons to minimise the risk of inducing a specfic drug resistant endoparasite. Consult your veterinary surgeon.

Thus, Fenbendazole and Oxfendazole come from the same major chemical origin. In this chart they are also shown with their trade names which further implies a generically different drug when in fact they are close relatives.So, too, with the macrocyclic lactones but to a lesser extent. So far, in practice, there is no cross resistance.

It is cynically observed that in the millenium there will be a varying level of resistance to all presently known, pharmaceutically safe wormers, just as already with some of the Benzimadazoles and adult forms of roundworms, large and small but not, fortunately, with the cyathostome larvae.

GENERIC	SUBGENERIC	TRADED AS	BY SUPPLIER
Benzimidazole	Fenbendazole	Panacur	Hoechst
	Oxibendazole	Equitac	Pfizer
Tetrahydropyrimidines	Pyrantel ombonate	Strongid P	Pfizer
	Pyrantel ombonate	Pyratape P	Hoechst
Macrocyclic lactones	Avermectin	Equalan	MSD Agvet
	Milbemycin	Moxidectin Gel	Fort Dodge

STOMACH BOTS
Stomach bots, a larval stage of the Horse Bot Fly which parasites the stomach wall during the autumn and the winter, without apparent ill effect, is also susceptible to Eqvalan. Tapeworms are susceptible to only a double dose of Strongid.

TAPEWORMS
Tapeworms are susceptible only to a double dose of Pyrantel Embonate. In recent years more attention has been paid to the potential pathogenicity of tapeworms. These have an indirect life cycle whereby the eggs develop to larvae in summer-pasture grass mites; these are ingested with grazing. The larvae escape on digestion of the mite and colonise on the wall of the distal ileum and the rim of the ileo-caecal valve to become adult there. Either from secreted toxins or from metabolites liberated on their death, both of which are absorbed into the gut wall and onto the gut's neural controls, or merely through adverse stimulation, a morbidity develops in the ileum and the caecum, causing impaction of the former and/or intussusception in the latter, leading to serious colics, some requiring surgery.

WORMING CONTROL STRATEGY
An essential control is pasture hygiene which necessitates thorough and complete picking up of horse faeces:
- Once a week from November to March.
- Twice a week from April to October to maintain pasture larval numbers.

Worming strategy involves:
- Correct selection of the appropriate wormer.
- Tactical changes to minimise risk of emergence of resistant strains.

Both require dosage rates accurately related to the horse's body weight.

ECTOPARASITISM AND OTHER SKIN DISORDERS

Insects cause reduction in health by being:

(a) Seriously annoying – such as to interfere with grazing, and/or exhaust the horse by it 'gadding' away from some insect types' flight noise.

(b) Irritant on the skin – as with lice and mange mites that induce constant rubbing, even self-mutilation.

(c) The antigenic source of hypersensitivity skin reactions – from biting and sucking insects which inject allergenic saliva onto the keratin and dermal layers.

Prevention is by:

(a) Repellants: these show marked lack of success because the horse is a sweating animal which 'washes off' any applied chemical and dilutes any sprayed chemical; and it is frequently exposed to cooling and cleansing washes following hard work, which add to the above.

(b) (Ecto)-Parasiticides: these are a matter for veterinary discussion. The chemicals used for both therapies have a risk to the handler and also to the horse(s).

Lice can be controlled by strategic dressings applied three times at 10-day intervals

from December/January. In out-wintered horses it is sensible to do this as a matter of course. The horse is the only source of lice which 'live' as adult or nymph through spring, summer and autumn to be activated by winter conditions on the winter coat.

Some blood-sucking insects and dermal invaders will succumb to Ivermectin medication.

Reference to Stable Management, Section III, shows that at daily groomng the horsemaster was advised to take the opportunity for a health check including changes in the skin (and coat) such as lumps, bumps, minor injuries and fly bites, and for evidence of ectoparasitic activity e.g. lice, mange mites, Sweet Itch, ringworm and mud fever.

Most horsemasters will at least be suspicious of lice activity, they cause severe pruritis or itchiness. So too does mange mite infestation, particularly by those that burrow into the skin. This 'scabies' is comparatively uncommon whereas the lesions produced by the leg mange Chorioptis mites could be the result of several other types of inflammation. Psoroptic mites result in self-inflicted injury. The common sign of itch is also seen with Sweet Itch, Anal Pin worm infestation and some feed allergies. Differential diagnosis is important and includes:
- Seasonal incidence.
- Management (feed) changes.
- Allergy in the individual horse.

It usually requires veterinary help.

What is more important is to recognise the earliest changes before self-mutilation and/or secondary bacterial infection. These can be catalogued as follows as being associated with

- Prurities, i.e. itching dermatoses
- Hair loss, i.e. alopecic dermatoses.
- Scaling and crusting, i.e. dry/flaking dermatoses.
- Weeping or seeping, i.e. moist dermatoses
- Nodular lesions, i.e. skin-thickening dermatoses

Ringworm, perhaps surprisingly, is not an itchy condition; it shows moist scab formation and hair loss.

Rain scald is not itchy unless secondary bacteria attack, as in the mud fever form, whereas many of the allergic skin diseases are, classically sweet itch associated with the saliva of the Culicoides midge.

Plant nettle sting is seriously irritating to cause almost maniacal behaviour in some cases; the irritation is primary to the leaf's toxin. Similarly bee and wasp stings inject a primary toxic agent.

The more common biting flies are, for example,

- Horse fly.
- Stable fly.
- Black fly.
- Mosquitoes.

Some transmit viral infections and fungal infestation but development of a hypersensitive state following a first bite is rare. Swarm attacks can be fatal. Irritable behaviour will follow the pain of some bites, and restlessness, even evasive gadding, can be induced by the noise of flying insects.

The 'blow' fly will lay its eggs in moist wounds or other insect-induced morbidity – blow fly strike – resulting in marked myiasis or maggot invasion.

Nodular disease – e.g. 'lumps and bumps' – firm painless discrete subcutaneous nodules 5-20mm in diameter usually but not always along the back, the sides of the chest; quite often unilateral. Possibly due to insect bites resulting in necrosis of the dermal protein collagen. Old lesions may have calcified cores, no itch, no hair loss except perhaps initially. Saddle pressure may be contributory.

There are two very common dermatitic conditions related inasmuch as the same germ is involved. Dermatophilus congolensi is the bacterium. As with many secondary bacterial conditions following activation of skin commensal, opportunist germs, this one can survive only on the horse. When cast off with dead hair and scabs it may live for short periods but not significantly as to be a soil/environmental contaminant. It hibernates in the long coarse hairs of the mane, tail and feather in tiny dandruff-like flakes.

In the classical condition called Rain Scald it becomes activated in surface water in the hair following repeated wetting from persistent rain which is shed along the coat patterns to the ground. Consequently the inflammatory lesions are seen mainly over the back, quarters and posterior thighs. Horses always stand tail into the wind and so into driven rain.

The activated germ multiplies to invade the hair follicles with resultant inflammation, matting of the hair and eventual falling-out of the resultant plaque to leave a moist, sometimes raw surface. Stabling and artificial drying – not scrubbing with a coarse towel – brings about a remarkably quick recovery. In neglected cases antibiotic therapy systemically and topical antisepsis (see First Aid for type and dilution rates) will be necessary. A subsidiary type is called hunter's rash: it occurs on the front of hind cannons. It may be confused with the next disease.

In the second dermatitis, the lesions are restricted to the back of the heels, pasterns and sometimes the posterior fetlock. It results from the wetting and the excoriation of the skin from mud with breaking of the hair. An acute fissuring dermatitis develops particularly in winter-used horses (e.g. hunters) where, paradoxically, the limbs are daily washed down but only partly dried. Originally it was assumed that the Dermatophilus came from the mud but it is now accepted that the wetting actuates latent infection. Treatment is more difficult. Secondary staphylococcal infection and other commensals can create folliculitis, then furunculosis often with ascending toxic infection.

ALLERGIES

An allergy is a state of incorrect immunity; it is usually a hypersensitivity. It may be inherited; it is seemingly genetically determined, when it is described as an atopy. It is frequently acquired in the process of developing a resistance to a particular pathogen whereby it becomes neither fully susceptible nor fully immune but liable, on re-exposure, to exhibit unusual signs. These are presented in the

* Skin
* Digestive tract
* Respiratory tract

all of which are epithelial tissues, epidermal in the skin and mucosal in the other two.
In the horse they are frequently a reaction to

* Insect saliva, particularly subsequent attacks.
* Foodstuffs, usually the protein constituent.
* Fungal spores, bacterial infections.

They quite often become clinical away from their primary site especially with food allergies which present in the skin.

Skin allergies must be differentiated from contact sensitivities, e.g. 'nettle stings', which react the first time. Chemical and other physical contacts are similar.

COMMON ALLERGIES

The common horse allergies are the following.

Skin

Lumps and bumps from protein feedstuffs, usually on face, head and neck, but may be wider spread.

Focal reaction to insect saliva repeat bites localised to the arthropod midge's special feeding area as with Sweet Itch at the base of the mane and at the head of the dock. The resultant dermatitis is very itchy and so subject to self-mutilation. The primary lesion is sensitive to the sun's UV radiation which compounds the disorder.

Purpura haemorrhagica is a particularly serious, usually lethal, hypersensitivity to Streptococcal toxin liberated after a complete or a part recovery from e.g. Strangles. The classical ocdernatous lesions in the skin are associated with oral and internal haemorrhages.

Respiratory
The very common Chronic Obstructive Pulmonary Dis-ease (COPD) is the consequence of invasion of the air tracts' alveolar mucosal lining by the spores from fungal contamination of hay and straw – usually when these are harvested in wet conditions. The primary sensitivity when exposed to further contaminated inhalations reacts by liberating cellular toxins. These in turn cause broncho spasm, a constriction of the airway's smooth muscle component and a consequent airway narrowing or constriction. There is a coincidental production of a clinging, thick mucus which further obstructs the air flow. An equine form of asthma with certain important differences to the human form. A similar condition can develop from grazed herbage fungi: this is called Summer Grass Acute Obstructive Pulmonary Disease (SGAOPD). The affected horse may have acute flare-ups in COPD, with longer periods of a chronic state. The outdoors and selected hay or substitute is the ideal environment. Otherwise the respiratory functioning is variably handicapped. In stables, environmental control is difficult but is based on haylage and non-straw bedding for *all* horses in a yard.

PREVENTION OF HYPERSENSITIVITIES
Prevention of these hypersensitivies is directed at keeping the causal agent away from the horse, which may in fact be inherently susceptible. Determination of which foodstuff is responsible is difficult. When a grass protein is culpable it is usually only a matter of time, a week or so, before the growth pattern of the grazed material changes – with age – and the level of sensitising material drops sufficiently.

Sweet itch prevention depends upon stabling the horse – it is usually a pony or a pony cross – during the time the midge feeds. In this case it is the evening species, which loses its activity as the sun sets. From 4pm till dusk the horse, if boxed, should be safe. Daylight hours until 4pm are usually safe. Other midge species feeding at other times *and* on other parts of the skin are causing conflicting skin allergies.

Where necessary the wearing of a light sheet over the head, neck and to the quarters is very helpful.

An antiparasitic repellant lotion such as Benzyl Benzoate mixed with an oil such as olive oil or liquid paraffin prevents the midge from getting the necessary foothold on the coarse hairs of the tail and the mane and may repel some.

Purpura is another matter. It comes 'out' from the inside, usually 3-4 weeks post clinical signs of Strangles. Careful observation for early signs should permit expeditious veterinary attention. It can be fatal, especially if neglected .

COPD is incurable; once sensitised, always so. In the controlled absence of attacks the affected animal's respiratory system can return almost to normal, but it must be accepted that a lower performance is to be permanently expected.

Paradoxically, the contaminated hay (or straw) allows growth of the fungus during its drying-out period. When 'made' and fed, the handling of the hay and the pulling it out of the net or rack by the horse released millions of spores into the atmosphere near to the nostrils. If the hay is wetted (this usually requires bulk soaking for up to

12 hours) the surface tension between spore and hay fibre is increased sufficiently to prevent its liberation. Spores which are swallowed do no harm.

Hay which is made into haylage and quickly wrapped does not 'culture' fungi and so is safe to feed. Suspect straw should not be used. It is less dangerous than hay but is always a risk. Alternative bedding material is always advisable, especially for a known subject. Untreated wood shavings, shredded paper or peat moss are all safe substitutes.

Affected horses may, of course, have to be exposed at shows etc. to unselected hay and straw upwind of them. There is a medicated aerosol which, if given under veterinary supervision, will protect a susceptible horse during this time.

FUNCTIONAL AND METABOLIC DISORDERS

In the elite athlete especially, or in any horse which has suffered a previous metabolic disorder such as Exertional Rhabdomyolysis, liver malfunction or a hormonal disturbance, or which may have recently been exposed to viral infection, blood samples are taken for relevant laboratory analyses such as:

- Haematology – i.e. blood cells' numbers and ratios can be determined, for example, to suggest the possibility of a virus infection or subclinical parasitism.
- Metabolic profile – to assess: electrolyte levels (in association with a urine sample); enzyme levels in excess from liver, heart muscle or systemic muscle malfunctioning; and hormone levels.

Ideally, as used in elite competition stables, a basic picture is obtained from samples taken at the beginning of work of clinically healthy animals. A first sample, if taken during a suspected illness will reveal the ratios at that time but will not be more than presumptively helpful. Subsequent samples, especially for virus antibody levels or to monitor reduction of morbid metabolites, do help considerably in either case. A single sample, especially for haematology, when illness is suspected, can be misleading without this base line. Enzyme rises are more significant.

DEGENERATIVE DISEASES

Degenerative diseases imply an on-going condition presenting as a chronic state. They are mainly in the locomotor system and particularly in the articulation area of a unit of locomotion, i.e. an osteo-arthritis. Their prevention is no longer applicable but their management is within veterinary input which should be sought.

Dental: the 'degenerative' effects of 'wear and tear' on the molar teeth, have already been discussed. They constitute one very important feature of domestication.

- Excessive points and ridges on the inner aspect of the lower arcades and on the outer of the upper.
- Hooks on the first and the last of both arcades.
- Other morbidities.

These justify at least annual inspection and attention by a veterinary surgeon or a certified dental technician working under a veterinary surgeon. In a percentage of cases a full dental workup, if necessary under sedation and including specialised rasping and cutting, is required, not just a 'simple' rasping or 'floating'. Failure to do so can cause serious welfare considerations as well as interference with equitation. (See separate information on 'Teeth'.)

REHABILITATION[1]

A veterinary surgeon must have more than a passing interest in every aspect of horsemastership and horsemanship (Equitation). The undesirable effects of some questionable, perhaps incorrectly understood or misapplied, techniques and gadgetry to induce movements said to be natural for a horse but not necessarily for one encumbered by a less than sympathetic rider, is a case in point.

Horses are, of course, adaptable to become beasts of habit; such habits may not always be pleasant for them; some are said to be acceptable only because of low-grade pain-induced secretion of endorphins.

The interest becomes most important when dealing with the initial aftercare and, particularly, the subsequent rehabilitation of the convalescent horse as it is returned to work.

Man to horse communication, however transmitted, is not always done clearly and so is often misunderstood. Horse to man – especially when it is trying to tell 'how it feels despite what it ('my action', 'my behaviour') looks like' – is not always heard, even listened for, let alone fully understood. How far this impedes recovery, let alone impairs performance, remains an enigma in training and more so in retraining.

A frank lameness is one thing, as is an inflammatory reaction swelling. It is the more subtle deficits in locomotion which are, if perceived at all, put down to 'it's forgotten all I taught it'. Few trainers appreciate how true this belief is; only a few really understand what and why the horse has forgotten.

Reception of an aid and the response to it is not, and never was, a matter of teaching and learning. Of course these polarised features are important but it is more than a sensory message stimulating (somehow) a motor response. Rehabilitation is directed retraining to jog a subconscious memory system, as distinct from sharpening up obedience to a command. Most convalescences, whether from medical illness or orthopaedic injury, must begin only after the end of associated pain of whatever type. The horse begins the retraining with a memory of this pain. Don't we all? We may have the determination to put that out of our mind by self-will, as well as by skilled physiotherapy and 'man to man' discussion regarding the progress.

A horse will race in pain, or with the memory that it might be painful, because it is competing within a herd situation. It has no great desire, if any, to be first; it has instinctive fear of being last – first ahead of an imaginary predator. As a single competitor in most if not all competitive disciplines it is man and horse against the course, the time limit, with man as the thoughtful, or the selfish, stimulator.

In rehabilitation man the trainer may seek the assistance of (a) patience but perseverance; and (b) complementary therapies mainly to:

- Speed resolution of residual inflammation and discomfort, but no work as such during this time.
- Speed healing – physiologically difficult even impossible if full integrity of the tissue is required. Most tissues have an inherent healing time; even then a return to initial quality is not always possible. Some modes claim to improve this. Tendons are the most recalcitrant.

- Minimise low-grade inflammatory residual stiffness.
- Mobilise muscle tone and so the range and power of contraction and the ease and degree of relaxation – bilaterally symmetric.

Acupuncture is often high in the list of complementary therapies. Its practitioners, by and large, are trained in its use and knowledgeable of structure and functioning. By law only veterinary surgeons are allowed to use needle therapy.

Osteopathy and chiropractics are often associated disciplines to benefit from acupuncture's holistic 'freeing of energy flow'. Not understood in detail but usually satifactorily effected *as judged by results* subjectively and often objectively assessed (see skin sensory input below), especially in the locomotion system.

The more focused effects of electronic transcutaneous therapies said to reach many deeper parts and perhaps to have holistic inputs are mainly used on specifically known musculo-skeletal lesions. Improvement here at least minimises the unbalancing effects on other parts of the locomotor system.

Physiotherapy, and particularly whole-body massage techniques, has its practitioners, and quite rightly so. They too can detect direct and indirect disorders but also aim to reduce the associated spasms and simultaneously relieve the splinting and nerve-trapping effect of stagnation or oedema *before* the horse is put to work and on subsequent occasions. Post-exercise massage has also its use in aiding the venous and lymphatic return flows from the exerted muscles. It is a scientifically applied technique of what is now either forgotten or – thankfully for the groom! – an overlooked part of horsemastership: strenuous strapping. It is also particularly directed at spasmed knots in the origin ends of muscles known to be particularly overstressed in athletic work. Just as importantly it stimulates a variety of dermal sensory nerve endings, as well as massaging flesh, including those related reflexly to skin's functioning and to respiration and secretion, both involving thermo-regulation and 'emotion' via the brain centres.

This effect is said to be bio-electrical through skin sensory nerve endings. Thus a behavioural response to massage could be an 'emotional' or mood indicator in addition to being a pointer to local superficial discomfort and discomfort at other regions as well.

It is not generally appreciated that a significant part of the dermal sensory network's enervation is the receptivity through its many neural interconnections, which has therapeutically potent impulses. Much more than the simple 'rub it (the pain as felt through the skin level) better'! Recent work suggests that all transcutaneous input and homeopathic therapy ultimately has a sub-atomic effect called 'bioresonance'.

Massage therefore can be an (apparently simplistic) approach which can have much ramified (complicated) influences on the sensory inputs elsewhere, not least of all on those of proprioception.

Proprioceptor nerve endings are position sensory afferent receptors. A horse's neurophysiology can quickly become 'untuned' following a rest at grass and more especially at box rest enforced by injury or illness. A return to work requires this very important automatic system to be 'retuned' by careful and gradual return to those stimuli associated with work – from the word go.

What it subconsciously impeccably responded to when last fully fit has to be represented to it. Simultaneously such revision gives time for the memory of pain to disappear; this can take weeks even months before this fear disappears. Its conscious memory of and its subconscious receptive setting for this has to be eliminated. The horse must regain confidence in its postural muscles' proprioceptor messages and the motor responses to support it dynamically at foot fall and in flight. This is instigated by synchronised motor output of its propulsive muscles, by further feedback information. The integrity and stability of all joints have to be tried and not least those worst disordered originally.

Rehabilitation therefore is directed quite considerably at the neuromotor system as well as the direct motor (muscle) refittening exercise along a painless neural and physical route to fitness.

The positive reinforcement messages induced even when the horse is no longer lame but still unbalanced in action, and so too in subsequent proprioception inputs have to be subdued; this is obtained from:

(i) Progressive walking work on differing natural terrain – beginning on the level hard and on to firm, soft but not sinking or holding on the level; then uphill, downhill and across slopes (on changing reins).

(ii) This is followed after 3 weeks by first walking then trotting over some different (3-6 metre) surfaces once away and once back twice daily.

(iii) As natural walking progresses to include the trot in the exercising, these boxed off, in line areas of hard, soft, yielding, firm, hard, rough, smooth, are continued once daily for about 10 minutes for a further 2-3 weeks.

(iv) Later, work gaits increase on the natural, varied surfaces and will include grid work.

[1] Abridged and adapted from *Physical Therapy and Massage for Horses*. Demoix and Pailloux, translated by Lewis Manson Publishing 1996.

SADDLE FIT AND RELATED BACK PROBLEMS

In recent years much emphasis has been put on the possibility of a competition horse showing Poor Performance Syndrome (PPS). One possible cause is being 'wrong in the back'. This, of course, can be factual. One aspect of such morbidity is the 'ill fit' of the saddle and consequent bilateral or, more frequently, unilateral and, within that, lengthwise asymmetry of pressures.

Pressure gauge measuring devices have been used to refute or to confirm rider's suspicions and saddle fitter's findings. Unfortunately, such recordings fail in accuracy when it comes to dynamic imaging. Thermography will highlight 'hot spots' in the skin which can indicate dermal circulatory defects and can suggest deeper-tissue traumatic inflammatory response to over-pressures. Scintigraphy too will show inflammatory hot spots in soft tissues and in bone.

The back areas usually affected, as indicated by manual and visual assessment, later 'scientifically' confirmed or not, are:

- The sides of the withers over the Trapezius muscles.
- The dorsal edge and the caudal surface of the scapula from saddle point contact, as in too narrow an arch or from forward cut sloping points.
- The cranial thoracic area of the Latissimus dorsi muscle and through it to the deeper spinal postural muscles from stirrup bar contact.
- The lateral aspects of the dorsal processes under the 'seat' from too narrow a gullet.

- Over the caudal seat areas of the Longissimus dorsi muscles from saddle panel pressure, caused by the saddle being asymmetrically flocked, and/or an asymmetric rider's position, both with lateral displacement of the pressure.
- An unlevel saddle seat area causing a drop from rider's weight either on to the withers or on to the back muscles.
- Asymmetry in muscle development (or atrophy) in the relative areas of the horse, causing in addition saddle slip – laterally, caudally, at the cantle or cranially at the pommel.
- The selection of a wrong tree, especially at the twist and at the arch, or one which does not produce a level seat.

It is advisable that a qualified saddle fitter should examine horse and saddle with and without the rider up, at the halt and at the walk and at the trot:
(i) Early in the post-grazing conditioning period.
(ii) Some 6-8 weeks later when fat has been lost and muscle is developing.
(iii) Finally close to full fitness. (Event horses of higher ability show a significant change some 3 weeks before full fitness.)

Or at any other time following an altered symmetry of muscle development and/or loss of balanced action, either from ill-fitted saddles, or most importantly, from other causes such as:
- Low-grade chronic pain peripherally.
- Abaxial lesions especially, but not only, hind leg lameness.
- Unbalanced hoof capsules.
- Mouth discomfort.

Following more traumatic and sudden onset trips or slips there is the possibility of torque overstresses along the axial soft tissues and the bony vertebrae. The resultant morbidity can be:
- Painful in itself.
- Pain-producing from inflammatory pressure on the related nerves; and later
- Chronic arthritic lesions.

Cyclic disharmony often follows resulting in clinical:
- Myopathy (muscle spasm).
- Secondary overstress in compensatory musculature.
- Asymmetric action.
- Compensating rebalancing efforts in the axial and/or the abaxial units of locomotion; more 'guarding' may well follow.

In such situations a veterinary surgeon must take a broad (holistic) view of the various disorders, attempt to quantify them and to qualify them as primary or secondary, and then, and only then, consider the value of complementary therapies such as:
- Massage.
- Re-alignment by osteopathy or chiropractics to relieve neurogenic spasm and oedema.
- Other modes and therapies.

The originating cause in the periphery of the system may have:
- Healed.
- Reduced with or without diagnosis and treatment but left the unbalance effects in the spine.

Or, as is often the case:
- Not been suspected, especially in the absence of clear, overt signs, to the extent that the horse, rested or not, only temporarily responds to these therapies – or, if the unknown lesion is serious, does not respond at all.

When reasonably satisfactory, all-round healing has occurred, and judicious work can restart, management will consist of residual pain-relieving treatment, including:

- Analgesics.
- Electronic modes to improve healing and the removal of periodic spasm and oedema.
- Rehabilitation, to 'jog' proprioceptor memories.
- A controlled exercise programme.

7. FIRST AID

Accidents do happen. The blame is variously apportioned within 'Sins of commission or of omission' and their effect on 'occupational hazards' – the risks of using a horse; 'Act of God'; 'bad luck'; someone else's fault, etc. Some are related to the nature of the horse; for example, one which:
- Rolls and gets cast and then self-injured.
- Paws and so engages a fore leg in a too-low empty hay net or wire in fences, especially square netting.
- Tries to upset the pecking order and suffers bites or kicks as a consequence.
- Free-jumps hedges, fences or gates to join others.
- Escapes onto a road and slips over or becomes involved in a road traffic accident.
- Breaks into a feed store, gorges, gets laminitis.
- Escapes on to growing corn, gets indigestion – colic.
- Escapes to browse poisonous shrubs.

Some accidents are exacerbated by ignorant, if well-meaning, people first on the scene. Others are a reflection of less than optional horsemastership and equitation.

Most can be at least reduced to a chance event, even prevented by care and thoughtfulness. Nonetheless, the hazard risk increases with the level of athleticism. The outcome of such relates to:
- Initial site injured.
- Type of wound.
- Severity.
- Speed of recognition, assessment and action.
- The quality of the initial action or first aid.
- The subsequent management.

An accident is a one-off occasion. It is often of emergency action status. If dealt with efficiently the damage can be resolved, at least within reasonable limits. Sometimes it will become a crisis – that too will resolve; it may, however, devolve into a catastrophe because those present were:
- Unready.
- Ill-prepared.
- Slow to act.
- Inadequate in skill, experience and/or learning.
- Not called soon enough.
- Not directed to the occasion accurately enough.
- Uninformed of the whereabouts of professional help.

The aims and objects of First Aid are:
(a) To sustain life by minimising
- Bleeding
- (Shock)
- Infection

and by
- Assuring an open airway.

(b) To prevent worsening of the injury by efficient
- Restraint of the injured (excited) horse.
- Initial action to the patient on site, and thereafter back at the home stables, preferably by transport.
- Subsequent management.

(c) To promote recovery.
But with care for the helpers, other bystanders, other horses, not forgetting that, where relevant, the rider has priority or any other coincidentally involved injured person.

AT THE SCENE OF AN ACCIDENT
At a road traffic accident (RTA) it is essential to

- 'Secure your ground' – set up 2-way warning posts.
- Enlist help.
- Send for emergency service(s) as required.
- Secure the horse: if necessary have someone 'sit on its head'.
- See to injured humans.
- Do not start discussion as to blame or enter into it.
- Try to memorise the incident as you saw and now see it.
- Get names of any witnesses (in due course).

What follows is applicable to any occasion whether in stable, yard, field or at an event.
The horse and the helpers require freedom to work. They must attend to the horse: restrain, examine and consider. If the horse is mobile, even if on '3 legs', move it, as soon as possible, off the road into a field or a garden etc. or away from traffic of any sort including competing horses. Common sense will determine when 'as soon as

possible' is. Render first aid as assessed. The helpers ideally are:
- Trained, experienced, knowledgeable.
- Not so, and admit it – but are either willing, unwilling or a 'fainter'.
- Not so, but believe themselves to be either amenable to instruction (orders) or to know more than anyone else – a menace.

Make certain all accept one 'Chief' and the rest remain as 'Indians'.
When professional help arrives subordinate yourself and give an account of what has happened so far.

ACTION
If horse is on its feet:
1. Have it held with both hands on the bridle/reins or headcollar rope: instruct if necessary.
2. Unbuckle reins, take out of martingale rings and pass to head holder (don't tie or rebuckle).
3. Have the holder grasp two reins near the bit, loop rest over that arm and 'speak' to the horse.
If and when necessary, other restraints, in order, are:
4. Holder 'gentles' the neck and the muzzle with the other hand.
5. Second person pulls and offers grass (or other feed if available); or takes a one handed grip of the neck skin in front of shoulder or grips muzzle – from other side to first person – but holds bridle or halter cheek piece as well.
6. Have irons run up, girth loosened.
7. If cold (horse and/or weather), apply rug or equivalent.

'Chief' meanwhile has inspected for:
- Wounds.
- Bleeding – and makes common-sense decision as to when to control this. Apart from the 'sight' there is no great urgency if other action seems more pressing or important.
- Marked lameness, e.g. one leg 'off' the ground.
- Any other disorders.
- Weakness behind when gently moved over.
- Rapid, shallow respirations.
- Patchy or widespread sweating.
NOTE: These last three are signs of shock.

If the horse is down:
1. Continue to have head (i.e. flat of the cheek) sat on with sitter pulling horizontally on curb chain chin groove to maintain essential extended head and neck.
2. If breathing not laboured and movement is seen in all limbs, spread earth etc. under patient's limbs and trunk and forward of its fore end.
3. Have helpers stand back.
4. Warn head-sitter to be ready to stand clear on command.
5. Have reins held by another as before but far enough away from fore legs to be safe.
6. 'Chief' takes tail close to dock and says 'now'!

7. With head-sitter moved well clear and handler ready, give horse a sound slap on the rump and as it moves lift strongly at the tail.

8. If all efforts are unsuccessful let horse down and get head-sitter back in position.

9. It might 'just' be shocked and/or afraid or fatigued. Rest, to try again in 10 minutes.

10. It could have an injured spine.

NOTE: In human emergencies it is culpable to attempt to sit the patient up, let alone encourage them to rise. In the horse the risk of converting a fractured neck or back into a lethal (or hopeless) dislocated fracture with paralysis is always going to exist no matter who makes the decision. Spinal supports and a stretcher are not practicable. Sooner or later the risk of self-standing has to be taken unless a veterinary surgeon pronounces that euthanasia is necessary.

To have the horse down on the road when it is not unconscious is dangerous to all concerned.

If unconscious or patently otherwise unable to rise, it will have to be left until professional help arrives. If the police insist on moving it, it is their job and their responsibility.

Such unconsciousness is rarely the result of it being 'winded' in an RTA, though it could well be the case in racing or fast competitive sport especially if a fence fall is involved.

However, especially in hot/humid weather, cold water thrown over its head and into an ear (with bridle and tail holders standing by ready) will be worth trying in any situation. Remember a horse's natural response on discovering it is in a 'threatening' situation is Fright, Fight and Flight.

If down but 'coming to', it should be restrained by the head until it is obviously 'with it' and seems consciously moving at least three legs in a normal fashion. When allowed to rise as described before it will either stand still (shaking, looking anxious, may accept grass) or try to escape – with no thought for other horses, people or itself, other than to get back to its stable. It must be held and restrained especially if on a public highway: this is a priority. If in a field, make sure all gates are already closed.

When the horse stands:

1. If the horse stands but tries to evade any handling regarding first aid or for more
   detailed inspection: various types of restraint now become necessary such as lifting
   a fore leg, and/or applying a twitch.

2. If bleeding, apply pressure pad etc. (see later): now is the most sensible time to do so. All four limbs and all 'sides' of the animal must be inspected.

3. Move it to determine any lameness and severity of that.

4. Get it off the road even if one leg looks or is suspected broken: it will carry this.

5. Let it graze.

6. Use common-sensible horsemastership but no heroics.

THE 'ABC' OF FIRST AID

A

Approach, Assess, Act.

Airway

If a horse is up it is breathing.

If down, breathing can still be judged – but restrain. Meanwhile if breathing is noisy and distressed – stertorous – check nostrils for mud and blood obstruction, swab out with wet cloths. The stimulation may induce helpful sneezing.

If there is marked snoring and gurgling with bluish gums it may be 'swallowing its tongue'. This is a severe form of respiratory obstruction, possibly stress tension induced, due to a backward bulging of the tongue to displace the soft palate and so obstruct the naso-pharyngeal opening. Carefully grasp the tongue through the area of the bars on one side (the head-sitter stays put) and slowly pull it forward and out to the side, hold for up to 10 seconds or until horse voluntarily tries to retract it, then let go. If successful the noise will stop and the gums will quickly regain the pinkish hue. Repeat if necessary; especially if the horse is unconscious, try to keep the tongue out.

B

Bleeding

The following types of bleeding may occur

Closed: Subcutaneous (and deeper), i.e. bruising, no great urgency unless a fracture is suspected but that is a veterinary matter.

Hidden: As into major cavities: internal haemorrhage – such as in the skull, chest or abdomen. This is not a first aid problem!

Open: External, such as:

(a) Through a natural orifice from a hidden organ source, e.g.
* The nose, as from head trauma or lungs. No action feasible but remove any obvious clots.
* The mouth, but beware attempting to discover what is traumatised.
   Most, unless from skull, will stop.
(b) Through an unnatural opening – a wound. This may be
* Major as from large veins or arteries e.g. in neck, armpit or groin. Horse is rapidly unconscious, death follows quickly.
   (There are recorded incidents of a jugular haemorrhage being occluded until the vet surgeon, on duty at the event, i.e. on the spot, ligated the vein above and below the tear; first aid occlusion was by fist 'over' towel pressure.)
* Less than major. A first aid task.

Do not worry whether venous or arterial bleeding. Blood clotting starts immediately blood is exposed to the air, in fact once it leaves a blood vessel. This progresses with the physiological chain of events induced by blood-clotting factors in the blood and on the vessel wall. Once a clot gets established in a vessel at the

point of section or laceration it:
(i) Adheres to the vessel wall and opened edges.
(ii) Spreads backwards along that particular vessel.
(iii) Stops at the junction with a larger vessel.
(iv) The branch is sealed off.

In certain cases it will reopen, e.g. in a superficial vessel which has been punctured or lacerated and there is no cut end and the backward clotting is 'tunnelled' by the passing flow pressure.

Delay in clot establishment is occasioned and determined by the blood pressure to the area which reflects (a) heart and flow rate and pressure generally, and (b) the prior and recovery demand for blood in that area, e.g. high in recently exercised limb musculature and so on down the limb.

As exercise heart-rate and flow-volume subside the clot has a better chance to lodge in the vessel. Continuing bleeding can lead to a general fall in blood pressure. In so-called minor haemorrhages from the surfaces, such an amount of bleeding as to cause collapse and death is unlikely.

Nevertheless it is advisable to hasten clotting and so minimise bleeding to end consequent weakening and thereby:
• Prevent delay in the healing process.
• Help general recovery.
• Prevent a fall in general immune levels with a subsequent greater risk of infection becoming seriously established.
• Reduce the fear or at least the irritation to the horse.
• Make initial handling of the wound easier and more efficient.
• Lessen the upset to onlookers.

Techniques to control bleeding

In areas where there is little or no subjacent muscle, use a pressure pad either bandaged on as with leg wounds, or held on as with head and some trunk lesions.

In areas where the wound is over, and has penetrated into, the underlying muscle group, it may be:
(a) Shallow – mainly skin bleeding: use a hand-held pressure pad.
(b) Deep – blood welling up from the depth: use a packing.

In all situations the initial bleeding will have in itself washed the area and the skin edges to a great extent clear of infection. This will relate to what did the injury and what the environmental conditions are. For example:
• A kick is bound to drive 'dirt' into the wound.
• Wire lying loose in mud is 'dirtier' than taut fencing wire.
• A stake in the mud is more dangerous than a similar object projecting from a wall.

The dressing used aims to stop the bleeding and prevent further entry of infection.

Once the bleeding stops, first aid continues in order to reduce the primary infection and to stop further infection until a decision is made: is vet attention necessary? If the wound is over a 'vital area' the answer is YES. If suturing is required: this again is a professional decision. Is transport home advisable? Usually safer and wiser to say yes.

The Pressure Pad: This need only be clean as determined by being a 'new' material or laundered or still wrapped as, for example:

- An open-weave bandage (still rolled up in its foil covering until eventually required).
- A piece of animalintex, cut for size.
- A swab (usually bought as sterile in packets).
- A clean handkerchief.

It is folded, in the case of cloth, or, with animalintex, is covered by a folded (not necessarily so clean) material. A porous material such as open-weave bandage or a swab will form a surface framework for the clot to form.

In all cases it is pressed over and held onto the wound or placed over and bandaged on firmly. The aim is to staunch the flow, slow it down to allow clotting. The bandage as such, of whatever type, is left on (the horse is kept still) for some 15 minutes. Hand feed grass or hay meanwhile.

If blood continues to ooze through, either remove and reapply fresh material, or bandage, more firmly, over the top of the original. If it seems to have stopped, get the horse home where you then remove the pad and prepare to clean the wound.

Where pad is hand-held on, maintain this for 10-15 minutes. Be prepared to reapply a fresh pad and so on until bleeding has stopped. Ease it off slowly so as not to disturb the clot. Protect wound from contact with trailer or lorry side e.g. by tying head up tight with wound on partition side or attaching padding to keep horse 'off' the partition.

The Packing: The need to plug a gaping wound is not always necessary; muscle tissue bleeding clots quickly as a rule. Sometimes a biggish vessel is involved as judged by the ongoing flow.

Where the wound has started in the skin as in the trunk and especially in ventral chest wounds the skin itself can be compressed onto the subcutaneous bleeding and held in place by girth or surcingle. (Beware producing a bucking strap!)

Where packing is deemed necessary, usually with muscle wounds, a variety of materials can be used, such as:

- Gamgee but preferably not cotton wool.
- Towelling, or in dire emergency
- Shirt cloth.
- Underwear.
- Bed linen.

It should be soaked in cold clean water at least or if possible with antiseptic solution and, if possible, lubricated with antiseptic cream, 'udder salve' or any medicinal gel. Then it is slowly 'stuffed' into the cavity in narrow folds, if necessary, until the edge of the wound is reached. The horse should be kept warm, quiet and placated with hand-fed grass, hay or a little low-energy concentrate feed. It may need to be sedated, in which case the veterinary surgeon will take over.

Next-stage management of wounds

If suspiciously near a vital area, leave covered until veterinary help is (quickly) there. Otherwise:

1. Remove pad or packing.
2. Clip hair off edges of the skin wound after applying a bland cream or gel under the peripheral skin to trap the clippings.

3. Lavage the wound with:
- Hosed water at gentle pressure.
- Sterile saline or Hartmans solution as from commercial packs administered through the cut-off nozzle.
- Boiled water with 1 teaspoon salt to 1 pint and let cool; administered by a syringe or clean house-plant sprayer.

4. Continue until fluid runs clean. First aid 'in the field' to clean a non-bleeding but dirty wound may also be done with clean hosed water or better still with the prepared salt solution mentioned above.

5. Antiseptic lavage using:
- Concentrated Hibiscrub diluted as directed by your veterinary surgeon. A 'safe' solution for wounds is 1 part in 40 of water. This is Chlorhexadine.
- Concentrated Pevidine scrub diluted as directed by your veterinary surgeon. A 'safe' solution is 2 parts to 15 of water. This is Povidore.

Syringed into or onto the wound and allowed to dry on. If wound is onto a tendon do not use Pevidine. If a vital site is involved use only Hartmans or sterile saline, *not* hosed water, antiseptics or home-sterilised saline. Leave specific treatment to the veterinary surgeon.

NB: Wounds suspected of still being contaminated may be left by the veterinary surgeon for several days intensive cleansing befor suturing is attempted.

6. If, after appraisal of the area penetrated, the horsemaster suspects the possibility of entry into a vital area – a joint capsual, a bursa, or a tendon sheath – the first aid
should be minimal:
- Control bleeding
- Cover and protect the wound, which is usually small, but get the patient transported to a vet. Time is of the essence, a matter of hours could make all the difference.

7. Top dressing as for limb wounds, using simple kit: *cold animalintex patch* to surround the area, shiny side down, covered with *gamgee* from coronet to knee and overlapping around *non-elastic tail bandage* or similar working upwards on first winds.

8. Leave until vet arrives and decides on further management.

9. If doing it all yourself, leave on for 12 hours, remove, re-examine, re-assess, re dress *or* get professional help.

Non-coverable body/head wounds as well as limbs should be assessed by a veterinary surgeon regarding possible suturing. If not suitable or necessary, an astringent, antiseptic spray, e.g. Savlon, or herbal applications, e.g. Aloe Vera gel, are all that is necessary.

Wound sutures or clips are usually inserted immediately after initial cleansing, the sooner the better, and left for up to 7 days until infection is definitely under control.

C

Circulation

Circulation may fail from:

- Shock: keep horse warm.
- Haemorrhage: not necessarily obvious, as with internal bleeding.
- Brain damage.
- Heart rhythm upset.

An unconscious horse is most unlikely to regurgitate its stomach contents. Even if it did its lateral recumbency and extended head and neck are reasonable 'recovery positions'. It is very rare for even a conscious horse to regurgitate stomach contents. In only serious cases will the stomach oesophageal valve 'open' to allow this upper, and that usually indicates a (fatally) ruptured stomach.

It is worth trying chest pressures when respiratory (and cardiac) failures are seen or suspected:

1. Thumping 15 times (1 per second) over lower ribs just behind elbow (either side), then
2. Heavy two-handed pressure over the 'spring' of the ribs every 30 seconds for 5 times – alternate for 10 attempts.
3. Cold water into an ear has been known to work.

In competitive conditions especially with cross country jumping a horse may fall and lie winded: respiration will be erratic and variable in depth; the horse may appear to be unconscious.

1. Check for tongue swallowing (see 'Airway').
2. Loosen girth and surcingle (if present, loosen noseband(s) and curb chain).
3. Do not struggle to remove saddle as long as the girth is loosened but undo breast plate etc.
4. Unfasten reins and have them held (as before).
5. Warn bystanders of a 'sudden' recovery.
6. It will soon look and listen as judged by eye and ear movement.
7. On no account try to turn it over without professional help.
8. Check all four feet for studs and spread plates and warn handlers accordingly.
9. Ensure throat lash is secure.
10. Let the horse lie until movement begins in head, neck and limbs.
11. Have head-handler ready and warn him/her on no account to stand in front of the forward line of the horse.
12. Position handlers:
    - One level with the withers.
    - One level with the quarters.
    Describe what is to happen.
13. You will strike the quarters hard and be ready to grasp the tail close to the dock.
14. As (and if) the horse attempts to sit up:
    - The head-handler will guide, NOT forcibly pull, the head round.
    - The withers man will push there upwards and over.
    - The quarter-man likewise.
    You will 'strike' again if necessary.

15. If the horse 'goes' to get up:
- You will lift.
- The 'sides' men will help steady and be ready to pull the saddle off but both should beware of the horse's feet when it does get up.
- The head-man will go forward with the horse in a straight line at first either to help steady or to restrain it from escaping, in which case go in a wide circle.
  If no success, let it rest for 5-10 minutes and try again.
16. If any doubt about leg injuries (they are usually the underneath ones) await professional help but be aware of the horse voluntarily trying again.

BE PREPARED

It is advisable that you consult your veterinary surgeon before an accident occurs for his advice regarding materials and techniques for first aid as he would prefer. Ask him to plan this for:
- Stable.
- Transport.
- In one's pocket when hacking, hunting, etc.

Antibiotic powders and creams for topical (surface) use are contra-indicated, as are any powder or ointments which clog the wound in the first instance. Antibiotic treatment systemically is illegal without professional dispensing: injections must be given by him or under his direction.

All horses should be up-to-date with anti-tetanus toxin protection.

8. THE OLDER HORSE

There is little clinical or research evidence that age brings significant geriatric illness per se as it does in the human. From approximately 25 years and on there is an increasing risk of molar teeth loss mainly from complete eruption of the reserve crown with failure of the jaw bones to hold the short residual roots. A secondary problem is the development of gingivitis and subsequent inflammation of the socket. Caries, following dentine damage may lead to tooth fracture.

The overall loss of the architecture of the molar arcades leads to mastication difficulties and subsequent loss of condition. Management mistakes, such as failure to maintain a satisfactory worm control or to compensate for the increased energy requirements of a horse 'at grass' in the winter, are added factors which can lead to loss of condition.

Lack of foot care in the unridden horse is an additional welfare problem. Viral infections can be more lethal in the old horse. Where possible, suitable artificial immunisation should be maintained. All these can be taken care of by observant horsemastership and appropriate professional attendance. A pensioned-off horse does not deserve to be neglected. If the ongoing 'extra' costs are too much, then euthanasia must be considered.

In ponies particularly, a condition called Cushingoid disease is significantly common. This is basically a compounded metabolic dysfunction beginning with a tumour growth in the pituitary gland. The slowly developing signs are:

- Failure to completely change the seasonal hairs: the resultant, shaggy, curly hairs, seen mainly on the ventral aspects of the neck and the trunk, is called hirsutism.
- Loss of condition possibly masked by the retained coat.
- An increase in thirst (polydipsia).
- And in urinary output (polyuris).
- Secondary bacterial infections of the upper respiratory tract.
- Intermittent mild colic.
- Laminitis.

It is variably responsive to prolonged specific therapy.

Other neoplastic diseases are:

- Worsening melanomata, especially in grey animals. These, if abraded, are subject to 'fly strike' (maggot infestation) in the summer.
- Lymphosarcomata.

The inactive geriatric horse, pensioned off because of reduced athletic ability, can become more arthritic and in unacceptable pain.

Liver disease can occur from ragwort poisoning, cumulative in weedy, poor grazings as might renal disease following 'bastard' strangles. Both these can lead to ammonia toxicity of the brain.

9. THE END OF THE ROAD

Elective euthanasia is a comparatively easy decision for most owners faced with a severely injured or an incurably sick horse. A veterinary surgeon is usually on hand to give unemotional, objective advice to prevent unnecessary, hopeless continuation. He will be able to expeditiously 'do the necessary' and to arrange subsequent disposal.

A decision in other much less clear-cut circumstances is not so easy. There is often the private and personal feeling that one should not take a life when, to them, there is no obvious reason for not letting their 'friend' finish its unusable and perhaps geriatric days in retirement. Of course it is good to be able to go on seeing the 'old boy' in the field – the grass is green, the summer sun is warming. But is it really content to graze and to doze? And what about winter time?

PENSIONING OFF

A pensioned or turned away horse must be inspected:

- Daily for signs of illness or injury; made to move regarding checks for lameness.
- Weekly for bodily condition, the coat and the skin and the state of the hooves.
- 4-6 weekly by the farrier, dependent on ground condition.
- Twice yearly by the vet for dental care; deterioration, especially in the old horse, is a common cause of pain and loss of condition. The vet will advise on worming.

The environment must be monitored regularly for:

- Safety of fencing.
- Overgrowing nearby bushes which might be toxic.
- Grass too lush or getting too short and sparse.
- Constant (and in winter, unfrozen) water supply.
- The field becoming poached and muddy – more areas for feeding supplementary hay and concentrates.

You should also consider whether the horse requires a companion – not necessarily a horse. In practice its use as a nursemaid for youngsters is often a justification for pensioning a horse off. It all costs time and money but the care must not be neglected.

Most importantly, before pensioning a horse off, you must ask yourself is it fair, let alone humane, to do so? Veterinary advice is essential irrespective of the reason for the pensioning off. This is also the time to discuss and to decide on the action to be taken when the ultimate end of the road is well in sight:

- How should it be 'put down'?
- Can it be buried in the field? There is no legal reason against this if the field is owned; if it is rented, permission must be sought.
- Who takes it away and how much will this cost?

If the reason for a younger horse being unusable is not because of lameness with ongoing, if low-grade, active pain, and especially if pensioning off is impracticable – grazing has to be rented, no time to monitor and so on – there are options other than euthanasia.

Sale (or donation) to an equine unit which runs horses at grass and in yards dependent upon seasons. These become donors of hyper immunised blood for human medical diagnostic use. Patently they are well cared for and can be visited; and, if perchance time heals the cause of the original loss of use, a horse can be bought back.

Some Homes of Rest will take in animals able to 'run at grass', not in discomfort but otherwise unusable, if the owner is genuinely unable to meet the costs of private pensioning off. A contribution is always acceptable!

Provided it is fit to travel, it can be taken to an authorised horse slaughterer. Such an option is not acceptable to all owners but it is a practicable solution and the 'end' is certain and known.

Please do not send it to market or advertise it as 'free to a good home', when you yourself know that it shouldn't be worked.

EUTHANASIA

There are two methods of euthanasia:
(a) The bullet: It is quick, efficient and clean; the slaughterman is efficient (through practice). Your vet can also carry it out.
(b) A vet must be there for the intravenous method.

Horses have often seen 'needles', if only for vaccination. Not all take kindly to seeing the man in the green coat with a syringe and they may well prove reluctant to stand quietly. The dose must be given slowly and in full; a willing and efficient helper is needed. No horse has experienced a gun (some may be head shy to anything, but even these will stand to eat some titbits). It is over in a flash. Vets' guns now have a 'noise reduction attachment' so the report is no longer loud and emotive.

The author believes that the owner has the moral obligation to be present to soothe the horse even if not to hold it. As a vet and as a horse owner, he opts for the gun. He realises that some people just can't face that method and he would accede to their wishes. What is important is that the geriatric and/or in discomfort animal should be put down at its home.

Disposal of the body can be, as mentioned earlier, burial sufficient to have 3 feet of soil above – a JCB job. Permission from the District Council, and if relevant, from the owner of the field, is required. Alternatively you can arrange removal by the local knackerman: his fees will relate to the method of euthanasia, as the flesh from an injected horse cannot be fed to dogs. So too if removal is arranged by the local hunt – if they still run a 'flesh house'. Both will charge for the ultimate rendering of unused or unusable remains.

SECTION V

TACK AND EQUIPMENT

Like any sport, there is an enormous amount of gear available to those who want to get involved with horses and riding even at an amateur level. The fact is, you don't necessarily need even a fraction of what is available. One or two items are essential from a safety point of view, others are advisable for extra comfort or performance; but a large number are unnecessary for all but the professional, specialist or serious competitor.

Although it is sensible to keep the cost of equipment to a minimum while you find out if riding is the sport for you, even a beginner will need to invest in a couple of basic safety items such as a hard hat and proper boots suitable for riding, i.e. those with a sole which will slide in and out of the stirrup with ease, and a heel which is chunky enough to prevent the foot slipping right through. Other items, such as a pair of jodhpurs, gloves or a weatherproof riding jacket, are not essential but can make all the difference to comfort in the saddle. Of course, if you do not wish to actually ride and your interests lie in breeding or showing, the requirements are different again.

If there comes a time when you wish to buy your own horse, the expense of clothing it and buying suitable tack is a major consideration, and may well end up costing you almost as much as the horse itself. However, certain items of tack or clothing are often sold along with the horse, saving you the trouble of kitting it out from scratch.

188

1. BASIC SHOPPING LISTS

Like the rider's, the horse's wardrobe can be simple, containing only the most practical essentials, or it can be extremely diverse and expensive. The basics are outlined below.

For the ridden horse:
Essentials:
* Saddle with numnah, girth, stirrup irons and leathers (normally sold separately) and/or driving harness.
* Bridle and suitable bit.
* Headcollar and lead rope.
* Rugs for stable and turning out, depending on the type of horse and what you intend to do with it.
* Travelling equipment, e.g. tail bandage, protective boots or bandages, poll guard.

Useful extras: Lungeing equipment (cavesson, line and long whip); items needed for specific disciplines, e.g. martingale, breastplate, different bit for cross country, spare reins, girth and stirrup leathers, spare numnahs to allow for washing.
Luxury items: Smart woollen day rug or cooler kept for 'best', trailer or horsebox, second discipline saddle such as dressage.

For the rider:
Essentials:
* Hard hat.
* Boots suitable for riding.
* Jodhpurs.

Useful extras: Additional pair of jodhpurs, body protector, gloves, warm coat, jumping and schooling whips. If you look after your own horse and do the stable work yourself, you will certainly need waterproof boots as well as some that are suitable for riding.
Luxury items: Specialist breathable equestrian jacket, show jacket and breeches, long leather boots. For competition, dress needs to be appropriate to the class you have entered. There are a number of dress codes for the rider as well as the horse, and these are listed in individual rule books. Jackets, jodhpur colours, spurs, buttonholes, shirt colour, stock or tie, gloves, whip and boot type can all vary. For cross country, it is often mandatory to wear a body protector as well an appropriate standard of hat.

For the stable:
If you are a horse owner and look after the horse yourself, you will need a certain amount of practical stable equipment too.
Essentials: A suitable fork for straw, shavings or rubber depending on your horse's bedding; yard brush, shovel, stable barrow or muck sack, grooming kit, hay net, water and feed buckets, rodent-proof feed bins, tack cleaning kit.
Useful extras: Rake, small skip for droppings, additional hay nets; boots, gloves and

overalls for mucking out, grooming, clipping etc.
Luxury items: Clippers, pressure hose.

2. CHOOSING EQUIPMENT

The following points should always be considered when buying items of
saddlery or horse clothing:

1. **Comfort of horse**
    Any equipment that goes on the horse must fit well and be properly
    adjusted. Pain and discomfort from ill-fitting equipment is common,
    and naturally causes severe resentment in the horse. It is likely to result
    in a loss of performance and apparent bad behaviour, particularly in the
    case of a badly fitting saddle, bridle or inappropriate bit. (For fitting
    guidelines, see part 3).

2. **Comfort of rider**
    Tack must be suitable for the rider too, especially in the case of a saddle. You
    cannot ride well or stay balanced if you are hindered by your equipment.

3. **Safety and condition of goods**
    Considerable strain is placed on most items of horse equipment during use and
    it is essential that the stitching, workmanship and materials are up to the job.
    Poor-quality equipment is dangerous, and it is always better to buy good-
    quality second-hand than poor-quality new. Stitching should be even and firm,
    leather should be smooth and pliable (although new tack may be stiffer
    initially) with no evidence of cracking. Metal items such as stirrups and buckles
    should always be made from stainless steel, never nickel which is too weak and
    prone to wear and breakage. Bits are commonly made from stainless steel,
    although there are other materials suitable for bitting such as the 'horse-
    friendly' copper-based varieties.

4. **Suitability for purpose**
    Equipment should meet the required criteria for your needs in terms of design
    and quality – a fine leather show bridle is not suitable for cross country riding.
    If you intend to use it in competition, check the tack requirements and
    restrictions for your discipline.

5. **Budget**
    Good-quality tack and leather goods are not cheap but it is worth buying the
    best you can afford.

6. **Personal preference**
    You're investing a considerable amount of money kitting out your horse, so buy
    things you like! However, keep an open mind and don't get obsessed with
    having a particular make or model; it may not be the right choice for you or
    your horse.

SPECIALIST TACK
Although they may all look pretty similar to the untrained eye, there is a huge
difference in style, type and quality when it comes to saddles, and this will be
reflected in the price. A wooden or more likely, synthetic tree is the 'skeleton' inside

every saddle, and determines its eventual type, shape and size. The rest is just padding. Some trees have metal strips inserted which allow a certain 'give'; these are called spring trees and are thought to allow both horse and rider more comfort and freedom. The stirrup bars are riveted onto the tree. It is the original tree which must be fitted to the horse, not the final padded version of the saddle, although some modern saddles have an adjustable tree where a small key can marginally alter the width.

The cut and design of a saddle helps the rider to maintain a particular riding position. For most people, a general purpose saddle allows them to do a bit of everything in comfort and security, but it is essentially a compromise between the dressage saddle at one extreme and a jumping saddle at the other.

A dressage rider needs and appreciates the extra help a specialist dressage saddle gives them in terms of placing them in the correct position; the seat may be deeper, the panels longer and flatter, and the stirrups and girth straps positioned differently to a jumping saddle, which is designed to accommodate the rider who is maintaining a forward position for shorter periods, i.e. during a cross country or show jumping round. An endurance saddle must be the ultimate in comfort as the horse has to wear it (and the rider sit in it) for hours at a time. Any soreness or bruising can lead to elimination at any one of the stringent veterinary inspections en route. With the tiny racing saddle, the rider's comfort and security comes way down the list as he is unlikely to sit on it for more than the immediate duration of the race, which is perhaps just a few minutes at a time. However, the saddle must be very light-weight.

As well as suiting the rider's purposes and the particular discipline, the saddle must suit the horse. An excellent fit is imperative, as described below, but a particular cut of saddle may also flatter a horse by showing off its shoulder in the show ring for example, hence the specialist showing saddle.

CHECK THE RULE BOOK

If you wish to compete, consult the relevant society's rule book to check on tack restrictions.

For dressage, the horse may not wear a martingale or any kind of leg protection in the arena. It may only wear an ordinary snaffle bridle for Preliminary and Novice classes, an ordinary snaffle or double bridle for Elementary to Advanced Medium, and a double bridle for Advanced. When a snaffle bridle is used, it must include a drop, flash or cavesson noseband. In the dressage phase of a horse trial, a Grackle noseband is also allowed. Bits may be: an ordinary snaffle with unjointed, jointed or double-jointed mouthpiece; eggbutt snaffle with or without cheeks; rubber snaffle; snaffle with upper cheeks or hanging cheek snaffle. All parts of the bit coming into the horse's mouth must be made of the same type of metal, and rubber bit guards are not allowed.

For show jumping, standing and running martingales are permitted and there is no restriction on bits provided they are not misused. For the show jumping phase of a horse trial, standing martingales are not allowed.

Endurance tack is above all practical and comfortable, and many riders favour synthetic. A recognised form of bridle must be used.

NUMNAH OR SADDLE CLOTH

Although considered unnecessary by traditionalists – and indeed, it is incorrect for some showing classes – it is common practice to put a numnah or saddle cloth between the horse and the saddle. It keeps the underside of the saddle clean, soaks up sweat and can have a cushioning effect which is appreciated by the horse. Modern technology has targeted the humble numnah and it is now possible to buy a wide variety that claim to have spectacular shock-absorbing effects. However, the numnah is only as good as the saddle and rider which sit on top of it, and putting too much cushioning between the saddle and the horse's back can actually produce additional pressure unless the saddle is wide enough to accommodate it.

Numnahs and saddle cloths must be kept clean, which in summer may mean changing daily. Sheepskin is a traditional choice of material as it is a natural fibre with 'spring', but the horse can become hot beneath it and it does not respond so well to regular washing and drying as cotton or a synthetic material.

THE GIRTH

Traditionally these were made of leather or webbing, but as technology moves on, more 'horse-friendly' designs from soft, absorbent but extremely strong and durable materials have emerged. These are much cheaper than leather and can be thrown in the washing machine; however, many people still like the look and performance of a leather girth.

Many girths, both leather and synthetic, have elasticated insets that are supposed to make them more comfortable for the horse. This is a matter of opinion; it makes it very easy for the rider to unwittingly tighten them far too much, and there is a legitimate argument that suggests the last thing a horse needs as it lands over a fence or exerts itself in any way, is for the saddle to move! The more stable and securely it is fastened to the horse's back under such circumstances, the better.

When riding at speed in a high-risk situation such as racing or cross country, a second girth (called an over-girth or cross-country surcingle) is often fastened over the entire saddle for added security.

IRONS AND LEATHERS

These take a lot of strain and should be of the best quality. It is not just the leather but the stitching on a stirrup leather that must be strong. Stirrups should be solidly made from stainless steel, and they must fit the foot correctly so that it can neither slip through nor get stuck in the case of an accident. Rubber treads can improve grip and may be bought separately.

REINS

Basic reins are usually of plaited, laced or plain leather and can come in a variety of widths depending on the size of the rider's hand. Finer reins are suited to the show ring or the curb rein of a double bridle or Pelham.

Rubber-covered reins are popular as they offer excellent grip when poor weather or sweat can make leather reins slippery; however, it is often forgotten that rubber's primary use in life is to deaden 'feel' and vibration, so it is not advised for schooling or dressage when a great degree of subtle contact with the horse's mouth is needed. The other common type of reins are called Continental reins, which are made of soft webbing which is light, easy to handle, and gives good grip and 'feel'.

When mounted the spare loop of the reins should not be in danger of catching on the rider's foot; however, it should be sufficiently long to allow the horse to stretch its neck fully over a fence for example.

RUGS
Here more than anywhere else, the choice of materials, weight and design can be endless. See part 6 for further information on types, choice and fitting.

FLY FRINGES
There are various types of masks or fringes designed to reduce the irritation caused by insects. Some are simple lines of knotted string which hang from the browband to protect the eyes, others are made from a fine mesh netting which fits over the muzzle or face. However, careful fitting is needed to ensure the horse does not find them more irritating than the flies themselves! They should be well clear of the eyes and fitted so that insects cannot actually crawl under the edge and become trapped inside. From a safety aspect, it is important that the fringe will rip off quickly and easily if the horse gets it caught, while rubbing its face on a fence for example.

SAFETY CLOTHING
While not all organisations insist on competitors wearing a properly fitting, approved hat, most do, and it is certainly advisable from a safety point of view. Hats should conform to BSI standards in the UK, or be ASTM/SEI approved in the USA. They should have a properly adjusted safety harness and be properly fitted by a knowledgeable retailer.

Depending on the shape of your head, the front of the hat should sit midway on your forehead, between the hairline and the eyes, and should not be loose enough to jerk forward over your eyes in the event of a fall. Once a helmet has sustained a blow, its ability to withstand further impact may be compromised even though it appears undamaged, so riders are always advised to replace hats after a serious fall. For the same reason, you should take care not to drop the hat onto a hard surface.

For appearance's sake, some hats are already covered in a velvet material in the style of the old hunting caps. For others, it is possible to buy an elasticated or tie-on covering called a 'silk'; this may be made from velvet or various synthetic materials, and you can choose from a wide range of colours. For showing or competing, a sober colour to match your jacket is best, although for cross country events it can match the rest of your outfit.

3. FITTING EQUIPMENT

TIPS BEFORE YOU START

1. Horse language for small, medium or large is usually 'pony', 'cob' or 'full' size respectively.
2. Consider asking for expert advice from a qualified expert or experienced horse person, and be prepared to pay for it if necessary.
3. Use common sense in following the fitting guidelines below.

Observe your horse's reactions and decide for yourself if it is comfortable.

4. When buying a saddle, bear in mind that saddlers are craftsmen, not necessarily horsemen or trained saddle fitters.

5. The best-fitting gear in the world is not going to help a horse which is unsound or in pain. The horse should be regularly checked for discomfort by a vet in the first instance and by an equine dentist.

6. For items such as a saddle or girth, fit will be affected by the horse's condition. While slight weight variances throughout the year are to be expected, the horse should not be grossly overweight or very thin when you buy new tack.

7. Beware of buying tack and equipment with a new horse. It can seem like a good deal to get the complete package, particularly for a first time buyer, but do not assume that it all fits or is of good quality. A vendor should charge considerably more if the horse's tack and rugs are included, so check it's all worth having first!

8. Be prepared to change your tack when you change your horse. Many people are fond of their own saddle and may well have spent a considerable amount purchasing it, but the horse's comfort comes first and ill-fitting tack or the wrong bit will not get your relationship with a new horse off to a good start.

9. If you wish to add another hole in a strap in order to improve fit or versatility, it is relatively cheap and much easier to buy a proper hole punch for leather, than to purchase a new piece of tack or to take your tack to a saddler. These can be adjusted according to the size of hole you require, from a small one on a bridle cheekpiece, for example, to a much bigger one on a stirrup leather or roller.

Factors affecting fit:
- Horse's conformation (including that of its mouth and head), movement, muscle development and state of maturity.
- Size and weight of rider.
- The manufacturer. Just as one make of shoe may suit you better than another in the same size, some goods fit certain breeds or types of horse better than others.
- Material, cut and design of item and its intended use.

THE HEADCOLLAR

Because this is an everyday item in daily use, it is important that it fits well, especially if the horse wears it for extended periods. It is useful to have more than one in case it gets lost, broken or mislaid. Lead ropes are usually around one metre long but longer ones can be useful, especially if you are leading an unpredictable animal or one inclined to rear: a short lead rope may cause you to become 'sucked under' and unable to hold on whilst maintaining a safe distance. Some webbing lead ropes have a hand loop at the end which should not be used. If you need extra security or grip, make a large knot in the end of the rope as a stopper in case your hand slips.

Checkpoints:
- A leather headcollar will break more easily than nylon in an emergency, which is advisable if the horse is to travel or be turned out in one.
- The headcollar must be comfortable and allow a finger's width under each strap, with three fingers' width between the noseband and face.

- Young horses' heads grow extremely quickly. If a foal slip or small headcollar is left on, it must be checked for fit every few days. In a matter of weeks, it could be putting severe pressure on the youngster's head.

THE BRIDLE

These generally come in pony, cob or full sizes but it may be necessary to make up a full bridle with a mixture of sizes in order to get a comfortable fit for a horse with a particularly long, narrow head, for example.

Checkpoints:
- The headpiece and browband should not pinch the base of the ears.
- The browband must be wide enough to avoid pressure across the forehead, yet not so long that the headpiece could slip back. Two fingers' width between the horse's forehead and the browband is usually about right.
- The cheekpieces should be adjusted so that the bit sits comfortably at the right height in the horse's mouth, and they should not 'sag' significantly outwards when a contact is taken up on the reins.
- There should be room for the width of your hand between the horse's cheek and the throatlatch.
- A cavesson noseband should sit two fingers' width below the prominent cheekbone on the horse's face; a drop or flash may be lower but never below the end of the nosebone, or it will restrict breathing by pressing on the soft part of the nostril.

PARTS OF THE BRIDLE

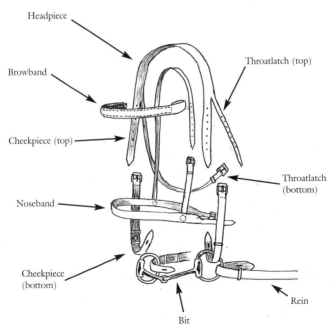

Headpiece

Throatlatch (top)

Browband

Cheekpiece (top)

Throatlatch (bottom)

Noseband

Cheekpiece (bottom)

Bit

Rein

- You should be able to fit two fingers between a cavesson noseband and the horse's face, one finger with a drop. They are simply to stop the horse opening its mouth wide, not to prevent it moving its jaw completely!
- The reins should stretch at least as far as the waist of the saddle but should not be so long that there is any danger of the rider's foot becoming caught in the loop.

THE BIT

Fitting depends on the type of bit, the conformation of the horse's mouth, the thickness of its tongue and to some extent the type of noseband that will be used with it.

Bit sizes usually go up in centimetres or half-inch increments. The bit should be placed in a slight curve, as if it were lying in the horse's mouth, and measured along the length of the mouthpiece from cheek to cheek. The type of cheeks may influence the size slightly – you should allow a little more space between the horse's lips and the cheek rings with a loose ring than with an eggbutt, to guard against pinching.

The thickness of the bit mouthpiece and its weight will also vary. Which you choose will depend on the type of horse, the shape of its mouth and thickness of its tongue. A thick mouthpiece must have sufficient room to lie comfortably in the horse's mouth, which is unlikely if it has a small mouth or thick tongue. A thin mouthpiece exerts a sharper pressure but can be more comfortable for a horse with a small mouth.

With a curb bit such as a Pelham or Weymouth, the length of the cheeks dictates its severity. A long curb will provide considerable leverage and is therefore more severe than a curb with shorter cheeks.

See part 4 for more details on bits and bitting.

Checkpoints:
- There should be room for one little finger between the cheek and bit ring (about one centimetre) on each side of the horse's face.
- Look for one wrinkle at each corner of the mouth with a jointed bit.
- A straight or mullen mouth bit should fit snugly into the corners of the horse's mouth.
- The bit should be high enough to lie across the bars of the mouth and not to bang on teeth.
- The horse should look comfortable with the width and type of bit chosen.

THE MARTINGALE AND BREASTPLATE

There are two main types of martingale; both are designed to prevent the horse raising its head above the angle of control. The standing martingale runs from the girth to the cavesson noseband; also attached to the girth, the running martingale splits into two straps with rings at the end, and these run along each rein. Both types of martingale are held in place with a neckstrap.

Some types of breastplate can be combined with a martingale. Breastplates prevent an otherwise well-fitting saddle slipping too far back if the horse is herring-gutted, narrow-chested, very fit and lean or has big shoulders and relatively weak quarters; or they can be used for extra security when riding cross country.

Checkpoints:
- With both running and standing martingales and a hunting breastplate, there should be a hand's width between the girth loop and the horse's chest, and between the horse's shoulder and neckstrap.
- A racing breastplate should not be tight across the bottom of the horse's windpipe.
- The rings of a running martingale should reach into the angle between the horse's neck and jaw when detached from the reins.
- A standing martingale should be long enough to allow it to be pushed up along the jaw and the horse's gullet when in position (i.e. attached to the noseband and girth).

THE SADDLE

Although there will be variances according to the type of saddle, the principles of fitting are generally the same. Obviously, a racing saddle which is only on the horse for a very short period has different fitting criteria from an endurance saddle which must remain comfortable for several hours at a time, but both types must support the rider and have sufficient clearance of the horse's spine, shoulder blade and withers to allow free movement.

It is the tree on which the saddle is built that must be fitted to the horse's back and shoulder. It is no use padding out an incorrect tree size with flocking to make it appear to fit, just as a thick pair of socks can't make up for over-sized shoes. The fit of the tree, the tree points and the balance of the saddle will be incorrect and will hinder comfort and performance. Likewise, removing flocking to make a narrow saddle appear wider will only result in discomfort for the horse, unless the saddle was over-flocked in the first place!

Generally, saddles are sold with narrow, medium or wide trees, although reputable manufacturers may have several widths or even make the tree and saddle to measure. Saddle size is commonly measured in inches from the pommel to the cantle and standard sizes are 15ins to 18ins in half-inch increments. Once you have decided which make, size and shape of tree suits your horse best, you need to decide which seat size and panel length will allow the rider to sit securely, comfortably and effectively.

The rider's length of thigh from hip to knee should be comfortably accommodated by the panels when they are riding at normal stirrup length. The rider's seat should have space for one hand between it and the cantle, and when viewed from the front, back and side, the rider should be able to maintain a correct balanced position in the deepest part of the seat easily, and not look or feel 'perched' forward, thrown back or seated to one side. Of course, any of these can be rider faults anyway and are not necessarily due to the saddle!

If you have a particular reason for using a special saddle pad or numnah, allow for this when fitting the saddle. Thick fluffy pads do not make life extra fluffy and comfortable for the horse, or make up for a poorly fitting saddle. A thick numnah will make the saddle fit more tightly in the same way as a thick pair of socks inside your normal shoes will. If the saddle fits well, it's best to use only a thin cotton numnah to absorb sweat and keep the saddle panels clean.

PARTS OF THE SADDLE

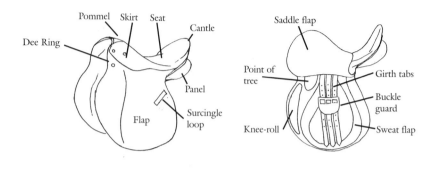

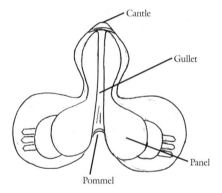

Checkpoints:

- Look for a clearly visible channel of daylight through the length of the gullet when the rider is on board, to indicate sufficient clearance of the spine and withers.
- Ease your fingers between the knee roll and the horse's shoulder to check shoulder movement is not being restricted. The shoulder blade will rotate back around three inches when the horse moves, so do not place the saddle too far forward.
- Ensure the back of the saddle does not extend onto the horse's loins.
- The entire panel should be in even contact along the horse's back, with no obvious concentrations of dirt on the panels at any one point if the horse is ridden without a saddle cloth.
- With a new saddle, ride without a saddle cloth for a few weeks to allow the leather to warm and mould to the horse's back.
- See the horse on the move and when jumping without a rider. The saddle should look as if it follows the contour of the horse's back, not be perched on top of it. It should not bounce up and down or lift clear of the horse's back without the weight of rider.
- Warning signs of poorly fitting tack or a painful back are white hairs, the horse hollowing, flinching, raising its head or swishing its tail when you tack up or approach with tack.

TYPES OF SADDLE

General purpose.

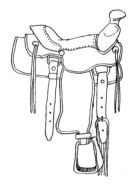

Western saddle.

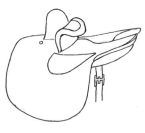

Side saddle from off side.

Side saddle from near side.

- Always use a mounting block or get a leg up to protect your saddle and ease strain on the horse's back.

NOTE: Occasionally, particularly on small ponies, the saddle can tend to slip forward, despite being a good fit. A crupper is an adjustable leather strap that attaches to the back of the saddle and runs around and under the base of the dock. The fit should be snug enough not to rub but not tight enough to pull when the saddle is in the correct position. You must ensure that the strap does not chafe the horse's skin, particularly on the underside of the dock, and some extra padding around the strap may be necessary to prevent this.

THE NUMNAH OR SADDLE CLOTH
Generally available in pony, cob and full size (small, medium and large respectively), an incorrectly fitted numnah may crease and ride up under the saddle, creating pressure points. Specially shaped numnahs are available to fit specialist saddles.

Checkpoints:
- Any numnah should be pulled up into the gullet of the saddle before the girth is tightened to avoid pressure along the spine and over the withers.
- It should be bigger than the surface area covered by the saddle, with a couple of centimetres visible all the way round once fitted.
- Tie loops to the girth straps to help hold it in place.

THE GIRTH

This can be leather or synthetic, but must be clean and broad to ease pressure. Elasticated girths are popular and are said to be more comfortable for the horse, but as already mentioned, they are very easy to over-tighten and under some circumstances they can also allow too much movement of the saddle when the horse least needs it, for example when landing over an obstacle or travelling over undulating terrain.

Choose a well manufactured girth for safety, with good-quality buckles to prevent damage to your saddle. You will need a couple of girths to allow for cleaning and repairs. It should be long enough to reach at least the third hole of the girth straps on each side of the saddle, but not so long that it only fastens securely to the top hole on each side. Some girths (such as the Atherstone or Balding) are narrow behind the elbow; this shape was designed with the horse's comfort in mind, but the narrower a strap is, the greater the pressure beneath it, so ensure that any shaping is minimal. Wide girths distribute pressure best.

Checkpoints:
- If your saddle has three girth straps, it is usual to attach the girth to the first and third.
- The girth should be long enough to reach half-way up the girth straps on each side. Get into the habit of changing your regular holes from time to time so that you are not always putting strain on the same area of the girth strap.
- Tighten the girth up gently, one hole at a time. You should be able to get the flat of your hand between the girth and horse's side before and after mounting, unless you are about to go cross country, in which case tighten it as much as possible for security! (Note the points about elasticated girths above, however.)
- Stretch each of the horse's forelegs forward in turn to 'iron out' any loose skin underneath the girth which may pinch.
- If the girth is a shaped one that narrows behind the horse's elbows, check that the tapered part is in the correct place on both sides.
- Check you can just get the flat of your hand under the girth once you are mounted. With the rider's weight in the saddle, it often needs tightening a hole.
- With a dressage girth which fastens near the rider's foot to avoid bulk under the leg, you may need help to tighten it once you are on board.

THE STIRRUPS

There should be at least 2cm between the side of the stirrup and the widest part of the rider's boot. However, they should not be so wide that the foot could slip right through to the ankle. Leathers should slide easily through the slot at the top of the stirrup to allow stirrup length to be easily altered.

Checkpoints:
- Go for stainless steel, not nickel, which is brittle and breaks easily.
- Purchase correctly fitting treads with the stirrups to reduce the chance of the foot slipping out or through the stirrup and to increase comfort.

4. BITS AND THEIR ACTION

There are literally hundreds of bits on the market, with thousands of variations in size, weight, shape, material and action.

Whichever you choose, the bit must be:
- The correct size, in length and thickness.
- Properly fitted.
- Crafted by a reputable manufacturer – there are many cheap copies about which are both unsafe and detrimental to the horse.
- In good condition.
- As mild as possible whilst still allowing the rider good communication and control.
- Permitted within the level or discipline at which you are working.

TYPES OF BIT

1. Bits can be made in combinations of metals, plastics or rubber; for competition, the parts of the bit entering the horse's mouth must all be of the same metal.
2. The bit rings are usually round, egg-shaped or 'D' shaped
3. The rings can be can be fixed, as with the eggbutt, or loose.
4. The mouthpiece can be one or multi-jointed, completely straight or slightly curved (known as 'mullen').

The main 'families' of bits are:

Snaffles: Although these are generally seen as the simplest and mildest form of bit, there are hundreds of different varieties, some of which are very severe. With the exception of the gag snaffle, they are used with a single rein. A simple jointed snaffle has the general effect of flexing the poll and lower jaw, and encourages the horse to raise its head.

Double bridles: A curb bit and chain, with a second rein, is added to the snaffle to allow finer communication between horse and rider. In order for both bits to fit inside the horse's mouth, each one is generally thinner and lighter than usual. When used together as a double bridle, the snaffle is known as a bridoon and the curb as a Weymouth.

In addition to the snaffle action of the bridoon, the curb or Weymouth will exert pressure on the poll, curb groove and bars of the mouth. This produces greater flexion of the poll and lower jaw.

Pelham: This is a single bit used with a curb chain, which attempts to simulate the effect of a double bridle. Pelhams usually have an unjointed mouthpiece, which some horses prefer. Two reins should still be used so that the rider can activate curb or snaffle action as required.

A bitless bridle or hackamore: This is sometimes considered to be 'one of the family'. It works by exerting pressure on the nose and poll, activated by single reins attached to long cheek pieces which create leverage. Steering is by the reins exerting

TYPES OF BIT

Loose-ring Bradoon.

Pelham.

Egg-but snaffle.

Kimblewick.

Fulmer.

Breaking bit with keys.

Double brindle (Weymouth).

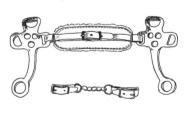

Hackamore.

pressure on the side of the horse's face through the cheek pieces. It can be a useful alternative for regaining confidence or rehabilitating a horse which has suffered mouth injuries or bitting problems in the past; but it is very severe and in the wrong hands may do more harm than good.

POINTS OF CONTROL

Depending on the bit shape, type and which 'family' it belongs to, it can act on one or several of the following points of control in and around the mouth and head:

- First lower premolars.
- Bars of mouth.
- Upper jaw – wolf teeth, if present..
- Corners of lips.
- Tongue.
- Roof of mouth.
- The poll.
- The nose.
- The curb groove.

FAULT-FINDING

When it comes to their equipment, riders are conscious of the dangers of worn, weak leather and rotten stitching, but rarely check the condition of their bit closely enough. This is unfortunate since there are hundreds of poorly manufactured bits for sale in tack shops everywhere. They are usually cheap copies that have been mass-produced abroad, with none of the technology, craftsmanship or quality of materials that make a well-manufactured bit effective, safe and comfortable for the horse. Look out for cracks, sharp edges instead of smooth contours, incorrect welding, holes, gas bubbles and defects in the metal, for rings and cheeks that do not move freely and smoothly, and for jointed bits that don't fold into equal halves.

The best bits are designed especially for the job by expert loriners, and moulded with great care from high-quality materials. The price of the bit generally reflects this extra care – be suspicious of cheap bits. If you go for a branded product, it should be covered by the manufacturer's guarantee.

TROUBLE-SHOOTING

If your horse appears to object to the bit or to being bridled, ask yourself the following questions:
1. Is the horse comfortable in his mouth, teeth, head and ears?
2. Are you being strong or clumsy with your contact?
3. Does the horse object to certain pressure points being used?
4. Are you using a bit that exerts too much leverage?
5. Are you asking for a head position that the horse finds physically too difficult to maintain, either because of its level of training or due to conformational faults?
6. Is the bit suited to the conformation of the horse's mouth?
7. Is it a good-quality, well-made bit from a reputable manufacturer?
8. Is the bridle properly adjusted?
NOTE: 'Above the bit', 'behind the bit', 'leaning on the bit'; these schooling terms are explained in Section VI, and do not necessarily relate to the bit itself.

5. CARE AND MAINTENANCE

You may well find that your tack and equipment is worth as much, if not more, than your horse! It therefore makes sense to look after it. If properly cared for, tack can last the best part of a lifetime. As well as retaining its value, it also needs to be well maintained for the safety and comfort of both horse and rider.

TACK ROOM
Tack is expensive and easily damaged or stolen. A well-designed, properly maintained tack room is essential for its protection on both counts.

Size
You can never have too much space where horses are involved! Even the single horse owner will soon fill an average-sized room with tack, rugs and equipment, especially in winter when rugs may need to be spread for drying. Wall space for hanging tack and equipment is at a premium in a tack room; a rectangular room with a high ceiling maximises the floor to wall ratio; avoid large windows or wall-mounted cupboards if you can.

Security
To make theft more difficult, the tack room should have limited entry points. Access should ideally be through one door only, which should be robust and set into a solid frame. A minimum of two locks is standard for good security. Windows, if there are any, should be as high as possible and have security bars or grilles fixed to the inside. Interestingly, statistics show that many tack thefts occur through the ceiling or roof construction, the owner having taken great care to lock up all doors and windows! A sandwich layer of steel mesh reinforcement should prevent all but the most determined thief gaining entrance. The finishing touch is an alarm system which is clearly advertised outside. Don't leave equipment lying loose about the yard and be especially careful with gear at shows. Insurance doesn't usually cover losses under these circumstances; generally, there must be signs of forced entry into a locked building, which does not apply to a saddle left on a horse-box ramp between classes!

Temperature
Excessive heat, damp or cold are bad for leather, causing rotting and cracking; a reasonably warm atmosphere is also needed to dry synthetic items and rugs. Room temperature should be constant at about 20°C, with good ventilation to expel moist air and prevent a build-up of condensation and damp.

Facilities
The most important of these is adequate space, racks and hooks to hang tack and equipment. Semi-circular brackets on the wall will keep the headpiece of the bridle in good shape, and should be high enough to keep the reins clear of the ground. Saddle racks which support the saddles broadly along the underside of the panels, not through the gullet, can either be mounted on the wall or free-standing. Storage space for spare horse and human clothing is useful and protects it from dust and rodents. Most tack rooms are also used for tack cleaning, so a large sink with hot

running water and central tack-cleaning hooks are ideal. An electric socket is useful for a kettle or radio, to keep the tack-cleaner happy!

In a large yard, the tack room may also have a washing machine for horse clothing. The degree of hair and mud acquired may not do your own machine much good! Rug drying facilities may sound like a luxury, but can make a real difference to the life of both horse and owner during a long wet spell.

Last but not least, a hard-wearing, easily cleaned, non-slip floor is a must.

LEATHER CLEANING

Leather that has been properly tanned and prepared for use as saddlery should only require dirt and grease to be wiped off with a damp cloth or specialist cleaning product after each use, with occasional use of a saddle soap or conditioner which is the correct formulation and pH-level for leather. Well tanned leather should not need oiling. Any leather straps on boots or rugs should be treated in the same way as the rest of your saddlery.

TACK MAINTENANCE

The stitching and stress points on leather, such as the girth straps, stirrup leathers and reins, should be regularly checked for excessive wear, thinning, cracking or rotting. A saddler or leather worker can usually reinforce stitching or weak areas before they become a danger.

Check the fit of your saddle throughout the year and consider having it checked and reflocked if it does not meet the fitting criteria listed above. As most saddlers are very busy, you will usually have to book the saddle in for at least a few days and pay for this service.

BITS AND STIRRUPS

Clean after each use by rinsing with water. Never use metal polish on the bit mouthpiece.

TACK STORAGE

Clean tack should be stored at room temperature in a dry environment, protected from dust (plastic bags will do) and in the case of a saddle, properly supported on a saddle rack. After several weeks it is wise to check the leather and wipe it over with saddle soap or a similar conditioner, before returning it to storage.

SYNTHETICS

As well as most horse clothing, saddles and bridles are now commonly available in synthetic materials which are cheaper, more hard-wearing and do not require the same care as leather. Follow individual manufacturer's recommendations, but these are usually easy to clean with warm soapy water or scrubbing under a tap. They do not perish in the same way as leather, although stitching should still be checked. Smaller items can even be cleaned in the washing machine.

6. RUGS

Rugs come in a variety of materials and may be designed for indoor and outdoor use, or both. The weight and performance required depends on the horse, the weather and your system of stable management; a clipped animal out during the day in winter will need the ultimate in warmth and protection, while an unclipped, native pony with a field shelter should only need something basic to keep off the worst of the wind and wet. You can check the horse's temperature by feeling the base of its ears, which should be warm but not hot or clammy, and slipping a hand inside the shoulder of its rug. The horse should feel comfortably warm. If it feels cool to the touch or has cold ears, an extra layer can be added beneath the rug. This may only be necessary in occasional extremes of cold weather.

Traditional canvas and jute are probably still the cheapest and most basic designs, while at the top end of the price scale are lightweight, high-performance synthetics that keep your horse at a comfortable temperature all winter. Many now claim to be 'breathable'; this means that they prevent the horse getting damp and chilled by allowing body moisture to pass out through a one-way membrane, without allowing the elements back in. This allows the horse's skin to regulate its body temperature in the normal way even while it is wearing a rug. Breathable rugs come into their own after exercise or when travelling, when the horse is likely to sweat, yet needs the warmth of a rug, or for the working owner who may not be there to change the horse's rug if the sun comes out!

FASTENINGS

Rugs are held in place with breast straps, clips or Velcro at the front, and a fillet string loosely under the tail at the back. Cross surcingles that attach to the bottom edge of the rug, cross under the belly and clip to the opposite side, have pretty much replaced the traditional padded leather roller that fastens around the horse's body like a girth. If a roller is still used, there must be additional padding over the spine. The roller should be done as tightly as necessary to keep rugs secure but because the horse must wear it for extended periods, this should not be as tight as a girth. You should be able to fit at least one hand beneath the roller.

To prevent the rug from being blown about in windy weather, some turn out rugs have leg straps that thread between the hind legs to hold the back of the rug in place. Leg straps should be crossed through each other and must be correctly fitted so that the horse is unable to get a foot caught if it rolls or gallops about. You should just be able to fit the width of a hand inside leg straps or cross surcingles.

TYPES OF RUG

For the stable: A 'duvet' style padded rug with nylon outer is the modern replacement for wool-lined jute. These come in differing weights and thicknesses, and can have super-warm thermal linings and matching neck covers.

For turn out: Traditional canvas is being replaced by new lightweight synthetic rugs which are often suitable for stable use too, but the most important thing is that the rug is fully water/weatherproof. You will pay extra for breathable fabric which allows the horse to dry throught the rug and regulate its own temperature rather than remaining damp. A really good-quality, breathable turn out rug is expensive but worth it if your horse spends a lot of time outdoors. Neck covers are a good idea, especially for a clipped horse. In hot countries, reflective rugs have been developed to protect the horse from heat and protect its coat from the sun.

During exercise: If you need to exercise a clipped horse in very cold conditions, particularly if the going or the horse's fitness means that the work will be quite slow, an exercise sheet which fits under the saddle and over the numnah will keep the quarters warm.

After exercise and for travelling: A wicking 'cooler' which removes moisture from the skin while keeping the horse warm is ideal. To work properly, it should be made from a synthetic non-absorbent material; absorbent fabrics such as cotton simply hold the water in a chilly layer against the horse's skin. The traditional 'string vest' type of cooler allows the horse to dry off through the holes, but is only warm enough to be effective if a layer of insulating straw is used beneath it.

In summer: A cotton sheet will help to keep a stabled horse clean and protect it against flies. It can also be used as an easily washed liner under a heavier weight rug.

RUG FITTING

Rugs are sold according to their length in feet (these go up in three-inch increments) or metres. The depth from spine to belly and the fit over the withers and around the shoulders will vary according to the manufacturer, so go for a generous cut where possible. It is important that the horse's barrel and belly are sufficiently covered and that the withers and shoulders are well covered for warmth and comfort. Some designs of rug are not cut away over the shoulders and withers at all and extend right up the neck, for extra warmth and protection.

Measurements should be taken as shown.

FITTING A RUG

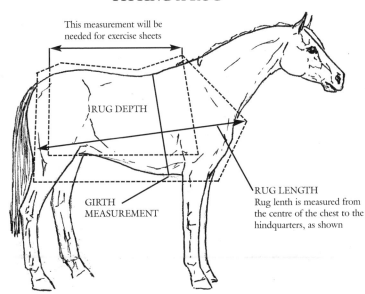

This measurement will be needed for exercise sheets

RUG DEPTH

GIRTH MEASUREMENT

RUG LENGTH
Rug lenth is measured from the centre of the chest to the hindquarters, as shown

TYPES OF RUG.

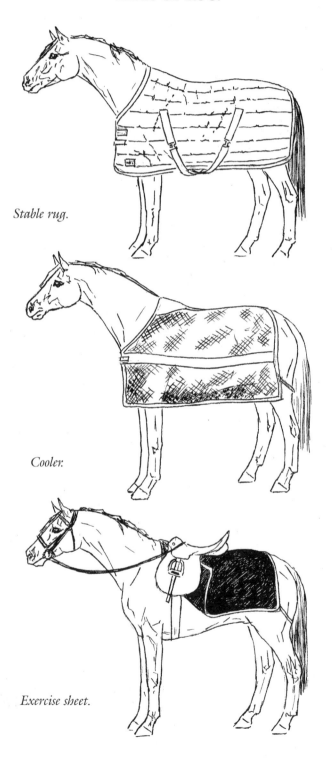

Stable rug.

Cooler.

Exercise sheet.

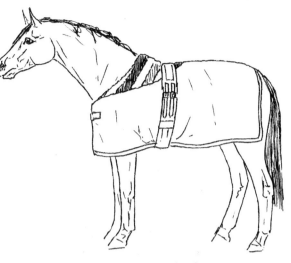

New Zealand
New Zealand with leg straps.

RUG MAINTENANCE

Every rug, no matter how expensive, will begin to lose performance quality if it is not properly cared for. While a horse will happily wear a rug which is wet on the outside, it should not be damp on the inside. This is a sign of the horse either getting too hot and sweating beneath the rug, or of a leak which needs repairing. Either way, the rug should be removed and dried thoroughly to prevent the horse from chilling. While repairs are done or a replacement is found, the horse will need to wear something else, which is why it is always a good idea to have a second rug on standby. As well as being useful in times of crisis, this allows rugs to be taken away and cleaned at regular intervals, which is necessary for the health of the horse's skin. Many synthetic rugs are machine-washable, if you can find a machine big enough to put them in! If not, it's a case of hosing them off and scrubbing by hand. Reproof waterproof materials and do minor repairs before storing clean rugs in sealed plastic bags for the summer. There are a number of special products designed for reproofing; rug manufacturers or outdoor clothing specialists will advise you on which is most suitable. Specialist companies who will clean, reproof and repair rugs, also advertise locally and in the equestrian press. Saddlers have the equipment for making large repairs.

Beware of damaging the membrane of breathable rugs with detergent. Specially designed cleaners are available from the manufacturers, or you may consider using the cleaners suitable for breathable outdoor gear from a camping shop.

7. LEG PROTECTION

WHEN AND WHY

By asking the domestic horse to deal with the unbalancing effect of a rider and perform movements such as circles, lateral work or

jumping, the chances of it knocking or stepping on itself are increased. A horse's natural movement or conformation defects can also result in it inflicting damage to its own legs, especially if it is shod, so it's safer to take the precaution of fitting leg protection before you start riding and it is definitely advisable when competing over fences. Protective leg wear is not allowed in a dressage test, however.

BOOTS AND BANDAGES

Bandages generally offer greater all-round support and conform well to the leg, but they require practice to put on correctly and can do more harm than good if they are wrongly applied. All bandages, with the exception of tail bandages and some specifically designed stable bandages, need a layer of padding underneath them such as gamgee, foam, or shock-absorbing pads. They usually fasten with tapes or Velcro.

For daily exercise, boots are quicker and easier to fit and keep clean than bandages. These are usually made from a combination of leather, neoprene, plastic or felt, with or without a shock-absorbing lining such as rubber or sheepskin. Fastenings are generally Velcro, buckles or 'hook and eye' type fixtures. Boots come in different sizes – generally pony, cob and full – and those intended for the back legs are usually longer, with four or five straps compared with the two or three usually found on front boots. It is important to put the right boots on the front legs to avoid intereference with the knee joint. All straps should face backwards and the pressure should be even.

TYPES OF BOOT

Knee boot: Protects against falls when the horse is being ridden or travelled.

Tendon boot: Protects the tendons at the back of the knee from being cut into by the toes of the hind feet when jumping or galloping. Can have an open or closed front.

Brushing boot: Protects the leg all round, from just below the knee to above the fetlock. May have tendon guard incorporated.

Overreach boot: Protects the front heel and back of the pastern from being trodden on by the back feet.

Travelling boot: Combines the effects of all the above, offering padded protection from above the knee to below the coronet when travelling. Should cover the heel to guard against overreaching.

Hock boot: Used for travelling to protect the hock joint from knocks.

Fetlock boot: A shorter boot which protects the actual fetlock joint from brushing injuries but offers no protection higher up the leg.

TYPES OF BANDAGE

Exercise bandages: Made from a stretchy crepe-like material and intended to support and protect the tendon area without restricting joint flexion. Because of the degree of elasticity, care must be taken not to apply them too tightly.

Stable bandages: Wider than exercise bandages and made of thicker wool or polyester material. They have some 'give' but are not elasticated. They are designed to protect and support the leg from coronet up to knee or hock.

Tail bandages: Made from a similar elasticated material to an exercise bandage, and used to smooth the top of the tail and protect against injury during travelling. An additional tail guard should also be used for longer journeys.

CARE AND MAINTENANCE

It is essential that all leg protection is kept clean to prevent rubs. Bandages can be washed in a machine and so can some boots, depending on the material; plastic and neoprene are easily scrubbed clean under the tap. Any leather on the boot, such as straps, should be cleaned and maintained in the same way as leather tack.

8. CLOTHING FOR TRAVEL

Horses have a knack of injuring themselves or treading on each other in transit, unless they are well wrapped up. They need:

- Full leg protection from above the knee or hock to below the coronet band, i.e. stable bandages with extra padding and additional knee and hock boots, or specially designed travel boots which cover all the vulnerable areas.
- A wicking rug (see 'Types of Rug') depending on the weather. Bear in mind that horses tend to grow hot while travelling.
- Tail bandage, with tail guard for longer trips, to protect the dock and keep the tail clean. Many horses lean on their tail for stability while travelling.
- A leather headcollar is better than nylon to prevent chafing.
- A poll guard if the horse is at all likely to toss its head.
- Horses can be travelled wearing their full tack if it is not too far and you need to mount up immediately at the other end, but use a saddle cover to protect your saddle from scratches and ensure that the horse still wears full leg protection and a tail bandage. The headcollar should fasten over the bridle; reins should be twisted up out of the way and secured with the throat lash close to the horse's gullet.

9. SCHOOLING EQUIPMENT AND TRAINING AIDS

There are many occasions when you may wish to lunge or long-rein a horse instead of (or as well as) riding it. Perhaps the horse is very young, has a sore back, is returning from injury or simply needs a break from normal schooling.

Traditionally a horse is lunged on a long line attached to a ring on a type of padded noseband called a lunging cavesson. The horse should respond primarily to the handler's voice commands, but a long lunge whip can help to reinforce these. Side reins which clip onto the bit from the saddle or roller can take the place of the rider's contact. The disadvantages of lungeing are that the false contact created by the side reins has no 'hand' at the end of it to reward or correct the horse, and the horse is restricted to going round the handler in various size circles until the handler stops and changes the rein.

Long-reining requires two lunge reins, one attached to each bit ring, which pass through a ring on the roller to hold them up against the horse's sides. The handler is still on the ground but has a rein in each hand and can guide the horse more accurately and make frequent changes of direction.

There are numerous gadgets which can help the trainer make the horse move in a correct outline and ensure proper muscle development, with or without a rider on board. Some are more useful than others, but all are a means to an end rather than an end in themselves. A horse which goes well with the aid of a particular gadget is not a well schooled horse.

10. FINAL CHECKS BEFORE BUYING EQUIPMENT

1. Are you and the horse completely comfortable with the clothing or equipment?
2. Is the design and quality suitable for your purposes?
3. Does the equipment meet competition criteria?
4. Do you really need it? Less is often more when it comes to tack!

SECTION VI

TRAINING AND COMPETING

These days, there is something for everybody when it comes to competing or simply enjoying your horse – dressage, show jumping, cross country, horse trials, endurance, Western riding, polo, showing, driving, side-saddle, vaulting... the list is almost endless.

If you wish to specialise in a particular sport or discipline, a good place to start is by contacting the relevant governing body, administrative organisation or breed society for information and a copy of their rule book; you may also find that in order to enter certain shows, you have to become a member. Some useful addresses are listed on page ??. In addition, there are many specialist books that go into the required detail about suitable breeds or types of horse, specific tack and equipment, training methods, performance criteria, show advice, etc. You can also make contacts, pick up information and gain an idea of what to expect, by attending shows as a spectator.

But whether or not you wish to compete, it is part of your responsibility as an owner to educate your horse and keep it in good shape. A fit, obedient horse is a pleasure to ride and own, is more likely to stay sound and will be easier to sell on to a good home when the time comes. The exact degree of schooling and training you need to put in, depends partly on the horse and partly on your interests, ambitions and ability, but a well-educated horse is always a happier, safer and more valuable one.

WHAT MAKES A GOOD TRAINER?

Whatever raw material you start with, the attitude and ability of the rider or handler and trainer, play an enormous part in ensuring the horse reaches its potential and performs to the best of its ability.

The good news is, it is not necessarily the most technically perfect riders who make the best trainers! A self-disciplined, thinking person who has the time and patience to tackle the horse's training in a logical way, foresee potential problems and handle them calmly and sympathetically when they occur, is likely to achieve good results. However, even if you have the knowledge and experience to undertake the horse's training yourself, most people still benefit from an alliance with a trusted and experienced instructor who can offer advice and support throughout, and a different perspective if required. (See 'Choosing an instructor' below.)

You can also derive food for thought from reading, watching others and attending the clinics or demonstrations of well-known competitors or trainers who visit your area. You don't have to agree with everything they do or follow their methods slavishly; just take on board what makes sense to you, and have a go at things that you instinctively feel might benefit your horse. Also bear in mind the following.

Training tips

- Research shows that training that is confrontational and based on punishment is less effective than training that works in harmony with the horse's natural behaviour. Always seek to place the horse in a situation where it can please you and be rewarded, rather than pressurise it into negative behaviour so it ends up being punished.
- Regardless of the competitive discipline, build the horse's confidence by using a logical, structured framework for your training.
- Good discipline and mutual respect are the cornerstones of successful training.
- Be completely fair and consistent. Establish definite rules so there are no grey areas to confuse the horse. This makes it much more unlikely that it will try to take advantage of situations or test your authority.
- A horse's education can start early in life, but make sure all training is appropriate. This often requires a lot of discipline for the trainer, never mind the horse! It can be tempting to ask too much from an intelligent, talented horse before it is really ready to give it, or to allow a difficult horse to have its own way over something; but you will be setting up a negative precedent for next time – and there will definitely be a next time!

While tradition abounds, there is no 'right' and 'wrong' way of training a horse. However, there are certain principles that apply and you will need to bear these in mind if your aim is to produce a contented, well-educated animal.

1. ASSESS THE RAW MATERIAL

Every horse can be improved with correct training: muscle can be built, fitness can be increased, suppleness and obedience can be developed; but the horse's basic conformation cannot be changed. Like it or not, looks are important, if only because a well put together animal is more likely to stay sound under the pressure of an increased workload. Even in a family fun horse, good conformation is highly desirable; for a top competition horse, it is absolutely essential. Regardless of training, even the most talented athlete in the world has first to make it to the start line in order to win, and to get there they must be physically capable of standing up to the months of necessary preparatory work beforehand. So while nothing in life is certain, especially not where horses are concerned, you can and should make sure you get off to the best possible start, and minimise potential problems by buying a horse with good conformation in the first place.

Talent and athletic potential are a little more difficult to assess at the buying stage, but with correct training, all horses should be capable of becoming fit and well-mannered enough to compete, if that is what you wish to do. Pleasure rides, local shows and the lower levels of affiliated competition are perfectly attainable goals for most horses and riders, especially if they set out with the intention of completing in good style rather than winning.

To reach the very top is a different story. The pressure is on to perform consistently well in good company at a high level, and both horse and rider must have a considerable degree of talent plus more than a little luck to achieve this. Money is also a major factor. While there are some heart-warming tales of cheap horses coming from nowhere to become world-class competitors, they are very much the exception to the rule and you will generally get what you pay for. Once a suitable horse has been acquired, running and maintenance costs are high if you wish to make an impression on the competition circuit and compete with any degree of success.

So before you attempt to train your horse, you need to know your goals and have a realistic expectation of what can and cannot be achieved with training. The trainer will always be working within the confines of the horse's natural ability, both physical and mental, and these limits must be respected. You cannot change a horse's natural character, and there is no doubt that some horses are more trainable than others.

Attitude and temperament are all-important, especially if you are not a very experienced trainer, and you should also consider this before you buy. If a horse is quick and nervous by nature, you may be able to build its confidence to a certain extent with patience and calm training, but at the end of the day it may still not be the right horse for you – especially if you too are nervous by nature! You cannot create your ideal horse out of unsuitable material, and it is useless to try and push it in a direction in which it cannot or should not go.

On the other hand, it can be the most talented and intelligent horses who are more difficult to train. Like precocious children, they need constant stimulation and careful handling to prevent them taking matters into their own hands. They are quick to recognise and take advantage of a lack of confidence or ability on the part of the trainer, yet resent an approach which is too authoritative or heavy-handed. Striking the correct balance requires a skilled, experienced and tactful trainer.

So the first step towards effective training is to assess the horse's suitability (both physical and mental) for its intended job, at whatever level it will be required to reach, then to be honest about your own ability. It is up to the rider and trainer to be realistic and ensure that they either understand the horse's limitations and work within them, or nurture its talent and make sure its potential is realised.

2. UNDERSTAND THE HORSE'S WORLD

Natural equine behaviour holds the answer to many aspects of successful horsemanship, as forward-thinking trainers such as Richard Maxwell and Monty Roberts have proved. An understanding of the horse's basic needs and natural instincts can help prevent and cure many problems related to their handling and training.

Horses instinctively seek the safety and security of a group with a strong leader, and this is to our advantage as we seek to train them. Horses are ready and willing to accept any leader as soon as that individual (horse or human) earns the right to call themself the boss by proving to be strong, intelligent, reasonable and reliable. After all, the safety of their herd and the continuation of the species depends on having a decent guy in charge!

Good discipline and mutual respect are the cornerstones of successful training. Fortunately for their human handlers, horses are used to discipline within their natural herd system. Horses live in herds, because there's safety in numbers, but there's only one way to all get along together harmoniously in such a close-knit community, and that's if everyone minds their manners and respects others. Wise brood mares are certainly not indulgent mothers. They don't let sentiment get in the way of discipline, because they know it is in their youngster's best interests to learn to read the body language of others and respect their personal space. Any horse which doesn't play by the rules will be driven out of the herd and made to feel insecure on the outskirts until it has learned its lesson, and returns contrite. Because it presents a real threat to life and limb, being alone is the ultimate punishment for a preyed-upon animal. Remember this when you're planning your stable management system; even though the threat of hungry big cats is unlikely in your livery yard, your horse still has a deep psychological need for friends, and will be far more relaxed and content in the company of others.

Psychology really is an indispensable tactic when it comes to handling and training horses. The use of physical force is undesirable for many reasons, not least because the horse is so much stronger than a human and you'll soon be fighting a losing battle. That apart, physical force is not appropriate, necessary or effective when training a flight animal like the horse. However, it's obviously vital to establish your authority in some way, and again, by understanding horse behaviour, we can learn the most effective way to do this.

In the name of survival, a mare can't afford to physically hurt her youngster in order to discipline it; if it respects her, her very expression and body language are usually sufficient to get the message across. She is also completely consistent. Every time it makes a mistake, she corrects it. As soon as it behaves correctly, it is rewarded. Without using any violence, it's completely clear to the youngster from day one what is acceptable behaviour and what is not. The success of your future relationship with the horse, not to mention your personal safety, depends on establishing your role as leader using similar tactics.

How assertive you need to be depends on the horse's character. You may need to be more forceful and even reassert yourself from time to time with a bolder individual, such as an entire male whose hormones constantly urge him to challenge, while more submissive horses may never question your authority but may take longer to gain trust and confidence.

Horses are born with the instinctive behaviour patterns of a flight animal. So when the time comes for you to climb on a young horse's back and cling onto its withers in the manner of a preying big cat, it's not surprising if it either runs off or bucks to remove you! Physically and mentally, horses are designed to run from danger or discomfort, rather than turn and face it. Thousands of years of evolution guarantee that only when the flight option is closed to them, i.e. they are trapped in what they perceive to be a threatening situation, will they fight back. Only very occasionally is a horse born which is nasty by nature, and any which appear to be so have probably been conditioned to become so, rather than born that way. Unfair demands, unreasonable treatment, pain and misunderstanding very quickly build resentment and sour a horse. What humans label 'bad behaviour' in equines is invariably just the horse reacting in a perfectly natural and instinctive way to something it perceives to be threat. You may know that you mean no harm, but does the horse?

Obviously the horse destined for life as a domestic animal must overcome its instinctive fears. Careful preparation and sympathetic handling can 'recondition' the horse's reflexes to a certain extent and most well-prepared horses happily accept their riders and learn to enjoy their work. The rider must also learn to recognise the difference between a horse which is genuinely struggling to control its instincts and one which is actually using them to take advantage of a situation, and react accordingly.

3. CHOOSE THE RIGHT TIME TO TRAIN

While it is certainly possible to keep improving and training an older horse for as long as it remains sound and healthy, the optimum training time for equines is from birth to about the age of four. This is the most influential period, when a horse is most ready and able to absorb information and accept new experiences. In other words, the horse's mental and physical growth patterns are linked, and as physical growth tails off at around the age of four, so does its capacity to learn and accept new experiences. There is also some evidence that horses 'learn how to learn' at an early age, and the more stimulation they encounter as a youngster, the more receptive they will be to future training at any age.

A new-born foal has a very steep learning curve because it is essential for its survival in the wild that it learns as much as it can as quickly as possible. The domestic horse may not face the same threats to life and limb as a wild one, but it doesn't actually know that, when it hits the ground at birth! Its natural flight instinct continues to make the horse extremely sensitive to its environment, which is in many ways a disadvantage for an animal destined for domestic life. It will be in a permanent state of severe stress unless it quickly 'desensitises' and comes to terms with its new life.

This is why it is good practice to 'imprint' a foal with human smell, touch and sound by handling it all over as soon as possible after birth, preferably within a few hours. This is also a good time to put on the first foal slip, a type of soft mini-headcollar. The foal's instincts will still tell it to fight and struggle, but it will struggle far less and give in much more easily than if you wait for a few days (or even worse, a few years), by which time it has built up its strength and a real sense of independence. Remember, you are doing it for the horse's sake as much as your own; it is your responsibility as an owner to do all you can to help it overcome its instinctive fears and become comfortable with the humans who are going to play such a big part in its life.

While it is never too early for this type of handling, at such an age we are talking entirely about mental stimulation rather than physical exertion. Anything you can do to increase a horse's acceptance of its role within the human way of life, will undoubtedly make the later process of riding and training it much easier and less stressful for all concerned. As part of its very basic early education, the foal should at least learn to lead independently from its mother, tie up to be groomed, stand obediently to have its feet picked out or be attended to by the farrier. Further training is dependent on the horse's age and strength, but there is no reason why a strong, confident foal can't learn to load and unload from a horsebox and trailer, cross water and small ditches (perhaps behind its ridden mother if you have a safe environment in which to do so), walk over small logs and poles and observe traffic and other future hazards from a safe distance. A foal may even accompany its mother to shows to be shown in-hand, which can be very useful if you intend to compete in ridden or in-hand classes at a later stage.

Although ridden work isn't appropriate until the horse is at least three years old, and even then it should not do anything strenuous until it is skeletally mature after the age of five (except in the case of Thoroughbred racehorses which are broken as yearlings and raced as two-year-olds), there is a lot more you can do in the early years to prepare the youngster for its future as a working animal. For example, it can learn to wear the necessary equipment such as rugs, boots, and even a saddle and girth. It may not be ready for the weight of a rider, but it can prepare for ridden work by learning the basics of lungeing, long-reining, in-hand work, being led out on hacks with other (ridden) horses and a small amount of loose jumping. If you make sure it enjoys itself and that every new experience is a positive one, by the time it is ready to back you'll have a confident, self-assured youngster who accepts anything and everything calmly.

The young horse's five-year diary

Under one day old: Handled all over by humans several times, wears first foal slip.

One day to one week: Handled all over and has foal slip taken on and off daily, leading in and out of the field and stable alongside mother with a helping hand behind quarters.

One week to one month: Leading independently but within sight of mother, will pick up feet for brief moments and accept grooming brushes all over. Socialising daily with other foals of a similar age.

Between one and six months: Stands obediently and lifts all four feet up for the farrier to trim, will load into a horsebox or trailer with mother, accepts hazards such as traffic and water, accustomed to stable procedures such as worming and the sound and feel of clippers (although it should not actually be clipped).

Six months to one year: May be weaned, so needs to lead well and load away from mother, learn to tie up and wear a rug and other items of clothing.

One to three years: Can be introduced to a bridle, saddle and girth (without the weight of a rider), learn the basics of lungeing, long-reining, in-hand work, and be led out on hacks and a small amount of loose jumping.

Three to five years: Backing and schooling on the flat and over poles, hacking quietly in company and alone, confident past hazards such as traffic and water. Possibly attend first ridden show, either to take part in a small class or just to look around.

4. LEARN HOW HORSES LEARN

Horses learn by four methods.

(a) By *habituation*. The horse's senses are 'flooded' with certain stimuli until it gets so used to them, its natural 'flight' response decreases or stops; for example, accustomising a horse to vehicles by turning it out in a field by a road or riding it amongst traffic. Learning by habituation can also work negatively, such as when a horse becomes unresponsive to a 'nagging' rider's leg aids.

(b) By *sensitisation*. This is a form of learning by habituation, but rather than becoming immune to certain stimuli by over-exposure, the horse's sensitivity to them is increased; for example, training the horse to move away from very slight pressure from the leg, or to lift its feet as soon as you touch the fetlock.

(c) By *association*, when the horse associates certain behaviour with reward or punishment, for example, receiving a smack when it bites, or being praised for jumping a fence. Horses cannot associate punishment or reward with a particular behaviour pattern unless it happens at exactly the same time. For example, you need to smack as soon as you feel it prepare to stop at a fence in order to be effective, not after it has done it. This also complies with the rules of fair play, as it still gives the horse a chance to put its mistake right. The horse's ability to learn depends on you giving it the motivation to make the correct decision.

(d) By *observation*, i.e. watching the behaviour of other horses. For example, when a foal stops drinking milk and experiments with nibbling at grass and hard feed like its mother.

5. RIDING BASICS

Sitting on a horse is something that many people try at some point in their lives, whether it's on a friend's pony, a beach donkey or a holiday trek; however, this is not really riding. For those who wish to explore the art of equestrianism further and become really proficient, many years of learning and practice lie ahead. For some, good progress is often related to circumstance – if you live in the country or on a farm, the opportunities generally present themselves more readily than for a city centre dweller. However, there is a huge network of riding clubs and schools across the country which present opportunities for anyone who wishes to learn to ride and further their equestrian knowledge.

Riding can be very physical and horses are living creatures who respond to the nature of their handlers, so the beginner who is naturally balanced, fit, supple and confident will have a head start. However, almost anyone can learn to become a reasonably competent rider with a combination of some theory, regular lessons and many hours in the saddle on different horses.

CHOOSING A RIDING SCHOOL

Everyone needs lessons, even those riders who have gone from hiring a riding school animal to the expense of buying their own. Just because you have something to ride whenever you like doesn't mean you should stop having lessons. As in any sport, lessons from a qualified professional may be expensive but they are necessary in order for your riding to be safe and enjoyable, and to enable both you and your horse to achieve your potential.

The size and standard of riding schools varies enormously. In the UK, many schools are visited and approved by the British Horse Society and licensed by the local authority, which publishes a list of those who have reached the required standard in terms of horse care and tuition. This can be a good starting point for selecting somewhere to ride, although if a centre you like isn't approved, don't be put off if it meets your criteria.

The ideal centre should be:

- Able to provide well-schooled horses in good physical condition, with well fitting, safe tack.
- The right size for your needs. Large yards can be less personal and more expensive; however, they may have better facilities and a wider range of horses and instructors.
- Well maintained and tidy.
- Within your price range. It's important that you can afford to go regularly, or else you will find it hard to make real progress. The cost of a lesson depends on how many people you share a class with, the training level of your instructor and/or horse and the facilities available.
- Able to offer the level of instruction, horses and facilities you require. If you wish to pursue a particular equestrian sport (such as Western riding or side saddle), you will probably need to find a specialist centre and pay accordingly.
- Conscious of good safety standards.
- Convenient to reach from your home or work.
- Staffed by friendly, qualified people who will take a genuine interest in your progress.

CHOOSING AN INSTRUCTOR

A good instructor is a valuable source of support and advice on all aspects of horse management, not just riding. If you can find yourself a true professional who knows what you want to achieve and understands you and your horse, you are well on the way to riding success!

Instructors are usually either members of staff at a training establishment or riding school, or travelling freelances who will come to your home or arrange to meet you and your horse at a suitable location. If you are considering the latter, you may need to add travel expenses and the cost of hiring an arena to the price of the lesson. People who compete in a particular equestrian sport may refer to their instructors as 'trainers'. These are specialists, often with considerable competition experience rather than formal qualifications.

Word of mouth followed up by a trial lesson is as good a way as any to find an instructor, but to gain the most benefit it can help to ask yourself the following questions.
- Do I like the instructor?
- Do they appear pleasant-mannered and professional?
- Do I feel inspired and motivated after a lesson, or tired and demoralised?
- What is my aim? Am I getting closer to achieving it through my lessons?
- What type of character am I? Do I give my best through bullying or cajoling?
- Can I afford to travel to lessons or must I find a travelling freelance?
- Can I afford regular lessons?
- Do I want a specialist trainer for my particular discipline?

Ask the potential instructor:
- What are their qualifications?
- To what level do they teach?
- When are they available?
- How much do they charge? Does this include travel or facility hire?

You should not be embarrassed about asking these questions. The instructor is a charging you for a professional service, and should appreciate how important it is for you to find the right person. A new instructor should be just as keen to quiz you about your aims and past achievements, and to spend time assessing you and your horse.

Although you are a paying customer, to be fair to the instructor and your horse you should commit yourself to having regular lessons for a reasonable period of time, such as a minimum of six months. Improving a horse and rider is a long-term project which requires commitment from you both.

EARLY LESSONS

MOUNTING AND DISMOUNTING
To reduce strain on both the saddle and the horse's back, it is always a good idea to use a mounting block, especially if the horse is big or the rider stiff. The horse must also learn to stand still while the rider mounts up, tightens the girth and alters stirrups. This may seem a small and unimportant discipline, but consider the horse's instinct to take flight when a big cat attempts to leap onto its back: each time a horse avoids completing this manoeuvre in a disciplined manner, it is moving closer to its instincts and further from your authority. Any subsequent attempts at control such as asking the horse to move around a gate, will then have to begin from a point of disadvantage in terms of respect from the horse for its rider. Mounting discipline therefore plays a small but significant role in the overall training of a horse. If the discipline becomes slack, it can quickly degenerate into a bad habit and anyone who has ever hopped after a moving horse, desperately trying to swing their leg over as it gathers speed, will know just how annoying and potentially dangerous this is.

The rider should keep hold of the reins while mounting, dismounting and altering tack.

Steps to mounting:

(i) Tighten the girth and pull down the stirrups, keeping hold of the reins. The correct length of your stirrups is roughly the length of your outstretched arm, so adjust them before mounting by placing your knuckles at the stirrup bar and pulling the iron into your armpit until the leather is taut.

(ii) Put the reins over the horse's head and position the horse alongside a mounting block if possible. The reins should be held in the left hand on the horse's neck, with the left rein running between the third and little finger, and the right rein through the palm of the hand. Ideally both reins should be the same length, but if the horse is likely to fidget then make the right one a little shorter; if the horse does move off as you are trying to mount, it will at least swing its quarters towards you rather than away.

(iii) With your back to the horse's head, turn the stirrup leather towards you and place the left foot in the left stirrup. Hold the waist or cantle of the saddle with the right hand, grasp some mane with the left and push off from the right foot, taking care not to jab the horse in the ribs with your left toe. Do not make the common mistake of pulling on the cantle of the saddle with your right hand and the pommel with your left, as over a period of time this puts a lot of stress on the saddle tree.

(iv) Swing the right leg clear of the horse's quarters and into place, but do not sit down immediately.

(v) Lower yourself gently into the saddle and place your right foot in the right stirrup.

Steps to dismounting

(i) Halt the horse and take both of your feet out of the stirrups.

(ii) Keeping hold of the reins in the left hand as described for mounting, place the right hand on the pommel for support. Incline the upper body forward to allow your right leg to swing clear over the horse's quarters.

(iii) Twist so that you lie briefly on your stomach over the saddle.

(iv) Drop to the ground onto both feet.

(v) Run the stirrup irons up the leathers to prevent them swinging, and loosen the horse's girth a hole or two. Some people prefer to loosen it just before they dismount, because the weight pressing down on the saddle makes it easier.

Although it is usual to mount and dismount on the left, it is useful and beneficial for both horse and rider to do it equally from both sides.

THE RIDER'S POSITION

Once on the horse, the rider must adopt a correct position. From the rider's point of view this is one which is safe, secure and comfortable, and which puts them in the best place to give signals or 'aids' to the horse without losing balance. From the horse's point of view, a good position is one which allows it to carry the weight of the rider comfortably and efficiently, with the minimum disruption to its own balance.

Beginners face a dilemma. To be secure and relaxed in the saddle requires practice on horseback. However, the horse is a living creature who will respond to the beginner's inevitable tension, imbalance and lack of co-ordination by tensing and

The rider's position.

moving forward less freely, which in turn makes it harder for the rider to sit softly. Any gripping or stiffening on the part of the rider makes matters worse and a vicious circle of stiff rider/stiff horse begins. There isn't really any way round this, other than using a comfortable, balanced and forgiving horse for short but frequent lessons; however, it is unfair for such a horse to be penalised for its generosity by doing more than its fair share of beginner classes.

The first stage of training the human body to sit easily and correctly on a horse is to practise on the lunge. Lungeing can be done with or without a rider and is of great benefit as a gymnastic exercise for the horse. However, it also allows the rider to concentrate on their balance and position without having to worry about steering or control of the horse.

Ideally, lungeing for the rider's benefit should be done by an experienced handler on an obedient and well-balanced horse in a quiet, enclosed space with a good, non-slip surface. It is recommended that the rider uses stirrups and a general purpose saddle and possibly a neckstrap in order to feel comfortable and secure in the early stages. As they become more secure and confident, riding for short periods without stirrups is good for developing strength, balance and the much sought-after 'independent seat' – this means that the rider's body is independent of their hands, and that they are in no way using them to stay on the horse or help their balance.

TYPES OF POSITION

Different riding positions or 'seats' have been adapted for various situations. In dressage for example, the emphasis is on a high degree of discreet communication with the horse mainly using the rider's legs, seat and weight; the dressage position is therefore very upright, with longer stirrups dropping the rider into the centre of the saddle and into closer contact with the horse's back and sides. This position maximises the physical points of contact between horse and rider, and allows the rider to feel, follow and influence the movements of the horse's back and give more diverse, precise aids. A specialist dressage saddle assists by having longer flaps, a deeper seat and the minimum of bulk between horse and rider. For example, it does not have thickly-padded knee rolls, and the girth is designed to fasten down by the horse's elbow rather than under the saddle flap beneath the rider's leg.

In the 'light' seat (also referred to as the forward, jumping, two-point or cross-country position), the opposite is true. In order for the rider to stay in balance over the horse's centre of gravity at speed or over fences, and so that the horse has the minimum interference from direct weight on its back, stirrups are much shorter. This closes the rider's knee, hip and ankle joints into a more acute angle, and allows them to incline the body forward and raise the seat from the saddle to a greater or lesser degree; the weight is taken on the knees, thighs and heels, which provide a firm but flexible support over which the upper body hovers. At one extreme the seat can be completely clear of the saddle with the upper body parallel with the neck, as with jockeys and show jumpers, or at the other, it can remain close to the saddle and lifted by only a few centimetres, such as when riding over ground poles or cantering over rough ground out hacking. The light seat is also useful for relieving the under-developed muscles of a young horse, particularly in canter.

Being in a forward position is not always a good thing, however; it can be less secure for the rider if the horse shies or misbehaves, and is unbalancing if used unnecessarily, as it tips the horse onto its forehand (see Equine Balance and Movement, below). Any forward incline should come from the angle at the front of the hips closing naturally with the motion of the horse, as he takes off over a fence for example, not through the rider dropping the shoulders or rounding the back; and should be as little as necessary to stay in balance with your horse.

The general purpose saddle has a more forward-cut flap, bigger knee rolls and a flatter seat than the dressage saddle, to allow the rider to adopt a lighter seat where necessary. A specialist jumping saddle is a further extreme for greater comfort and security at speed or when jumping, but like a specialist dressage saddle, is not ideal for everyday riding as it forces the rider to adopt a very particular position which will not always be appropriate to the situation.

EQUINE BALANCE AND MOVEMENT
Some understanding of equine balance and movement is necessary to prevent the rider hindering the horse more than is absolutely necessary, and to enable the rider to carry out particular exercises to improve strength, suppleness and co-ordination.

THE HORSE'S PACES
The four basic equine gaits or paces are walk, trot, canter and gallop, although in rare cases a particular breed may have a natural 'fifth' gait such as the Icelandic running walk or 'tolt', or an artificial pace developed through training, such as in racing trotters. Of the four usual gaits, however, each one can be subdivided depending on the speed, length of stride or degree of collection required; examples of these 'paces within a pace' might include a 'collected', 'working', 'medium' or 'extended' trot.

NOTE: When schooling a horse, it is common to refer to the 'inside' and the 'outside' of the horse. This is not meant literally! Rather, the side of the horse that faces towards the centre of the school is known as the 'inside' and the side facing outwards is known as the 'outside'.

Walk: This is a 'four time' movement, i.e. it has four well-defined 'beats' or footfalls. Walk can be 'free', 'collected', 'medium' or 'extended'. The sequence of footfalls that makes up the four beats of walk is:
(i) Outside hind.
(ii) Outside fore.
(iii) Inside hind.
(iv) Inside fore.

Trot: This is a two-time gait, i.e. it has two well-defined beats. It can be 'collected', 'working', 'medium' or 'extended'. The rider can choose to sit or rise to the trot; rising is the most basic method and is less tiring for both horse and rider. For rising (or 'posting') trot, the rider allows their seat to be pushed forward and up from the saddle for one step by the motion of the horse, using the knee, lower leg and stirrup for support, then sits softly back down for the next step. It is easier to remain balanced with shorter stirrups. To be strictly correct when working in a school, the rider should sit as the outside shoulder comes back, and rise as it goes forward – this is called 'riding on the correct diagonal'. Assuming that the horse is worked for the same amount of time on both reins, this ensures even muscle development. When changing the rein, the rider should also change the diagonal by sitting for two beats before beginning to rise again. A horse which is particularly stiff or one-sided will feel more comfortable on one diagonal than the other, and will try to manoeuvre the rider into sitting onto its preferred diagonal, i.e. its stronger side.

In sitting trot, the rider remains seated and allows the lower back and pelvis to match the sideways/forward and the upward/downward motion of the horse's back, absorbing the 'bump' of the movement rather than avoiding it by rising. Any tension or stiffness will prevent the rider from sitting softly on the horse's back and cause resistance. Longer stirrups are desirable so that the rider can sit as deeply as possible with the legs hanging heavily down, rather than being pushed upwards by the opposing force of the stirrups. Good sitting trot requires a secure, balanced and supple seat from the rider and a supple, strong-backed horse, and is therefore quite an advanced skill.

The horse springs from diagonal pairs of legs in trot, so the sequence is:
(i) Outside hind and inside fore together.
(ii) Inside hind and outside foreleg together.

Canter: This is a three-time gait and has four variations – 'collected', 'working', 'medium' and 'extended'. Because of the three-beat nature of this gait, plus the particular sequence of footfalls, the horse's balance is slightly shifted to the side on which its 'leading' leg falls. Thus, to make schooling or riding around a turn easier for the horse to balance itself, it is preferable to make the horse canter with the 'leading leg' to the inside of the turn.

The sequence of footfalls that makes up the three beats of canter on the 'correct lead' around a circle or school is:
(i) Outside hind leg.
(ii) Inside hind and outside foreleg together.
(iii) Inside foreleg, which appears to be 'leading'.

In 'counter canter', a more advanced movement, the inside hind leg initiates the movement and the outside foreleg is the last to touch the ground. This requires good balance, suppleness and a higher degree of training.

Gallop: This is a four-time gait and speeds can be over 30mph in racehorses. To gallop, you need a lot of space and it is usual to adopt a slightly forward seat, with the rider's weight out of the saddle to release the horse's back. Many horses do not know how to let go and gallop properly with a rider on board, and simply offer a faster canter. The sequence of footfalls that make up the four beats of gallop is the same as in canter, but the diagonal pair do not move together hence adding a fourth beat:

(i)   Outside hind leg.
(ii) Inside hind.
(iii) Outside foreleg.
(iv) Inside foreleg.

NOTE: Don't expect the horse to keep a proper gallop up for long; it is very demanding and not something they use in the wild unless escaping from great danger.

POSTURE AND BALANCE

In the wild, the horse's centre of gravity is thought to run roughly through its withers to the ground. When free, it has perfectly good balance and can move at speed over rough, undulating ground and jump obstacles with ease. If you watch your horse play in the field, its quick spins and sliding stops may be hair-raising to see, but it is most unlikely the horse will fall over. Its head and neck are great balancing aids, which is why it is important not to restrict their movement in ridden work, particularly when the horse is jumping with the extra unbalancing effect of a rider on board.

From the moment it is backed, the horse must alter its posture and balance in order to compensate for the added weight and movement of the rider on its back. Its centre of gravity must change, just as yours does when you carry a child in your arms, a heavy bag on your shoulder or a rucksack on your back. In order to stay balanced and upright, you adopt a posture which counterbalances the load; with a rucksack this means inclining your upper body forward to take the weight, or leaning through the left hip to counteract the weight of a heavy bag on your right side, for example. If you carry the same load in the same way on a regular basis, your posture will eventually change and muscles strengthen to support the new position. It's a similar story with the horse.

To counterbalance the effect of the rider and to allow the horse to carry the weight more comfortably and efficiently at all paces, the horse's centre of gravity must move backwards and it must transfer weight from its forehand onto its hindquarters. Its back should lift up to support the weight of the rider, and the natural side-effect of this is that its head will drop down. Try it yourself!

Go down on all fours and feel how much stronger and comfortable your back is when you pull in your stomach muscles and arch your back upwards, rather than allowing your back to hollow and stomach to sag down. Note also how the position of your back affects your neck and head position: it is possible to force your head down while your back is hollow, but it is very uncomfortable; while your natural inclination, when the stomach and back are lifted, is to realign your spine by dropping your head forward and down.

This is the most desirable way for the horse to carry the weight of a rider, and when a horse holds itself in this position it is said to be working 'in a good outline'. As the horse becomes more advanced in its training, its ability to maintain this lifted, round shape will increase. The joints of the horse's hindlegs will start to flex more deeply and the quarters will drop, lifting the back and forehand even more while providing greater power and 'spring'. This is called 'collection' and is the equivalent of the semi-crouched position you would adopt if you needed power and forward propulsion, when climbing, sprinting or jumping for example.

OUTLINE

The horse's silhouette when viewed from the side is referred to as an 'outline', and it is one measure of how well the horse carries itself. It can also give an indication of the level of the horse's training. A mature, well-muscled horse at an advanced stage of training should be capable of working in a collected outline, where the quarters are being used to a considerable degree and the forehand lifted as described above. A good outline for a novice horse should still show the horse moving forward, lifting his back, engaging the hind leg and accepting the rider's aids, but to a lesser degree, with the overall effect being longer and lower.

Physical fitness takes time to develop. It takes many months to change the horse's shape, and years before it is physically able to work in the collected outline you see in top-class dressage competitions. There are no true short cuts and the rider can only be patient and ensure that they follow an effective, structured schooling programme under the supervision of a good trainer. Horses are generous by nature but like the rest of us, will find ways of evading work that they find difficult or boring. It is up to the rider to exercise good judgement and prevent evasive habits from creeping in.

- A hollow outline, with stomach muscles sagging down, means a weak back.
- A good novice outline is best described as 'long and low'.
- A more 'collected' outline is only suitable for the more advanced horse. The ridge of stomach shows how the horse is using his abdominals to lift his back up and support the weight of the rider.

AIDS

As explained above, the horse must be encouraged to work in a way that makes it biomechanically easy for it to perform under the weight of the rider. The rider can make changes to the horse's outline and 'suggest' how it might carry itself better by using a series of aids. The more the horse becomes used to working in this way, the greater will be its physical strength and mental understanding of what is required (see 'Schooling', next). The rider has several ways of communicating their wishes to the horse including:

- Voice.
- Hands.
- Legs.
- Seat.
- Weight.

While horses can be trained to respond to the voice and undoubtedly come to recognise certain words, messages also pass from horse to rider in coded form: different patterns of touch from the leg, shifts of bodyweight from the rider or pressure from the seat and hands come to mean different things to the horse.

These are called the 'natural aids' and when a horse is listening and responding well to its rider it is said to be 'on the aids'. The rider must develop the 'feel' to know just how strong a particular aid needs to be in order to be clear to the horse, and how often it needs repeating; for some horses it will be very little, for others quite a lot. The rider must also develop co-ordination in themselves so that they can use one aid independently from another, or a combination of aids, for best effect.

There are number of items or schooling gadgets which are known as 'artificial aids' (for example the whip or spurs) which can be used to enhance, reinforce or refine the rider's natural aids as part of the training process. The aim in schooling the horse must always be to get it responding to the most subtle natural aids as quickly, calmly and obediently as possible by regular practice.

6. FITNESS AND EXERCISE

SCHOOLING

You can direct the educational process and encourage the horse to work in a better outline, with correct schooling. Schooling is simply the name used for any time spent furthering your horse's education or preparing it for a specific performance, either on the flat or over fences, in or out of the arena or stable. Schooling can be done almost anywhere, depending on the weather and ground conditions, although most people find it helps their concentration and that of the horse to set aside a specific area to act as a 'school room'.

The aim of ridden schooling is to develop the horse's physical ability to carry a rider and to increase its understanding of the numerous school movements and exercises which, when done correctly, will help the horse to use its body more efficiently, i.e. lift its back up to take the weight of the rider rather than hollowing away from it, and use the hindquarters to push forward rather than pulling forward from the forehand as it is naturally inclined to do.

Of course it takes time for the horse's balance, body posture and musculature to adapt to this 'unnatural' way of going, and that is why it is so important only to school for short periods and to allow the horse to stretch frequently, particularly with a youngster. Being tired but satisfied is one thing; being stiff, sore and exhausted is another and creates reluctance and resentment.

And schooling is not just for the horse. If you were to be completely comfortable carrying a heavy rucksack, not only would your fitness need to improve and the relevant muscles strengthen, but it would also be important that the rucksack was evenly packed and firmly balanced in the correct place on your back to avoid discomfort and injury. This is why it is important for the rider to develop a balanced and secure position, light seat and sympathetic hands (see 'The rider's position'). The aim of the rider is not so much to 'help' the horse carry out its work, although skilled riders may accomplish this to a degree, but to ensure that they can stay out of its way and interfere as little as possible, thus allowing the horse to get on and perform as nature intended. Every horse can do perfect transitions in the field!

USING A SCHOOL

A marked area set aside for training horses on the flat or over fences is usually referred to as a school, manège or arena. It should have a suitably soft, flat, non-slip surface and may be covered in sand, rubber chippings or one of the many special all-weather surfaces available. It can be covered (i.e. indoors) or uncovered. Sizes vary, but arenas are usually at least 20m x 40m to allow for effective schooling and to conform to the dimensions required for dressage.

For courtesy and safety, it is important to abide by certain 'school rules' when sharing an arena with others. These vary according to the establishment, but often include riders passing 'left hand to left hand' to avoid collisions, making way for horses which are performing more advanced movements such as lateral work, and informing other riders when you are entering or leaving the school.

School movements relate to 'co-ordinates' in the school, which are usually marked along the sides of the schooling area in big letters of the alphabet. There are also 'invisible' letters along the centre line of the school which indicate the point at which certain movements should be done in a dressage test.

MOVEMENTS AND EXERCISES

The half halt

This is a brief moment of collection where the horse is slowed and re-balanced by briefly closing the rein for a moment while the rider's legs remain on to send the horse forward; almost to 'bounce' the horse up into your hand. It has the effect of lightening the forehand and bringing the horse's hindlegs underneath its body, thus putting it in a better position to execute the next movement.

The half halt is basically a preparatory move, to get the horse balanced and attentive. A more advanced horse may respond to a very subtle half halt, such as the rider momentarily bracing their back against the movement, while a novice horse will probably require a less subtle check, perhaps a visible rein aid.

Half halts are commonly used:

- When riding a transition.
- To shorten or adjust the stride.
- To improve carriage or maintain collection.
- To gain the horse's attention prior to a new exercise.

Transitions

A transition is a change of pace, such as from walk to trot, or a change within a pace such as from working canter to collected canter. A progressive transition is where the horse works upwards through each gait logically, e.g. from walk to trot to canter. A direct or acute transition is much harder and requires a higher level of training for both horse and rider: the intermediate gait is bypassed, e.g. the horse goes straight from walk to canter, or trot to halt.

Transitions are the cornerstones of schooling. They require the horse to be obedient, co-ordinated, balanced and have its hindquarters engaged. This is why so much emphasis is placed on them in a dressage test.

Upward transitions: These are when the horse goes up a gear, say from walk to trot. Make sure the horse is going forwards in a round shape into a soft contact. Forward momentum is vital because you need balance and energy for a good transition.

See the guide to basic aids for a transition to each pace above. Prepare the horse by slowing the horse with a half halt (it may seem odd to slow down for an upwards transition, but it has a balancing effect), using your legs at the same time to push the horse forwards into the rein contact, then apply the aids. Keep as still and balanced as possible.

Downward transitions: These are when the horse goes down a gear, say from canter to trot. It's important not to just pull backwards with your hands to stop the horse, as you will encourage it to set its neck and jaw against you and pull right back! Unless you support the horse by using your legs as well, the transition will lack impulsion and the following gait will be unbalanced. Instead, think of containing the horse's energy by briefly pushing it with your legs into a 'non-allowing' hand. Rather than giving one continuous pull, squeeze and release the rein until the horse responds.

Transition timing: Ideally, you should ask for the transition as the horse's head reaches a particular marker. In the school this can be a letter, but out hacking you should also give yourself a start/finish point such as a tree or signpost to improve accuracy. The horse should respond immediately, and make the transition just as your leg is level with the marker. If it takes a little longer for your message to get through you may need to start asking earlier, but aim for as short a time as possible between applying the aids and the horse responding.

Transition tips:
- Practise transitions on the lunge or long reins first (using verbal commands). If the horse can't stay balanced on its own, it will find it impossible when it has got the weight of a rider to cope with.
- A good transition is the natural result of good preparation by the rider. If the horse is stiff or unbalanced beforehand, it will be even worse during the transition.
- Abandon a poor transition and start again – don't try and correct it.
- Give yourself a marker at which you execute the transition to improve accuracy.
- Use transitions frequently – don't sigh with relief and keep the horse cantering round and round once you've done one! It may exercise the horse, but it won't educate it. Try counting a certain number of strides at one pace before making the transition to another, e.g. three strides trot, six strides canter and repeat, so that the transitions are coming thick and fast and your horse has to engage its brain as well as its hindquarters!
- A common fault in upward transitions is to lean forward as if to 'urge' the horse on. This puts more weight on the forehand and makes it harder for the horse to do a good transition. Open your hips and shoulders, and even think of leaning back slightly.
- In downward transitions, resist the temptation to pull back and even think of pushing your hands forwards a little.

Lateral work
Anything that requires the horse to move its body sideways away from the rider's leg rather than in a straight line forward is referred to as lateral work. Lateral movements are the horse's equivalent of gymnastics and are used to improve

LATERAL MOVEMENTS

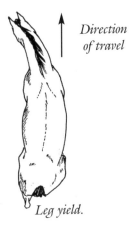

Direction of travel

Leg yield.

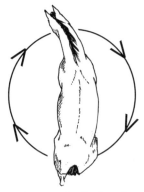

Turn on the forehand.

Half pass.

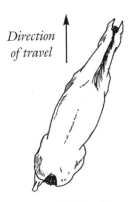

Direction of travel

Shoulder in.

Turn on the haunches.

Straight horse on two tracks.

suppleness, obedience, strength and hind leg engagement. They should be introduced as soon as the horse has learnt to work freely forward and accept a contact.

Lateral movements can be first taught to the horse from the ground – even asking it to step away from you in the stable is a start. Until this point the horse will only have understood the leg to mean 'move forward'. Patience is required to teach it that it can also mean 'move sideways', or depending on the movement, forward and sideways at the same time.

Common examples of lateral movements are::

Leg yield: When the horse moves forwards and sideways, flexed away from the direction of travel.

Half pass: When the horse moves forwards and sideways, flexed towards the direction of travel.

Turn on the forehand: When the haunches travel around the forehand in a small circle, while the forehand remains on the spot.

Turn on the haunches: When the forehand travels around the haunches in a small circle, while they remain on the spot.

Shoulder in: When the shoulders move to the inner track, so that the inside hind leg steps into the print left by the outside fore. The flexion is slightly away from the direction of travel and the horse is said to be on three tracks.

NOTE: When you learn a new dance or aerobics movement, you train your body and improve co-ordination one step at a time, then gradually speed up and link the moves together as you become more confident. Working on the same principle, when teaching the horse new movements it is a good idea to start slowly, in walk, then build up to trot or canter where appropriate.

SCHOOLING TERMS

Horsey jargon abounds when it comes to schooling and having lessons! Here are explanations for some of the most commonly used terms.

On the track: Keep to the well-worn track which goes around the perimeter of the school, or marks a ten or twenty metre circle.

Off the track: Work in the free space away from the track, towards the centre of the school.

Track left: Turn left.

Track right: Turn right.

Go large: Go all the way around the edge of the entire school.

Change of rein: A change of direction, from left to right or vice versa.

On the right rein: Going right, with the right hand towards the inside of the school.

On the left rein: Going left, with the left hand towards the inside of the school.

Incorrect bend: The horse's head and/or body is flexed in the wrong direction for a particular movement.

Above the bit: The horse's head comes above the angle of control, so there is no longer a straight line from the rider's elbow along the rein to its mouth.

Behind the bit: The horse's nose drops behind the vertical to evade the action of the bit, also known as 'overbent'. The contact will feel very light in your hand.

Leaning on the bit: The horse pokes its nose forward and the contact becomes very heavy in your hand.

Working from behind: The hindquarters are doing their job correctly, lifting and propelling the horse forward.

On the forehand: To avoid propelling itself from behind, the horse pulls itself along with the shoulders to a greater or lesser degree, resulting in a heavy, unbalanced feel.

SCHOOLING SUMMARY

Correct schooling aims to:

1. Encourage the horse to carry more weight on the hindquarters in order to balance itself and the rider.
2. Strengthen and supple the horse so that it is able to carry out its work and avoid injury.
3. Improve the rider's ability and co-ordination.
4. Improve understanding and communication between horse and rider.
5. Practise specific techniques needed by the competitive horse and rider in their chosen discipline, e.g. jumping, dressage.

RIDING OUT

However much you want to improve your horse, schooling in an arena every day is not the answer. Both horse and rider can benefit from the variety and relaxation of riding out (also called hacking) in the open countryside. Before riding on the road, however, you should be a competent rider. You should be able to control your horse and understand the rules of the road. When buying a horse, a major consideration should be whether or not it is well-behaved in traffic. Even if you only plan to hack off-road, a horse which is traffic-shy will be difficult to sell on in future.

While many areas have a network of bridleways and byways which you can use, it is becoming increasingly necessary in most areas to include some roadwork when riding, even if it is just to get to your local riding school for a lesson, to the farrier or from the horsebox park to the arena at a show.

Safety is paramount, for your own sake and for that of other road users. You should ride with the flow of the traffic, and when turning or crossing, observe other traffic and indicate clearly before moving to the appropriate position in the road.

Tips for riding on the road

- Avoid main roads and peak traffic times whenever possible.
- Use fluorescent and reflective gear for yourself and the horse.
- Make sure your tack is safe.
- Wear protective headgear.
- Beware of riding very fresh or young horses on the roads.
- Ride in company where possible, but not more than two abreast.
- Leave directions and an expected time of return with others at the yard.
- Show consideration for other road users and always thank them for theirs.
- Avoid riding in poor light, bad weather conditions or dangerous road conditions such as ice.

- Make sure you know the Highway Code (for horses) and any laws or by-laws applicable to horses and riders on roads.
- If leading a horse on a road, place yourself between the horse and the traffic to ensure the greatest possible control of the horse in the event that you need to restrain or prevent it from moving into the road.
- If possible carry a mobile phone for emergencies, or simply to let others know you have decided to extend your ride and will be back later than anticipated.

ROAD SAFETY
Riding up and down hill

When riding up and down hill, the rider should adopt a 'light' seat (see 'Types of Position' earlier in this section) to take the weight off the horse's back. The steeper the downwards slope, the less forward the rider should be. A soft rein should allow the horse freedom of its head and neck – its great balancing aid; the rider can help the horse maintain its balance by keeping it collected between hand and leg. This is essential if the horse has to move at speed or jump on an incline.

Different surfaces and hazards

It is good for the horse's balance and training, to learn to deal with a variety of surfaces and hazards, but when introducing a horse to anything new, allow it to take its time and gain confidence by following more experienced horses if necessary. Also, consider the safety aspects of riding over varying terrain and in different conditions, and carry a hoofpick with you.

- Ride only in walk with brief periods of trot on tarmac roads.
- Never ride on icy or slippery surfaces; if there is no avoiding the situation, dismount and lead the horse. It will cope better with only its own balance to worry about, and if it should fall, the impact and risk of injury to you both will be less.
- Over very deep or marshy ground, take the weight off the horse's back by adopting a light seat and give it as much rein as necessary. If it sinks or struggles excessively, jump off and lead it.
- Snow can be fun to ride through but it has a tendency to impact and ball-up in the horse's feet, and within a few strides the horse can be walking on icy 'stilts'. This is dangerous and unbalancing. It can be avoided by packing the soles with grease or, if you live somewhere that has a high snow fall and you frequently ride though the snow, your horse can be shod with special 'non-stick' pads under its normal shoes.
- Always ride slowly over stony ground, picking around the worst areas where possible. Traditional horse shoes give little protection against bruising of the soles or heels.
- When riding through water, first choose a shallow area with a firm, level bottom. There is no reason why the horse cannot trot or even canter through shallow water once it has gained confidence; eventually it may be required to jump in or out of water on a cross country course.
- If you encounter a ditch, allow the horse to take it at its own pace. It may be bold enough to jump from one side to the other; if the ditch is very wide or steep-sided, it is better for the horse to slither a little way down one side before launching itself. Check what is in the bottom!

WORK FROM THE GROUND

You don't always have to ride your horse to further its training and improve its fitness. As with any athlete, it can be very beneficial to vary your training by working the horse from the ground. The most common ways of doing this are lungeing and long-reining. These are most commonly used:

- In the initial stages of breaking and training a young horse.
- To vary an older horse's schooling.
- To improve the horse's obedience and response to the voice.
- When lack of time or poor weather prevents a long ride.
- If a certain type of injury, e.g. a girth gall, means the horse cannot wear its normal tack.
- When normal tack is away for repair.
- If the horse would benefit from loosening up or getting rid of excess energy before being ridden.
- In case of injury or tiredness in the rider.
- To tackle a ridden problem, which can often be more easily assessed from the ground.

LUNGEING

When lungeing a horse, the handler is positioned at the centre of an imaginary circle between five and ten metres from the horse. The horse works around the track at the perimeter of the circle. The handler controls the horse by means of a lunge rein attached to a special noseband, known as a lungeing cavesson, and by voice commands backed up with a long lunge whip where necessary. The rein should always be kept taut enough to avoid the horse's feet becoming entwined in it.

Equipment for lungeing.

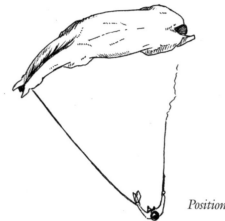

Position for lungeing.

Lungeing cavessons are made from leather or webbing and have one to three metal rings across the noseband; for lungeing, the rein should be attached to the centre ring. The noseband should be well padded to protect the delicate bones in the nose, particularly since a lungeing cavesson must be done up more tightly than a bridle to prevent it slipping into the horse's eyes.

The horse should wear:
* Boots on all four legs for protection.
* Its normal saddle with the stirrups removed or secured so that they do not bang about against its sides, *or* a breaking roller. If you do not wish to attach side reins there is no need for the horse to wear anything on its back.
* A snaffle bridle with the lungeing cavesson instead of the normal noseband if you wish to attach side reins to the bit, or the lungeing cavesson alone.

The handler should wear:
* A hard hat – horses are liable to kick out and 'express themselves' when on the lunge!
* Gloves.
* Non-slip boots.

LONG REINING
This is an alternative to lungeing and requires more practice. Instead of a single rein, two lunge reins are attached to the bit, or to each of the side rings on a lungeing cavesson; one on each side of the horse. They are held against the horse's side by the stirrups or rings on the roller. This allows the handler more control and precision, and simulates ridden work more closely without the rider actually being on board. The handler usually walks closely behind the horse or alongside the quarters, using the reins to ask for correct flexion and keeping them in contact with the horse's sides to simulate the leg aids. If the handler walks beside the horse, the far rein should pass around the horse's quarters, and care should be taken to keep it taut enough to avoid it becoming entangled with the horse's hind legs.

RUNNING UP IN-HAND

Simple as it sounds, getting a horse to walk or trot freely in hand takes some practice. If the horse is destined for in-hand showing, this is absolutely essential and must be addressed very early in the horse's training. It also applies to many ridden classes, where the horse is stripped of tack and run up in front of the judge to have conformation and action assessed in addition to ridden performance. In horse trials, a central part of every three-day event is the vet's inspection, where horses are trotted up the morning after the cross country in front of an expectant crowd to see if they are fit and sound enough to continue the competition.

Every horse should learn to lead freely and obediently beside their handler, even those who have no intention of competing. There are many occasions in its life when it will need to be 'trotted up' for viewing by a potential purchaser, or for inspection by a vet, farrier or therapist checking for lameness and incorrect action.

The horse can be led in a headcollar or bridle; obviously a bridle gives the handler more control if the horse is likely to get strong or excited. Horses are traditionally led from the left, although there is every good reason to handle and lead them equally from both sides. If the horse is to be led with the saddle on, the stirrup irons should be run up the leathers and the leathers pushed through the irons and secured, to stop them slipping down and banging against the horse's side or elbows.

Because the horse's head and neck are its great balancing tools, you will only get a true reading of its action if the reins or lead rope are slack, allowing true freedom of movement. The horse should be pushed away from the handler rather than swung around the handler on turns, for additional control and safety.

FITNESS PROGRAMMES

The process of fittening a horse is basically one of adapting his body to cope with a greater work load. This is done by stressing it enough to stimulate the body into building and strengthening, without over-stressing and causing injury. Too much is as bad as too little! However, whatever you do must be effective or you are wasting your time. As you may know, it's quite possible to wander around a gym half-heartedly for an hour and achieve very little, or put some effort in for the same amount of time at the same gym and have a very beneficial fitness session.

The age and previous fitness of the horse must also be taken into consideration. Young horses which have not yet been muscled up through correct training and are building the muscle for the first time will take longer to get fit than an older horse which has a degree of 'muscle memory' – however vague that memory may be! Elderly horses also gradually lose physical strength and muscle mass in the same way as humans, although like humans, this decline is much more gradual in an animal which has been kept fit and healthy throughout its life.

The starting point of any basic fitness programme always involves several weeks of gentle exercise to burn excess fat, tone muscle, strengthen joints and prepare ligaments and tendons for harder work. Once the horse has reached this basic level of fitness, incorporating short sharp periods of faster work will strengthen the heart and lungs. The final stage, where relevant, is technique training which will also fine-tune the specific muscles required most for a certain discipline, e.g. jumping. A 'pipe-opener' is also considered to be useful 'fine-tuning' at the end of a fitness programme. This refers to a sharp burst of fast work which will stress the lungs of an already fit horse to maximum capacity, thus clearing out and opening up the tubes and air sacs within. These air sacs or alveoli tend to become blocked with mucus, dead tissue and inhaled dust and rubbish from the horse's environment, which the horse will cough or snort out during strenuous exercise.

How fit is fit enough depends on what you intend to do with the horse, and the amount of time it takes depends on your starting point. If the horse has been completely 'let down' i.e. has been out of work for some time and is overweight and unfit, it will take about six weeks to reach a stage where it is able to hack actively. A further six weeks will then be required to put a harder edge onto this to make the horse fully fit for faster work; if you intend to take part in demanding competition at a high level, e.g. racing, polo or three-day eventing, the total fitness programme will take at least sixteen weeks and the horse may not reach its fitness peak until it has been to a couple of competitions and is well into the season.

A stabled horse is often considered to be easier to get fit, possibly because it is more convenient to have a clean animal in and ready for work at any time, and because its diet is more controllable; however, most stabled horses do not get more than a couple of hours work a day, compared to the field-kept horse which exercises itself gently for hours at a time. The mental aspect of getting a horse fit is also important – being turned out for at least a short period each day gives the horse a chance for both physical and mental relaxation, which will ultimately enhance performance.

BASIC FITNESS TIMETABLE

Week One: Walk on a hard, level surface, building up from half an hour to one hour over the week.

Week Two: Walk from one to one-and-a-half hours a day, introducing steady inclines.

Week Three: Active walk including hills for at least one and a half hours a day.

Week Four: Build up to two hours a day, introducing two-minute spells of trotting on a level surface.

Week Five: The horse should remain working two hours a day from now on but the work should become more demanding. Trot should total around twenty minutes, although still in two or three minute bursts, and can be done up inclines. Introduce a short, steady canter on level, soft ground.

Week Six: Continue as Week Five but increase trot work to a total of thirty minutes, and add further canters up inclines.

HEART RATES AND INTERVAL TRAINING

This is a relatively modern method of training horses which need to be aerobically fit, i.e. capable of extended periods of fast work, such as during racing, eventing or endurance rides, and is also used extensively by human athletes. The idea is that within one training session, several 'blocks' of hard work are interspersed with short recovery periods. The horse is alternately stressed with fast work then allowed to recover at a slower pace, before being stressed again. While not essential, a heart-rate monitor makes this method more precise and effective.

By monitoring the pulse rate, it is possible to stress the athlete's body (human or equine) to exactly the right level needed for optimum fitness without overdoing it and causing injury. In other words, it takes the 'how much, how hard, how often?' guesswork out of training. For effective aerobic conditioning, the horse (or human) needs to work at a certain percentage of their resting heart rate. Normally, the horse's heart rate can be calculated by feeling a pulse point or using a stethoscope, but it is not practical to use these methods on a moving horse. Instead, a special heart-rate monitor is used. Electrodes lie against the horse's skin to pick up the natural electrical impulses from the heart, and the pulse rate is displayed on a digital display clearly visible to the rider, similar to a wrist watch. The horse can then be worked hard enough to get the heart rate up into its optimum training zone. The horse can be kept working at this level for a carefully judged period of time, then allowed to rest until the heart rate drops again. Further short, sharp periods of work then raise the heart rate back into the effective training zone, followed by a further rests and so on. Some monitors can be pre-set to record the session, calculate improvements or sound an alarm if the heart rate is not within the target zone. The speed, number and frequency of work intervals can increase along with the horse's fitness. Generally, if a horse has not recovered to the required pulse rate after a ten minute rest, the programme is too hard for its stage of fitness and should be modified.

The horse's resting heart rate and the speed at which the heart rate drops in between intervals is also a good indication of fitness. The heart is after all a muscle, and will become bigger, stronger and more efficient with training, just like the other muscles in the body. The resting heart rate will therefore be lower and the heart should slow down and recover from exercise more quickly in a fit horse.

Approximate heart-rate guide
- Rest: 38-42 bpm.
- Walk: 60-80 bpm.
- Trot: 120-140 bpm.
- Canter: 160-200 bpm.
- Gallop: 210-230 bpm.

LETTING DOWN
Every horse needs a break, and time spent relaxing and recuperating in the field is particularly valuable for the competition horse. Peak fitness puts a considerable strain on the mind and body, and it cannot be maintained indefinitely. However, it is not beneficial for a super-charged equine athlete to be in hard work one day, then turned out on holiday the next. Once the horse has peaked and completed its season or the race or competition for which it was being prepared, its physiological systems need to be 'let down' over a period of days by reducing the exercise load and hard feed consumption gradually. This process is also called 'roughing off'.

INJURY AND REHABILITATION
If the horse has had a long break from work due to injury or illness, your vet should advise you on a suitable rehabilitation programme depending on the individual case. If a horse has been on 'box rest' i.e. completely confined to its stable to restrict movement after chronic injury, it is essential to start exercise again very gently, perhaps with just a ten minute walk in-hand building up to half an hour, before you even consider sitting on the horse. Think how wobbly your legs would be after a few weeks in bed!

Often horses become so stressed and fractious when kept on box rest, it does more harm than if they were left to wander gently around a paddock in the first place.

Another negative effect is that when the time comes for the horse to be turned out after a period of box rest, it is liable to bolt around and risk injury again. Turning a horse out to grass to allow an injury to recover is a better course of action than box rest, unless the particular injury requires immobility or the horse is naturally inclined to gallop and play about in the field thus aggravating any injury. However, most horses who are used to being out settle very quickly, particularly if they are in a relatively small enclosure with a quiet, sensible friend.

When the horse is ready to resume work, it may be that some form of physiotherapy or corrective farriery (also known as surgical shoeing) is required, alongside a careful fitness programme. Your vet will advise you. When rehabilitating a horse it is even more important that you stick to the principles of building fitness described above – start slowly, only building up the time and intensity gradually after several weeks of walking and gentle trot. You will need to keep a close eye on old injury sites as you go, so that any heat, swelling or weakness is spotted and dealt with immediately.

A long rest means that the horse may have changed shape by adding an extra layer of fat or suffering muscle wastage. Check that its tack still fits comfortably, as to get back in shape it must be encouraged to use itself as freely and easily as possible, without putting any undue stress on weak or injured areas.

Remember also that if the horse has been confined or rested for a long time, its manners may not be what they used to be! If you have any doubts, it is probably best to get the horse fit enough to lunge or long rein, so as to get rid of excess energy before you get back on board for the first time.

AVOIDING INJURY

Of course prevention is better than cure, and there are some situations in which the risk of injury is increased. All of them are avoidable by considerate riding, good management and heeding the advice of independent experts such as a vet or instructor.

Situations which may put a horse at risk are:

- When the horse is tired.
- When the horse is not fit enough to complete the task being asked of it.
- When the demands made are not appropriate to horse and/or rider's level of training and ability.
- When tack and equipment is unsafe or unsuitable.
- When a period of slow, steady work has not been done to provide the foundation of a fitness programme.
- Where poor technique or lack of confidence causes the horse to make mistakes.
- When horse or rider are unbalanced.
- When a sudden change of ground surface causes the horse to slip, flounder or jar.
- When the horse's feet are poorly shod or unbalanced.
- When the horse is genetically predisposed to injury.

7. JUMPING

Most horses have a degree of natural ability when it comes to jumping, as is apparent when a horse is loose-jumped, i.e. sent over a fence while loose in the school without a rider, but this ability needs to be trained if the horse is to remain balanced when jumping obstacles with a rider on board. Confidence building is also very important if the horse is to develop into a reliable and enjoyable ride. The key is to start small and build up, introducing as much variety as possible; a good place to start is by scattering ground poles around the arena to ride over as you school a youngster, and to encourage the horse to scramble over natural obstacles such as narrow ditches and small logs when out hacking with friends. It makes more sense to a horse to be asked to jump any solid, natural obstacles that are in its way rather than artificial coloured ones that spring up incongruously in the middle of a school.

Before jumping is included as a regular part of the horse's training, the horse must be reasonably fit and well schooled on the flat as already described. Jumping is one area where two novices definitely do not mix; while teaching a horse to jump, it is best to have a competent rider who will make the experience as easy and pleasant as possible for the horse.

Working over poles and along lines or 'grids' of fences will:

- Make the horse more supple and athletic.
- Improve jumping technique.
- Develop better rhythm.
- Teach the horse to think.
- Build correct muscle.
- Develop confidence.
- Help concentration.
- Quicken reactions.
- Add variety and interest to schooling.
- Aid impulsion and collection.
- Improve co-ordination.

As you can see, all of the above are desirable even in a horse which is not intended as a show jumper!

Jumping position.

POSITION: THE RIDER

See 'Types of position' (p.223). The rider adopts a light seat when jumping fences, to avoid getting left behind the movement and to allow the horse to lift off the ground and use its head and neck effectively. Over smaller fences, very little 'fold' is required; a common mistake is for the rider to 'throw' their weight forward thinking they are helping to free the horse's back. In fact, they are simply unbalancing the horse by putting all their weight on it forehand. To remain balanced and secure in the 'forward' seat or jumping position, you will need to shorten your stirrups from the length used for flatwork, between two and five holes. Take the cut of the saddle flap into consideration; when you shorten the stirrups, the knee should be comfortably positioned in the knee roll, not in front of or behind it.

Checkpoints

- Keep your leg on to encourage the horse forward but do not hurry it. The horse should come into the fence on its natural stride.
- Don't look down – focus your eyes beyond the fence.
- Let the rise of the horse's back close the angles between your thigh and upper body – don't try too hard to fold forward. The fold required is much less than you think until the fences are much higher.
- Allow your upper arms forward and give with your hands so that the horse has the freedom to use its neck and back.
- Keep your weight in your heels for security and shock absorption.
- Retain your light seat while the horse lands fully, to avoid slamming back into the saddle.
- Keep your hands forward while the horse lands fully, to avoid jabbing it in the mouth as it regains its balance.

Common rider faults

- Hurrying the horse out of its natural rhythm, or slowing it by 'hooking' it back.
- Throwing the upper body forward to 'help' the horse jump the fence.
- Dropping the head down on one side of the neck, known as 'ducking'.
- Dropping back too early in the air.
- Folding with the body but drawing back with the hands.
- Swinging the lower leg back.
- Looking down over the jump or on landing.

POSITION: THE HORSE

The rounded shape made over a fence by a horse jumping correctly is called a bascule. In order to use its body to maximum effect, the horse must sit back on its hocks and power itself upward and forward using its quarters, rather than trying to pull itself over a fence using its shoulders. The back should be loose, supple and rounded to allow the shoulders to lift and open, and the head to drop forward and down. Certain types and layouts of fences can build strength and technique, and are particularly good at encouraging the horse to jump in this way. It is important that the rider impedes the horse as little as possible, by developing a light, balanced seat and forward hands, as described above.

INTRODUCING POLES

With a horse which is new to jumping or needs its confidence building, start by working in walk, trot and eventually canter over and around a single trotting pole on the ground.

When the horse is quite happy, add a second pole at a distance of around 3m from the first, depending on the size of the horse and its length of stride. This will allow the horse to take a single trot stride between the poles. The distance between them can be reduced to around 1.5m and more poles added when the horse is confident and understands that it is to trot down the line of poles. The horse can also be lunged over trotting poles, and they can be raised by a few inches on small blocks if you wish to make the exercise more demanding. The horse should not wear side reins while being lunged over raised poles.

BUILDING GRIDS

A 'grid' is a line of fences with related distances between them which require the horse to either 'bounce' from one fence to the next (i.e. land with the front end and immediately push off again with the back end, with no stride in between), or to take one or two strides before the next fence. Depending on the size and number of fences, they can be very demanding for the horse but are excellent for developing strength and technique.

DISTANCES

It is important that you know your horse's stride length in order to set up poles and fences at the correct intervals. When the poles are the correct distance apart, the horse's foot should land in the middle of the space between them. If it appears to be stumbling or knocking the poles, the distances between them should be altered until it can work over them easily without breaking its natural rhythm. To help a horse (and/or rider) place itself in a good position for take-off before a fence, a 'placing pole' – a single pole placed on the ground – may be positioned one stride before the fence itself. Later on of course, you may wish to deliberately set poles at a longer distance to encourage the horse to stretch and lengthen its stride, or at a shorter distance than usual to make it collect and shorten.

When jumping a course, distances are worked out in terms of the number of 'non-jumping' strides a horse must take from landing after one fence to arriving in the correct place to take off at the next. If the horse needs to take six strides or less, it is called a 'related' distance. When the distance from one fence to the next exceeds six strides, it is called 'unrelated'. In competition, a standard distance is normally used, although this depends on the course builder.

Basic guidelines
- Trotting poles should be 1-1.5m apart.
- For a single trot stride, you need around 2.5-3m between poles.
- For a single canter stride, you need around 4.5m-5.5m between poles. Multiply this, depending on how many strides you want between them.
- A 'bounce' requires around 3-4.5m between fences.
- A placing pole should be around 2.5m-3m in front of a fence for a trot approach, 5m-5.5m for a canter approach.
- A horse takes off 1-2m in front of the fence.

SHOW JUMPS

Show jumps consist of coloured poles and fillers, that hang or are placed between two supporting wings. The poles fall easily and fences can be built to a specific height, width and tactical difficulty in accordance with the level of the horse's training.

Jumping a single show jump is relatively easy. The skill lies in jumping an entire course of around twelve or fourteen fences with varied changes of direction and only a few strides between each one, all designed to test control and concentration.

Don't expect a horse to jump as well at a show as it does at home. There will be a lot to distract it. Enter a smaller class than the fences you are comfortable jumping at home. Allow time to settle the horse, walk and learn the course, warm up and jump a few practice fences. Once on the arena, you will normally get four faults for a fence knocked down and three for a refusal. More than three refusals at the same fence results in elimination. There may also be a time limit. If there is not a clear winner after the first round, there will be jump off 'against the clock', where the course is timed, but a clear round is more important than a fast one.

CROSS COUNTRY

If your horse has been taught to jump correctly over poles, it should enjoy jumping rustic obstacles too. Horses soon learn that the fences on a cross country course won't fall down, and often respect them more and jump them better than show jumps. But it is not just the fences that present a challenge; dealing with undulating terrain, varying ground conditions and features such as water, ditches and variations of light and shade (for example, a jump set amongst trees) all add to the challenge of cross country riding.

Early in the horse's cross country training, fences should be low and inviting with level take-off and landing areas. Because they are fixed obstacles in a wide open space, safety is more important than ever. The fences should be well built, the horse's legs must be protected, tack should be double-checked for fit and wear and the rider should wear a body protector and safety helmet.

8. SHOWING

You don't have to ride to attend a show. There are such a variety of showing classes now available, suitable for all ages, types, breeds, abilities and even colours of horse. Classes may be ridden or in-hand, or be judged on the horse's performance in both. In some cases, the judge may also ride the horse. A show class is also a good place for a young horse to be introduced to the world of competition before it is ready for ridden work; the larger shows include in-hand youngstock classes for many of the breeds and types, often further divided by age, while at smaller shows you may just find one mixed class for one, two and three year olds.

Depending on the class you choose to enter, your horse should:

* Be controllable at all paces, individually and in company.
* Walk and trot up freely and obediently in hand so that its action can be assessed.
* Stand up quietly and squarely for the judges to assess its conformation.

- Stand quietly if the judge chooses to inspect its teeth, feet, or ears, move its forelock or tail to one side, or run a hand under its belly.
- Stand obediently in line while others take their turn.
- Meet the ridden requirements of the class, e.g. jump the required variety of fences, execute an individual show, remain well-mannered under an unknown rider (i.e. the judge), etc.

TACK AND TURNOUT

There is a huge range of headcollars and in-hand bridles currently accepted. Each breed class has its own preference, so check with the breed society. For ridden classes, decorative stitching is suitable for riding horse, hack and show pony classes, with coloured browbands for hacks and show ponies. Wide, plain bridles are more suitable for hunters and cobs. Double bridles and pelhams are suitable for hunter weight classes, while working hunters maybe shown in a snaffle, pelham or double bridle. A martingale is permitted, but you may not change tack between the jumping and showing sections of a working hunter class. For in-hand youngstock classes, use a leather headcollar or bridle for yearlings. Two- and three-year olds should be bitted, while brood mares should wear a double bridle and their foals a leather foal slip. Both mare and foal should be plaited. Hackamores are not acceptable in the show ring.

9. WESTERN RIDING

The tack, equipment, clothing and style of Western riding reflects the horse's past and present role as the essential partner of every hard-working cowboy or ranch hand, and is designed to make long hours in the saddle as comfortable as possible for both horse and rider. The Western horse and rider have to develop a number of practical skills in order to cope with daily life on a working ranch, and many of these skills are now shown at rodeo and Western riding classes. Traditional Western clothing and saddlery are still used for both work and competition.

The five standard events which make up today's traditional rodeo events have their origins in ranch work:

(a) Calf roping, where a calf is lassoed and tied as if to prepare it for branding.
(b) Saddle bronc riding, which dates back to the somewhat coarse methods used by busy cowboys to break in young horses in a short space of time.
(c) Bareback bronc riding, where the rider uses just one hand to hold a grip attached to a strap around the horse's girth and must hang on for an eight-second period.
(d) Bull riding, as above but on a bull.
(e) Steer wrestling, when a team of two cowboys race the length of the arena after a galloping steer; one keeps the animal on course while the other wrestles it to the ground in the quickest possible time.

Larger rodeos will feature other events in addition to the classic five described above, such as: team roping, where one cowboy lassoes a calf around the head while another ropes the legs; cutting, where a calf is separated from the rest of the herd by skilful riding; and barrel racing, where horse and rider gallop around a triangular course of oil drums as quickly as possible.

As well as the practical skills demonstrated by Western show riders, there is also the chance to be judged on looks and style such as in stock seat equitation, reining, trail-horse and pleasure-horse classes.

Stock seat equitation: Riders are judged on their skills and the horse's performance at walk, trot and lope (Western equivalent of canter). May also be required to show specific movements such as the sliding stop.
Reining: Tests the agility and ability needed for ranch work. Horse must demonstrate movements such as figure of eight, halts and turns on the forehand and haunches.
Trail-horse: Horse must show precision and care when negotiating rustic obstacles such as gates and narrow bridges.
Pleasure horses: Shown at walk, jog and lope to demonstrate suitability as well-mannered and comfortable hacks.

Traditional Western clothing and tack is used for all classes.

10. A-Z COMPETITION GUIDE
Nobody has to compete, but it can be fun and is a great way of increasing your experience and putting all that homework to the test. If you feel intimidated by horse shows full of experts on highly talented horses then no wonder – you're going to the wrong shows! While standards can and should be very high at the top level, the vast majority of local shows are small and low-key, run by riding clubs and similar organisations whose members are amateurs doing it for fun. Go along to any local show and you'll see people just like you, on horses just like yours. Here's a brief guide to some of the buzz words to make you feel more at home!

Affiliated
These are carefully graded competitions run by a national organisation. They comply with precise rules and guidelines regarding fence height in jumping competitions, or the difficulty of movements required in dressage, for example. You and/or your horse need to be registered as members of that organisation in order to take part, and any points or prizes you win are officially registered so that the horse can be appropriately graded. An affiliated horse can still take part in unaffiliated competition.

Against the clock
A timed jumping competition. Jump-offs are usually timed, although a slow clear round still beats a fast one with faults.

Ballot
Where the number of people wishing to compete exceeds the number of places

available, a ballot after the close of entries decides who is accepted. Competitors 'balloted out' of one event are often given priority next time.

Bell
This is used by the judges to indicate that competitors can start their jumping round or dressage test. They have a limited time to start once the bell has gone; this is usually between one and three minutes. Hearing the bell halfway through your round (dressage or show jumping) means you have made an error of course or have been eliminated. You should stop immediately and determine the problem from a judge or steward.

Class
Every show consists of different classes, which are listed and described in the show schedule. Horses may be divided according to breed, size, type, ability or even colour and age. There are also age limits for riders. Classes usually work up in difficulty throughout the day, from 'novice' for less experienced horses and riders, to the more advanced 'open' classes. Which class you choose depends on your interest and your horse's talents, but not all classes require competitive riding; many showing classes are in-hand only, and other fun classes might include Best Turned Out or Best Condition, for example.

Clear round
Also called minimus, this refers to the most basic level of show jumping competition where there is no timing or jump-off. There is no winner, but any competitor who jumps clear, i.e. without refusal or knocking a fence down, receives a rosette.

Collecting ring
An area set aside for gathering together competitors before they enter the arena, so that the stewards can call them in time for their class. It is also a warm-up area and may include a couple of practice fences.

Cool down
Cooling off after strenuous exertion is essential for the horse's well-being. It was once thought that warm water was preferable to cold for a post-race wash-down, to avoid cramping hot muscles, but research carried out on horses particularly prone to this kind of 'tying up' has proved otherwise. Cold hosing or even better, continual sloshing of ice-cold water over the major muscles of the neck, shoulders and hindquarters is the most effective way to cool off a hot horse after strenuous exercise.

After hard work the horse can be helped to recover by brisk walking and periods of slow trot for up to half an hour to keep the heart rate and circulation up a little. This helps the removal of toxins from the muscles and keeps freshly oxygenated blood circulating for better recovery. In addition, it helps unwind the horse mentally and prevents chilling or stiffening of the muscles. In practice, it is usual for the rider to dismount after a strenuous workout such as a race or speedy cross-country round, in which case the horse should have its tack removed and be walked in-hand. Depending on the weather, the horse may need a lightweight cooler rug for the latter part of the walk. This prevents chilling once the horse's pulse and respiration have returned to normal and it has stopped sweating profusely, just as a human athlete would keep tired muscles warm with a track suit once he had cooled down and had a shower after exercise.

Declaration
Even if you have entered a competition in advance, it may be necessary to 'declare' to the show secretary that you have arrived and definitely intend to compete.

Dress
Just as the horse and rider's training varies according to the discipline, so does correct turnout and tack. There are many variations of dress, which can alter not only between disciplines but also according to the level you compete at. It is best to contact the relevant association, breed society or show secretary for exact details of what is correct beforehand. As a general guide, the larger the show, the more formal the dress!

Electrolytes
If the horse has sweated heavily, an electrolyte liquid or powder can be used to replace salts, minerals and trace elements. These can be added to the feed or water (check manufacturer's instructions) but the horse should be accustomed to them beforehand and must also have access to fresh, untreated water as well as the electrolyte-treated water.

Entry
Can be done on the day at smaller competitions but is usually slightly more expensive than pre-entry, and there is always the chance that the class will be full. Pre-entry is usually required for dressage, and you will be given the specific time at which you are expected to compete in advance.

Faults
These are penalties for errors. A pole knocked down in show jumping is scored as three faults, although in some classes a time penalty may be imposed instead; a refusal counts as three faults. For dressage, see 'score'.

Feeding
Feeding is covered in Section III, but there are some specific guidelines relating to competition horses. As with any athlete, you get out what you put in. A horse with an unbalanced or inadequate diet will never be truly fit no matter how much exercise it gets, because it will not have the building blocks necessary to grow muscle tissue and provide energy. The more demands you make on the horse's body, the more 'high-grade fuel' it requires to provide the necessary energy and nutrients to build, repair and recover from exertion.

A horse should always have access to fresh water, even if it is about to compete. Depriving a horse of hay and water for hours before competing is old-fashioned and will actually cause more problems than it prevents, for example, colic and dehydration.

It's not just immediately before and after competition that a suitable diet is important, but throughout the horse's training schedule. It must put in the hours of training in order to be fit for competition, and as its training takes more out of it physically, its diet should alter accordingly. The basics of feeding should still be adhered to, however (see Section Two), and you must avoid the temptation to overfeed concentrates in an attempt to keep up nutrient and energy levels. A different type of feed will probably be required, with higher nutritional specifications, not just a greater quantity of 'low-grade fuel'. Feed manufacturers are fully aware of this and have many balanced feeds especially designed for harder-working horses, or those which need to put on 'condition' for the show ring.

Although you might imagine that a hard-working horse is always a hungry one, you may actually find that the mental and physical stress of being super-fit causes some to go off their feed. These types may need to be fed less more often, or at a different time, or changed to a more appetising mix, or perhaps just turned out to grass for a few hours to unwind and refuel. Provided the horse continues to drink water and eat roughage, i.e. hay, grass or haylage, its digestive system should still remain healthy even if it is picky about concentrates.

Fitness

Whatever you decide to do, it is only fair to ensure that you and your horse are fit enough to enjoy it. Fitness could be described as preparing the horse mentally and physically for whatever will be demanded of it. This may mean losing fat, strengthening muscles and increasing the efficiency of its heart and lungs for a cross country horse, or actually putting on fat for a show horse. Specific technique training may also be necessary if a horse is to be fit for a particular sport. In horse trials for example (also known as 'eventing'), one horse must compete in three disciplines – dressage, show jumping and cross country – so not only must the horse be fit and bold enough to tackle a stiff cross country course, but it must also be supple and obedient enough to do a calm dressage test.

Flags

These mark the fences which have to be jumped on a course. A red flag marks the right-hand side of the fence, and a white one the left, and competitors must jump between the flags to avoid elimination. Flags are also used by fence judges to stop a horse and rider out on the course or to indicate a hidden danger.

Hors concours

Literally means 'outside competition'. A horse and rider compete along with everybody else, perhaps just for the experience, but are not eligible for placing or prizes. Riders need to ask special permission to compete 'hors concours' and will often go last, when the competitors who are eligible for placing have finished.

Judge

Each class will have a judge, or possibly more than one, to decide on the outcome of the competition or settle disputes. At a cross country event, there may be a judge at each fence to send information about the progress of competitors back to a central control point.

Jump off

If there is no clear winner after a single show jumping round, those who 'tie' for places jump again around a different course. The horse with the fewest jumping penalties wins; if there is another tie, it is decided by time.

Optimum time

Before a competition starts, the judges or course-builder may decide on an ideal time in which competitors should finish the course. Competitors are penalised for every part of a second they come in after that time, but get no reward for being inside it. There may be an extra prize for the rider closest to the exact optimum time.

Passport

This is proof of the horse's identity and gives a full description, details of vaccinations, immunisation programmes and blood tests where relevant. It must be completed according to current regulations by a veterinary surgeon, who must not be the horse's owner. In order to enter many competitions and shows, or to stable a horse at a racecourse, any horse without a passport must have alternative identification and a current vaccination certificate completed by a vet.

Practice fence

Usually found in the collecting ring or near the start of a cross country course, these fences will be flagged with red on the right and white on the left to prevent head-on collisions between those warming up! Practice fences may not exceed the height of the fences you plan to compete over.

Prohibited substance

Like any athlete at a serious event, horses are not allowed to have certain performance-enhancing or pain-relieving drugs in their bloodstream while they compete. Some substances are permitted in stated amounts, others not at all. Doping is a serious offence but can be done in all innocence, as many banned substances come in innocuous forms and are on the shelves of many tack rooms; certain muscle rubs, tendon liniments, horse feeds, supplements or treats may specify that they are not suitable for use in competition. Drug testing is particularly widely used in the racing industry, where large amounts of money riding on the results makes fair play exceptionally important.

Qualifier

In order to qualify for a major championships, competitors may need to get through qualifying rounds at other events specified by the championship organisers.

Rules

Every competition has its rules, and it is up to the rider to find them out. Major organisations and breed societies have their own rule books, and it should be specified which set of rules a particular competition means to comply with; for example, the FEI rules (International Equestrian Federation) or the BSJA (British Show Jumping Association).

Schedule

The timetable of events at any particular show. Available from the organisers or secretary, it contains useful information about every class, such as course type, fence height, necessary qualifications or restrictions on entry, rules etc.

Score

A competitor's final score is judged by the number of penalties and points they have accumulated in the course of that competition. In ordinary jumping classes, penalties are given for knock-downs, refusals, run-outs or exceeding the time limit, so the fewer 'points' you finish with, the better! Showing is more subjective, and how well you do is largely down to the judges' personal opinions. Dressage is also subjective, with positive points awarded out of a maximum of ten for each movement; additional points are gained for the horse's paces and submission, and the rider's position and use of the aids. The total number of marks gained by the competitor is then subtracted from the maximum it was possible to gain, giving the final score in penalties or 'points missed', so the lower the score, the better.

Seasons

Different events take place in their relevant 'season' on the equestrian sporting calendar. Most equestrian activities (except for hunting and jump-racing related activities such as point to point and team chasing) start in spring and reach a peak through the summer – showing, show jumping, polo, endurance, dressage, driving, horse trials – and tail off in the autumn. Hunter trials are at the beginning and end of the hunting season, i.e. autumn and spring, and some events are divided into an indoor season in winter and an outdoor season in summer, such as show jumping.

Secretary

The fount of all knowledge at shows! The show secretary usually has a clearly marked tent or area where you register your entry and pick up your class number and results. A returnable deposit will often be required for your number.

Stewards

Show officials who see to the safe and smooth running of the show, and call competitors in time for their rounds. They may also assist a judge in directing competitors in the ring during a class.

Tack check

May be done by the stewards immediately before or after a competitor enters the arena, to ensure that all tack and equipment is legal and complies with the rules. Rules may change from year to year. Currently in the UK, permitted tack is as follows.

Dressage: Breastplates which stop the saddle sliding back are allowed, but not martingales. The horse may warm up in boots or bandages but these must be removed before he enters the arena. He may only wear an ordinary snaffle bridle for Preliminary and Novice classes, an ordinary snaffle or double bridle for Elementary to Advanced Medium, and a double bridle for Advanced.

A drop, flash or cavesson noseband must be used with a snaffle bridle (See Section V 'Tack and Equipment).

Bits may be: an ordinary snaffle with unjointed, jointed or double jointed mouthpiece; egg-butt snaffle with or without cheeks; rubber snaffle; snaffle with upper cheeks or hanging cheek snaffle. All parts of the bit coming into the horse's mouth must be made of the same type of metal (e.g. a stainless steel French Link with copper plate in the middle is not permitted). Rubber bit guards are not allowed.

Show jumping: Standing and running martingales are permitted, and there is no restriction on bits.

Horse trials: For the dressage phase, the rules are as for pure dressage above, but in addition to the drop, flash or cavesson noseband, a grackle is allowed. For the jumping sections, almost any tack is admissible, except a standing martingale.

Endurance: A recognised form of bridle must be used. Long distance enthusiasts often favour synthetic and/or bitless bridles.

Timed section

In some jumping competitions, particularly cross country, only a small section of the course is timed to decide the winner rather than the whole of it. It often includes some of the trickier fences fairly close together; in a hunter trial, it may include a gate which needs to be opened and shut, and a knock-down fence.

Trot up

The unofficial name for the official vet's inspection of horses before and during an event, which determines if they are fit to continue.

Vaccinations

Every horse should be vaccinated and for certain competitions (particularly where the horse is stabled overnight with others) you may have to prove your horse has a clean bill of health with an up-to-date vaccination certificate.

Walking the course

There is time set aside before the start of every jumping competition when competitors may walk the course and take a close look at each fence (on foot!). To give themselves the best possible chance of doing well they should also take note of start and finish timing apparatus, the situation of the judges, relation of the entrance or certain fences to the collecting ring, the exact line they intend to take between fences and any related distances. This is especially important on a cross country course where there is choice of routes for a particular obstacle; if you have a problem at the shorter, harder option, you may need to know your way around the 'long route'.

Warm-up

A proper warm-up before exertion minimises the effects of fatigue, reduces the chance of injury, increases circulation to the muscles and opens the blood vessels to allow toxic waste generated by exercise (such as the lactic acid which leads to cramp) to be more efficiently removed. In other words, it primes the horse both physically and mentally for its forthcoming performance. It is not just the muscles of the body which need to be primed either; internal organs such as the heart and lungs need to be adequately prepared for exertion to avoid undue stress and possible damage. Excessive sweating and excitement is not the same as a structured warm-up; while the horse's heart rate and body temperature are obviously raised, it will not enjoy the benefits that a true warm-up will provide and is in fact needlessly wasting valuable energy and reducing essential fluid, electrolyte and glycogen levels.

Weigh-in

Where a rider has carried a weight handicap during a race or cross country event, they are weighed-in immediately after the race with all their tack and equipment, to ensure that the horse finished the race correctly handicapped.

COMPETITION DAY TIPS

- Take your horse's normal food, hay and water with you.
- In most cases, any extra feed should be given after the competition to help the horse recuperate, not before to 'give him extra energy'!
- Allow the horse access to hay and water back at the box as soon as its breathing returns to normal.
- Consider using an electrolyte (see A-Z).
- If possible, turn the horse straight out to grass for at least an hour on returning home from a competition so it can wander round, roll and relax at leisure.
- Do not feed bran mashes; they are a sudden change from normal feed and are poorly balanced. Instead, feed plenty of hay and a small quantity of the horse's normal feed soon after competing, with the rest of the ration several hours later.
- If the horse is to have a day off following a competition, reduce the concentrate ration on that day and allow it to fill up on roughage instead to prevent 'tying up' (see Section Four).

When deciding on your timetable, allow time to:
- Enter your class if you have not already done so.
- Register and collect your number.
- Find the arena.
- Walk the course.
- Prepare the horse.
- Warm up well.
- Get from one class to the next, if you have entered more than one.

11. PROBLEM SOLVING

PHYSICAL PROBLEMS

As already discussed, it is better not to buy a horse which has physical problems or conformation defects in the first place. However, some weaknesses are actually the result of poor riding and training, and incorrect muscle development and imbalance can be improved. If you do find yourself with this kind of horse to ride or care for, the following advice can help.
- Warm the horse up well before the rider gets on, either by lungeing or loose schooling.
- Keep schooling sessions short and frequent so that the horse does not become sore or over-tired.
- Although it may be tempting to concentrate on strengthening a particular weakness, this is mentally and physically draining for the horse. Vary its work so that its overall fitness improves.
- Be especially careful to check that all tack and equipment remain comfortable as the horse makes progress and changes shape.

- Check that the horse's diet is providing it with all the nutrients it needs for growth and repair.
- Consider using a schooling device temporarily for riding or lungeing, to encourage the horse to work correctly and build new muscle.
- Consult an animal physiotherapist and see if additional therapy would enhance the effect of the horse's ridden work, e.g. massage or stretching.

PSYCHOLOGICAL/BEHAVIOURAL PROBLEMS

Many books have already been written on this subject, but as anyone who has had to deal with a problem horse knows, it is an area where the written word is of minimal help!

The fact is that a horse with behavioural problems can be frightening and dangerous, even for an experienced rider. Great skill and judgement are required if you intend to rehabilitate a problem horse, and the only way to do it truly successfully is to find the root causes and eliminate them logically, rather than trying to tackle the symptoms.

For example, there is no point forcing a horse over fences if it is refusing because it has a sore back or a lack of confidence in the rider. You may get it over a few, but you are heading down a tunnel with a dead end and all the time confirming in the horse's mind that it is not in its best interests to try and please its rider. Recognise that there is a problem immediately and give the horse the benefit of the doubt. Stop jumping, sort out the horse's back, regain its strength and confidence over small fences until it realises it doesn't hurt any more, and your problem will have solved itself without having a negative effect on your relationship.

The reasons for equine behavioural problems can be varied and complex, but about 99% of cases are pain-related, at least initially. Common sites of pain and injury are the neck, poll, brisket, shoulder, pelvis, mouth and teeth. The area where the saddle actually sits on the horse's back is very strong and is rarely the root cause. It doesn't take a serious fall or obvious injury to alter the horse's attitude to its work – it can make itself uncomfortable merely by slipping in the field or getting up awkwardly.

The horse is by nature a generous, non-confrontational animal, and if it becomes reluctant or even violent when ridden and handled, first assume it is not its fault. Think about it. It just doesn't make sense for a horse which has been perfectly well-behaved for years to suddenly start bucking or refusing to leave the yard. The nature of the horse is such that it will often keep trying to please even when in pain, and months can go by before a situation becomes so chronic that it can no longer bear it and reacts accordingly. The more generous and long-suffering a horse is, the longer a problem will go unheeded if you let it. So a so-called 'problem' horse is not behaving badly, it is behaving logically, and has been forced into getting its message across in the only way it knows how to.

Of course, mutual respect is another issue that will affect the horse's behaviour. The horse is a herd animal, and in the interests of its own survival it must always be certain of its leader's worth. If your problems with the horse stem from a lack of respect on the ground, e.g. barging in the stable, you need to reassert yourself and make it clear (without being aggressive) that such behaviour is absolutely not acceptable. Horses will not like you more for being a soft touch; like children, they are invariably more secure, happy and well-behaved when the boundaries are clear.

Problem checklist

- Always give the horse the benefit of the doubt.
- Remember that a so-called 'problem' horse is not behaving badly, it is behaving logically, so you need to be logical in turn.
- Seek to eliminate the cause, not the symptoms.
- Nearly all cases are pain-related. If your vet, or equine dentist can't find anything, keep searching for possibilities. Check your tack for correct fitting.
- Pain and fear override a horse's ability to learn. Getting frustrated with an apparent 'problem' horse's behaviour is cruel and a waste of time. It is futile to train a horse until you have eliminated these as a possible cause of any negative reaction to your training.
- When all other avenues have been investigated, check the balance of respect between you and your horse. If others have no problems with your horse, it may have the upper hand and be challenging your authority. Fair, firm, appropriate and consistent handling is the answer.

THE SHEFFIELD COLLEG
CASTLE LIBRARY